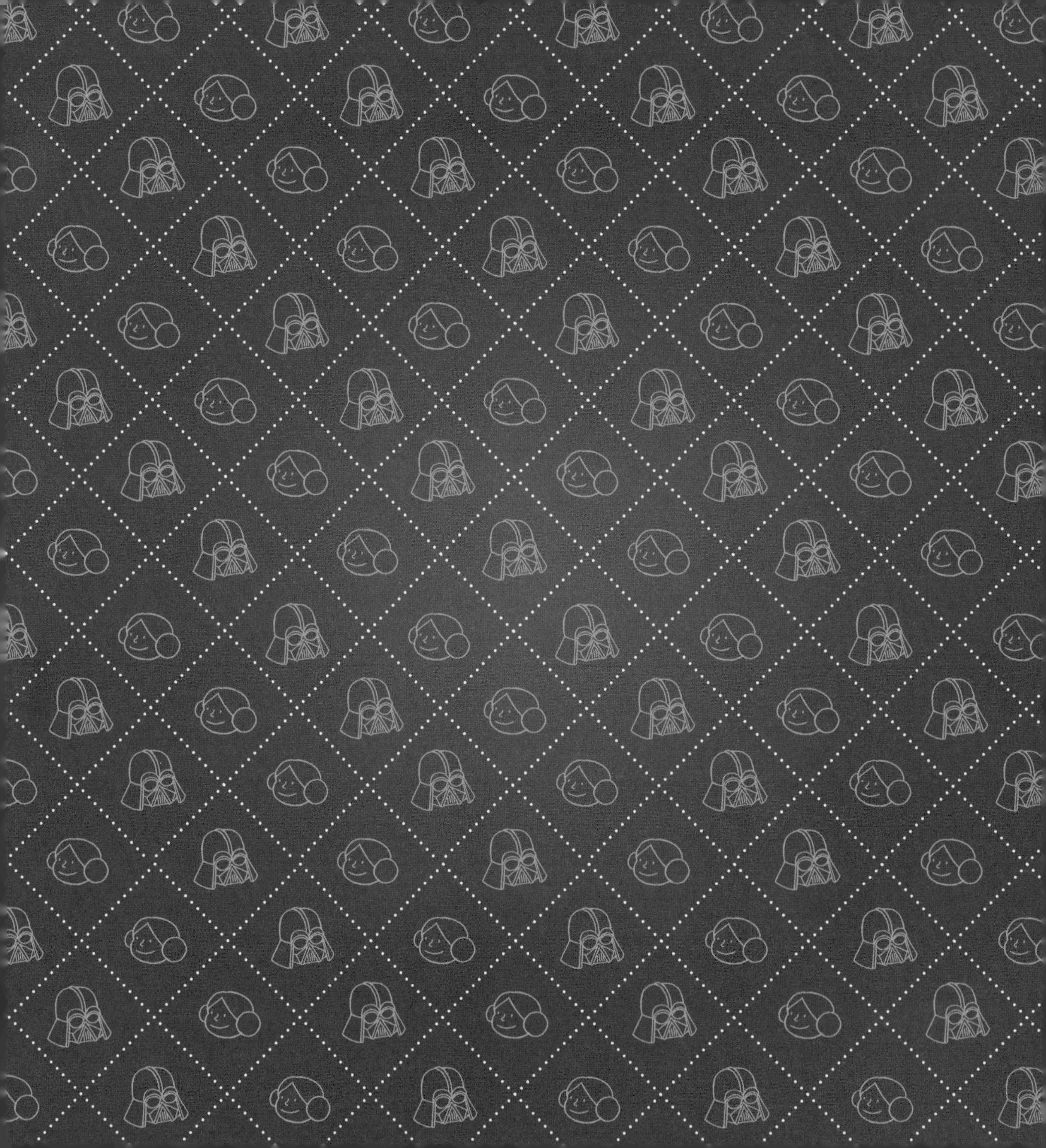

VADER'S ™
little princess

JEFFREY BROWN

CHRONICLE BOOKS
SAN FRANCISCO

THIS BOOK IS PART OF THE DARTH VADER AND SON / VADER'S LITTLE PRINCESS
BOX SET. NOT FOR INDIVIDUAL SALE.

BOX ISBN 978-1-4521-4487-0

THE LIBRARY OF CONGRESS CATALOGED THE ORIGINAL
EDITION OF THIS BOOK AS FOLLOWS:

BROWN, JEFFREY, 1975-
  VADER'S LITTLE PRINCESS / JEFFREY BROWN.
    P. CM.
    ISBN 978-1-4521-1869-7
1. LEIA, PRINCESS (FICTITIOUS CHARACTER) - COMIC BOOKS, STRIPS, ETC.
2. VADER, DARTH (FICTITIOUS CHARACTER) - COMIC BOOKS, STRIPS, ETC.
3. STAR WARS - COMIC BOOKS, STRIPS, ETC. 4. FATHERS AND DAUGHTERS -
COMIC BOOKS, STRIPS, ETC. 5. AMERICAN WIT AND HUMOR I. TITLE.
  PN6727. B7575V342013
  741.5'973--DC23
                2012050595

MANUFACTURED IN CHINA.

FSC www.fsc.org
MIX
Paper from
responsible sources
FSC™ C020056

WRITTEN AND DRAWN BY JEFFREY BROWN
DESIGNED BY MICHAEL MORRIS

THANKS TO STEVE MOCKUS, J.W. RINZLER, MARC GERALD, MICHAEL
MORRIS, AND MY FAMILY. SPECIAL THANKS TO RYAN GERMICK
AND MICHEAL LOPEZ AT GOOGLE FOR THE ORIGINAL INSPIRATION
TO MAKE DARTH VADER AND SON. MOST OF ALL, THANKS TO
GEORGE LUCAS FOR MAKING GREAT TOYS AND LETTING ME PLAY
WITH THEM.

10 9 8 7 6 5 4 3 2 1

CHRONICLE BOOKS LLC
680 SECOND STREET
SAN FRANCISCO, CA 94107
WWW. CHRONICLEBOOKS. COM

WWW. STARWARS. COM

A long time ago in a galaxy far, far away....

Episode Three and Three-Quarters:
VADER'S LITTLE PRINCESS

Darth Vader, Dark Lord of the Sith, continues to rule the Galactic Empire and is out to destroy the heroic Rebel Alliance. Meanwhile, he must raise his young daughter, Leia, as she grows from a sweet little girl - into a rebellious teenager....

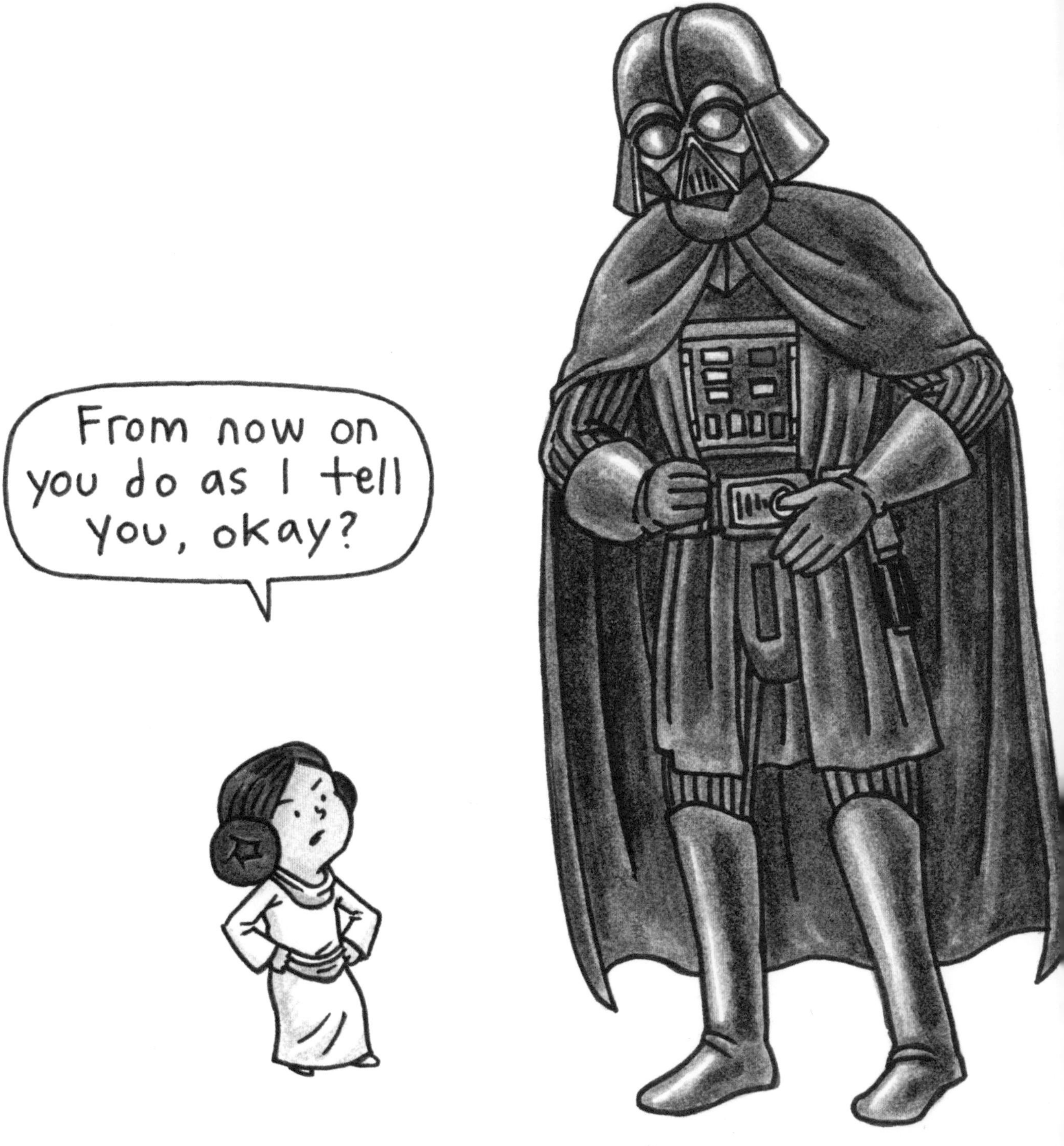
From now on you do as I tell you, okay?

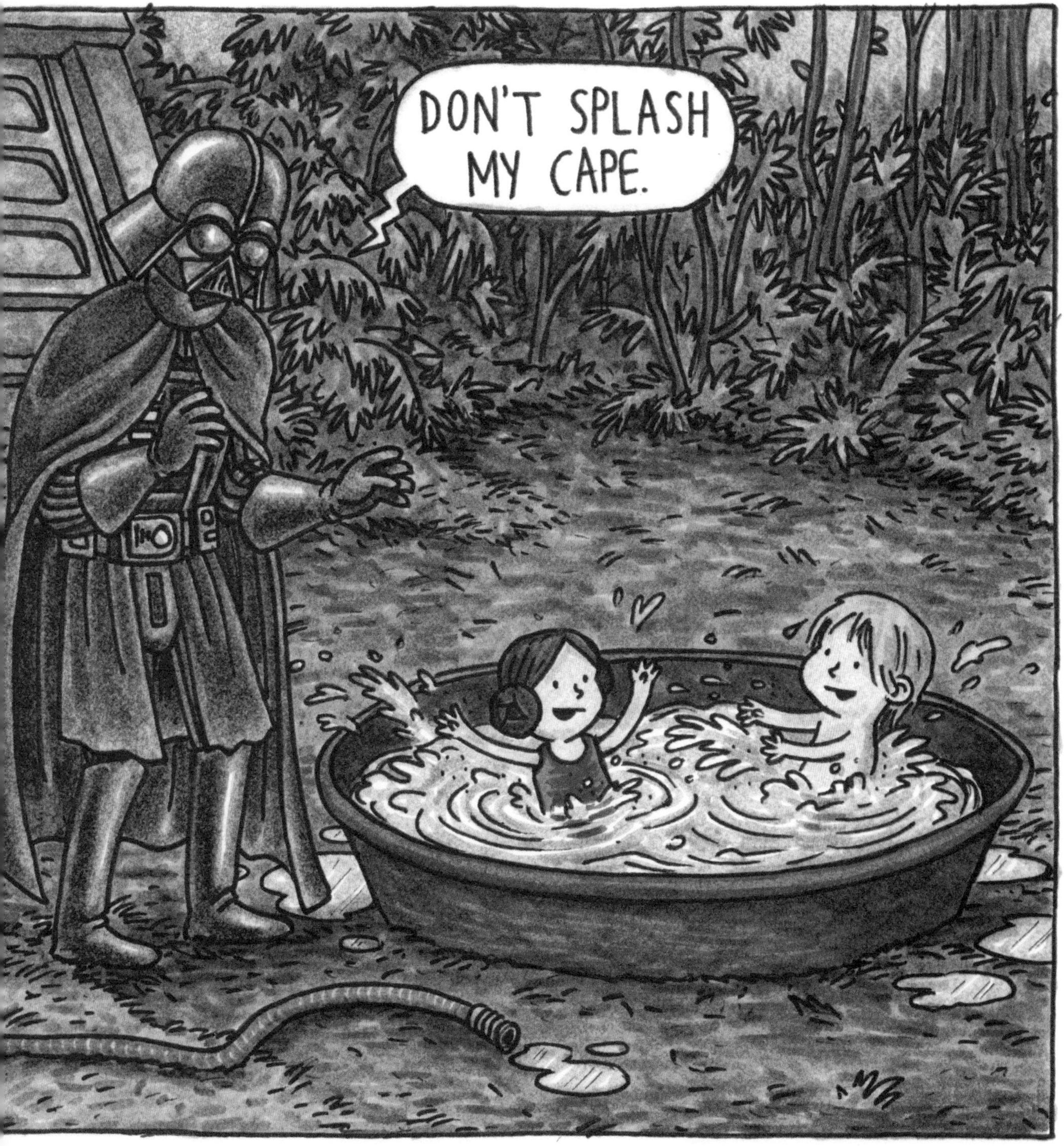
DON'T SPLASH MY CAPE.

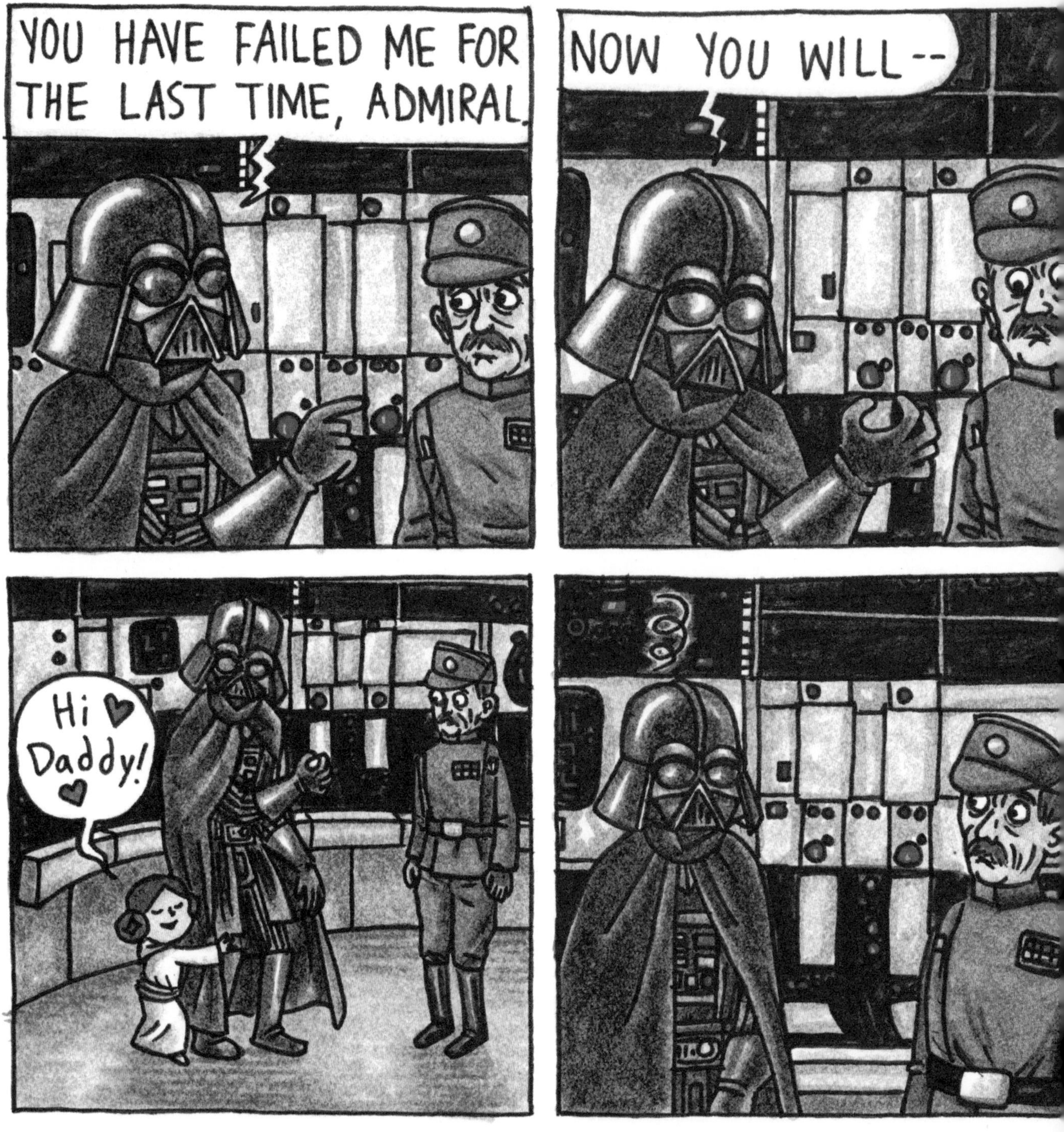
YOU HAVE FAILED ME FOR THE LAST TIME, ADMIRAL.
NOW YOU WILL--
Hi Daddy!

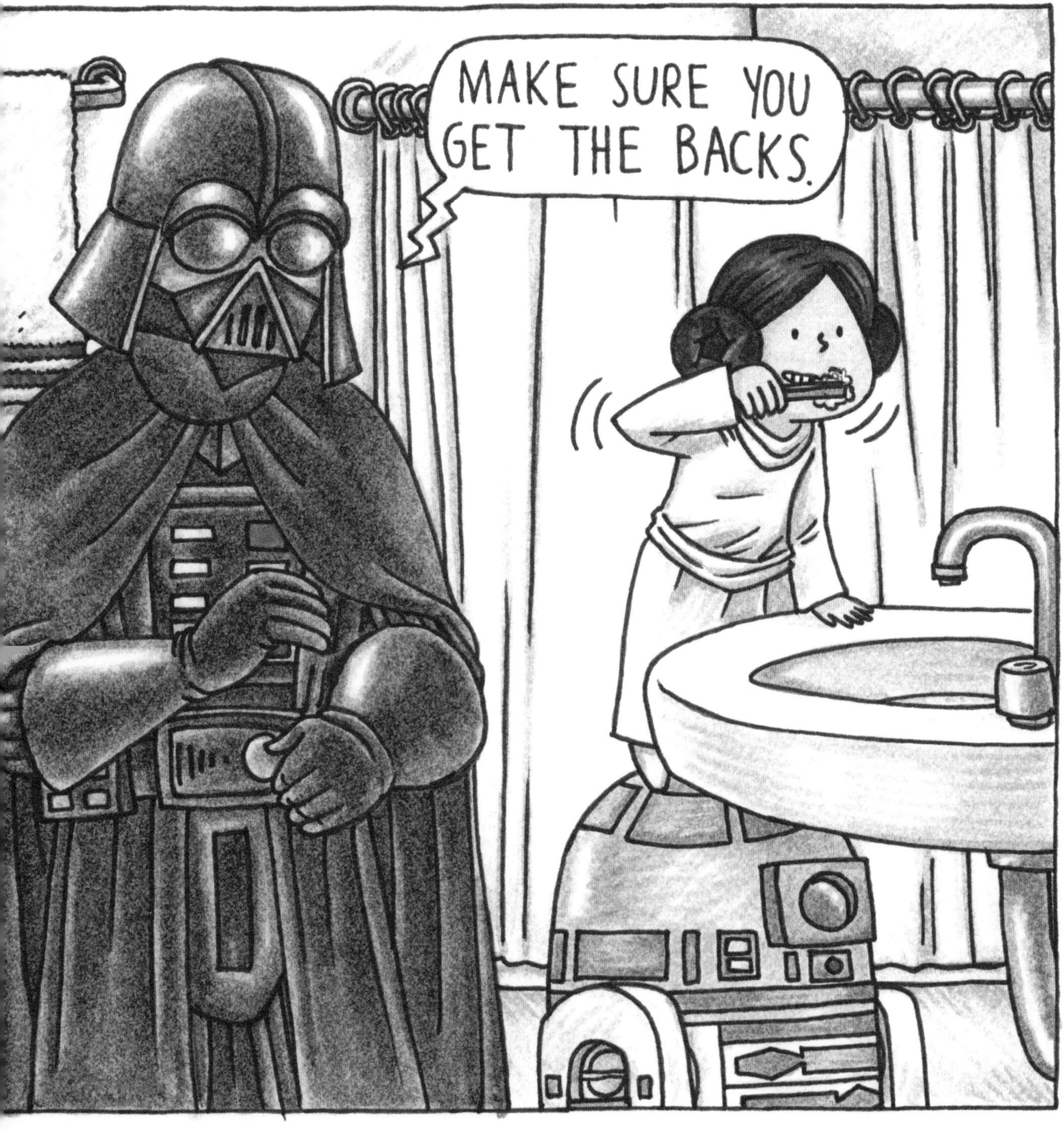
MAKE SURE YOU GET THE BACKS.

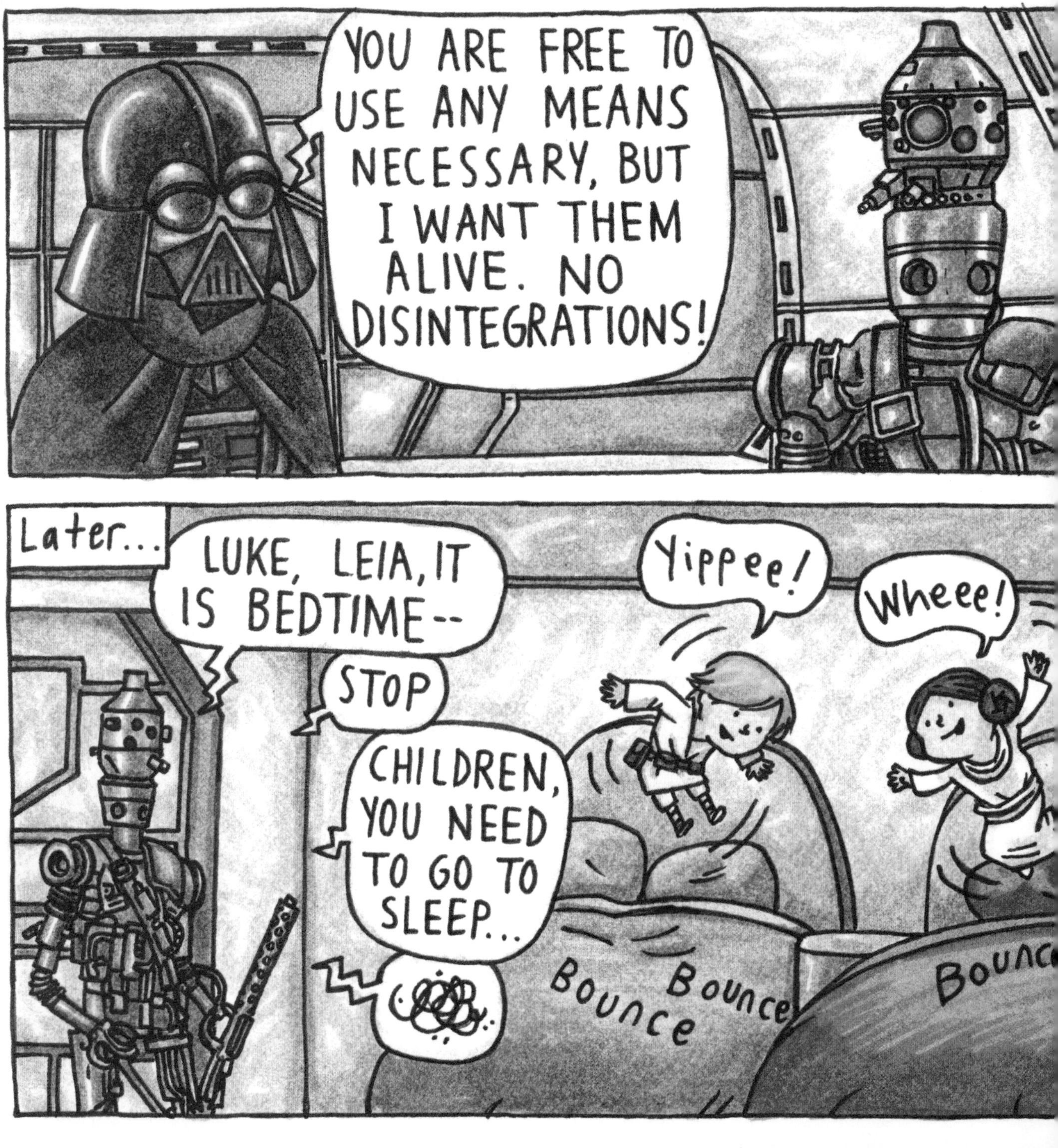
YOU ARE FREE TO USE ANY MEANS NECESSARY, BUT I WANT THEM ALIVE. NO DISINTEGRATIONS!
Later...
LUKE, LEIA, IT IS BEDTIME--
Yippee!
Wheee!
STOP
CHILDREN, YOU NEED TO GO TO SLEEP...
Bounce
Bounce
Bounce

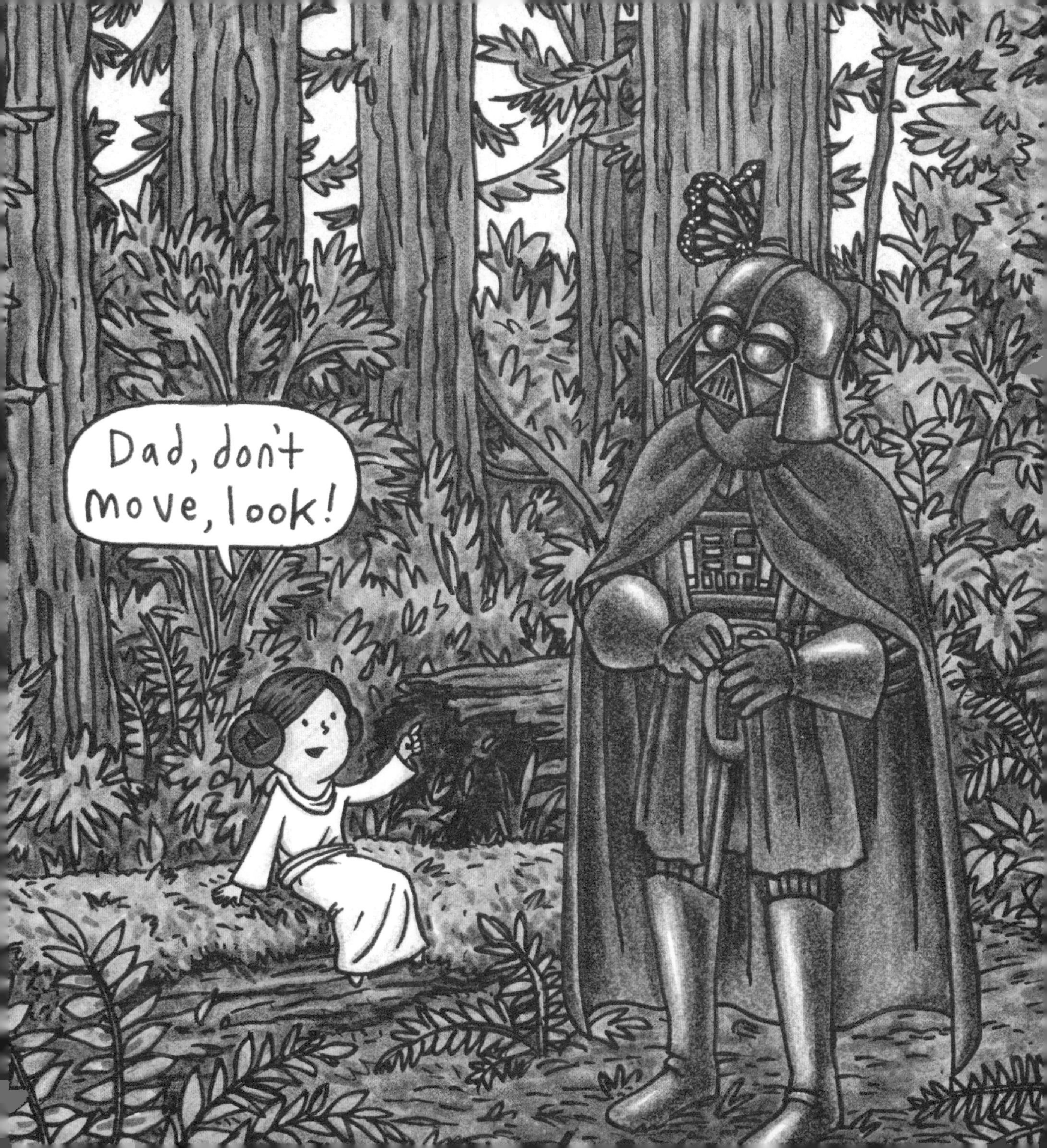
Dad, don't move, look!

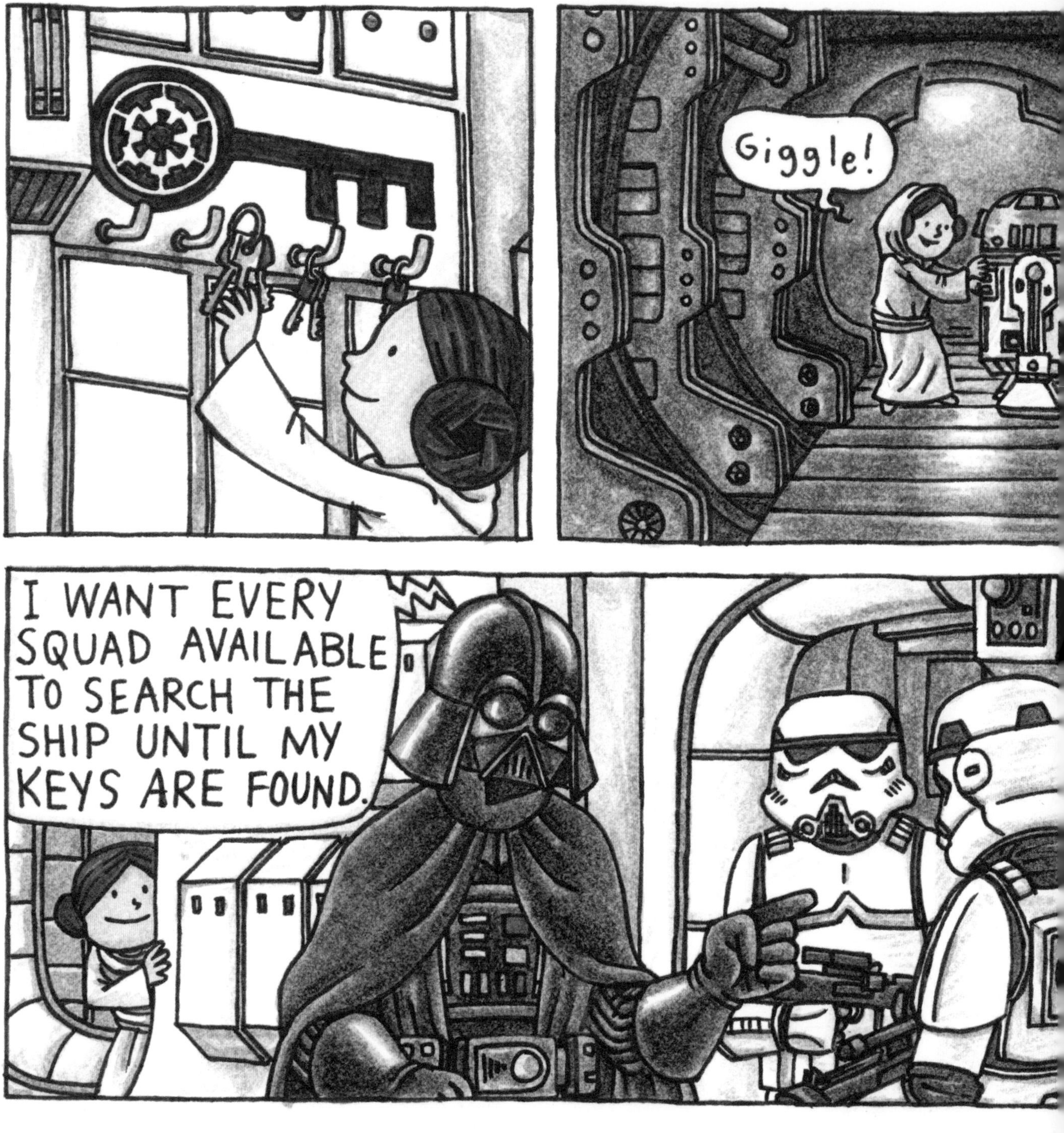
Giggle!
I WANT EVERY SQUAD AVAILABLE TO SEARCH THE SHIP UNTIL MY KEYS ARE FOUND.

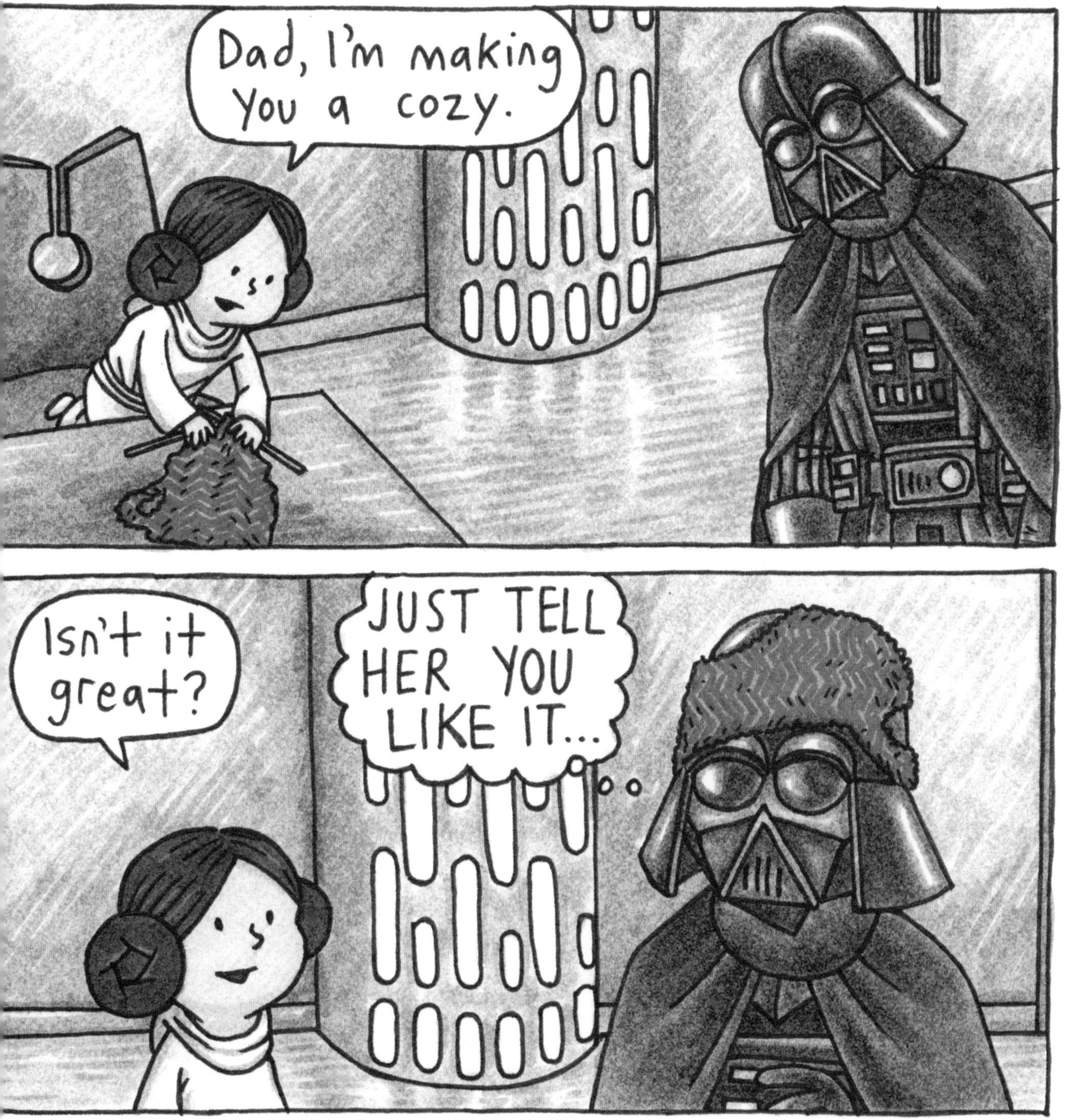
Dad, I'm making you a cozy.
Isn't it great?
JUST TELL HER YOU LIKE IT...

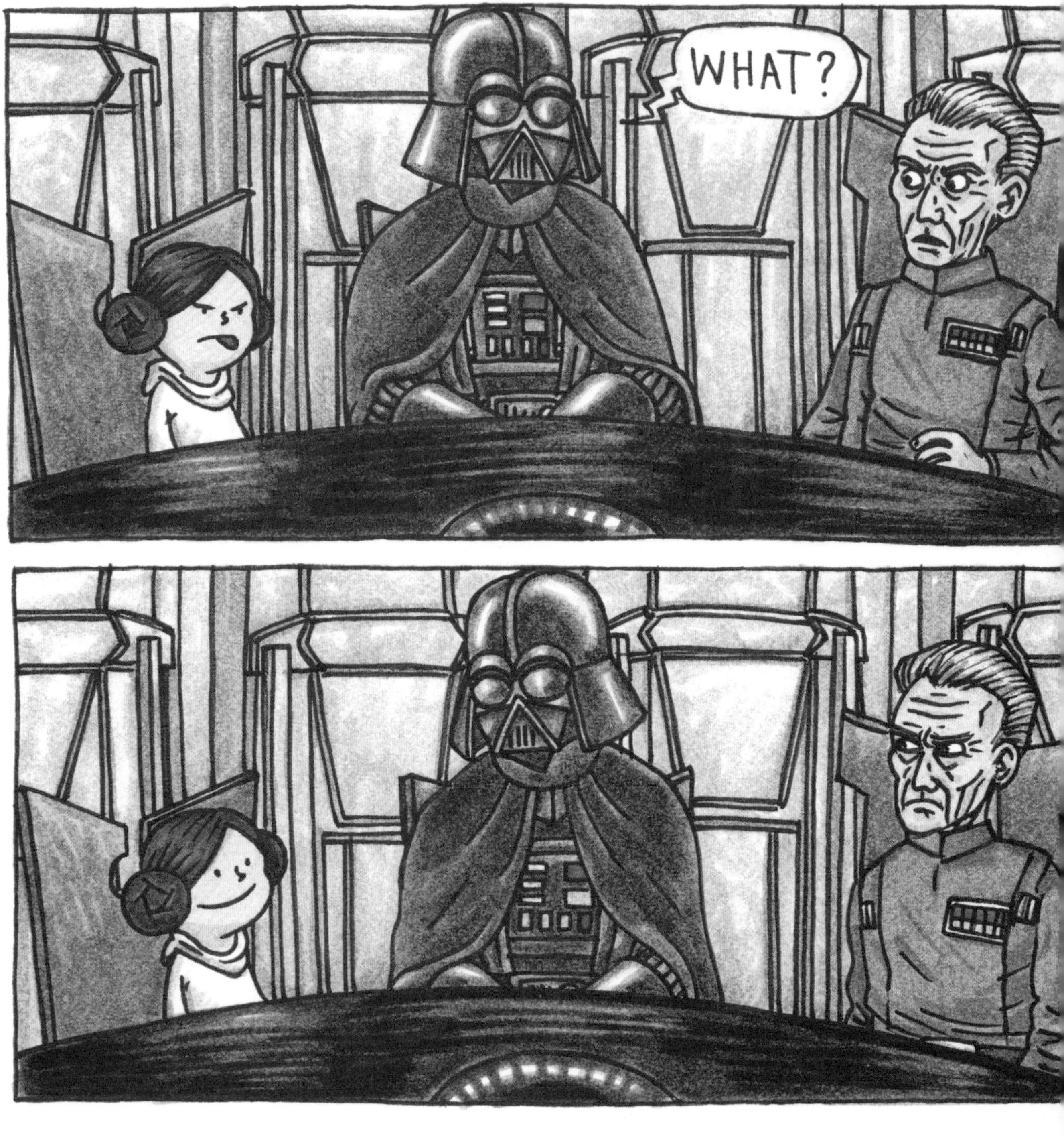
WHAT?

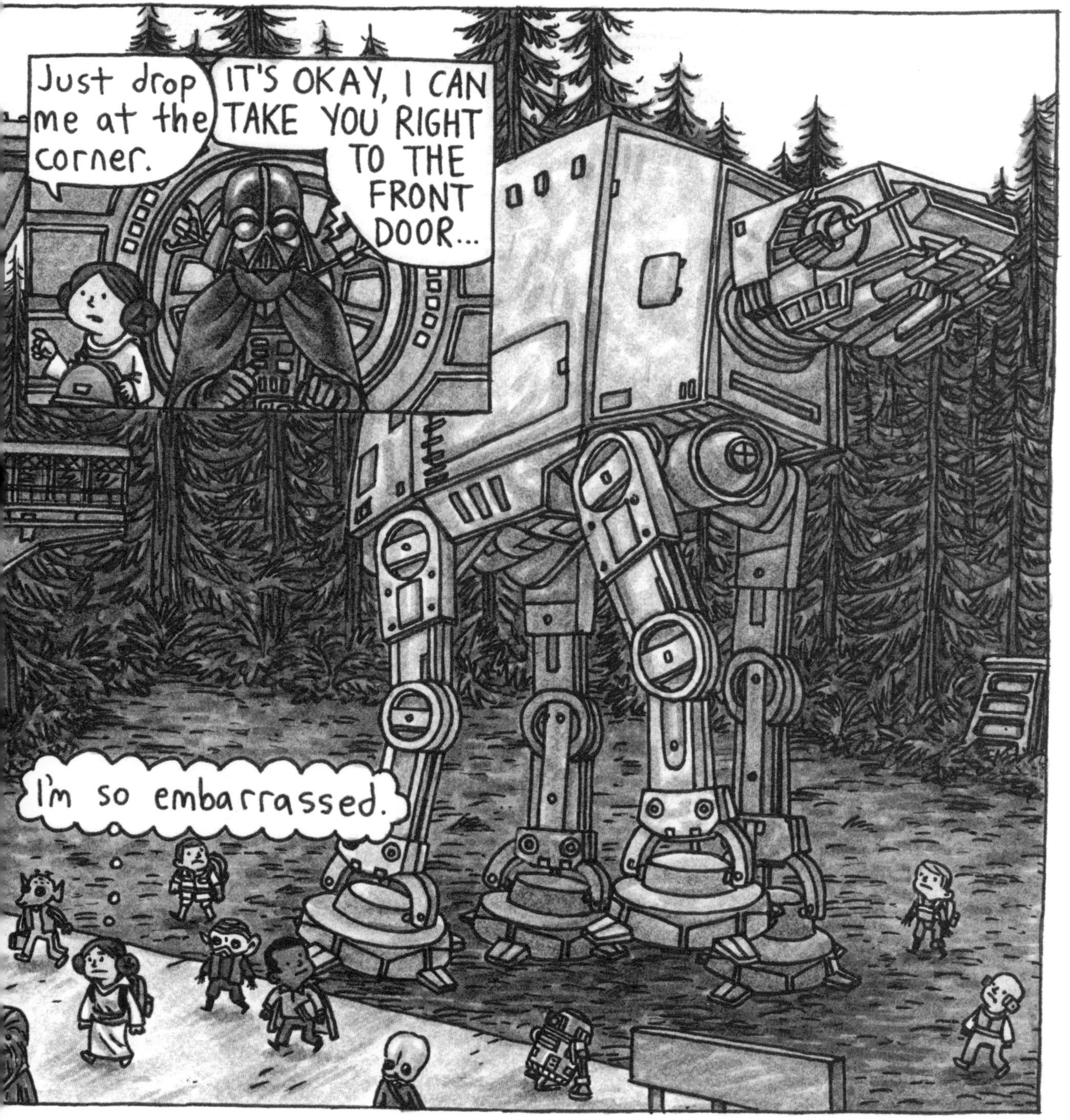

Just drop me at the corner.
IT'S OKAY, I CAN TAKE YOU RIGHT TO THE FRONT DOOR...
I'm so embarrassed.

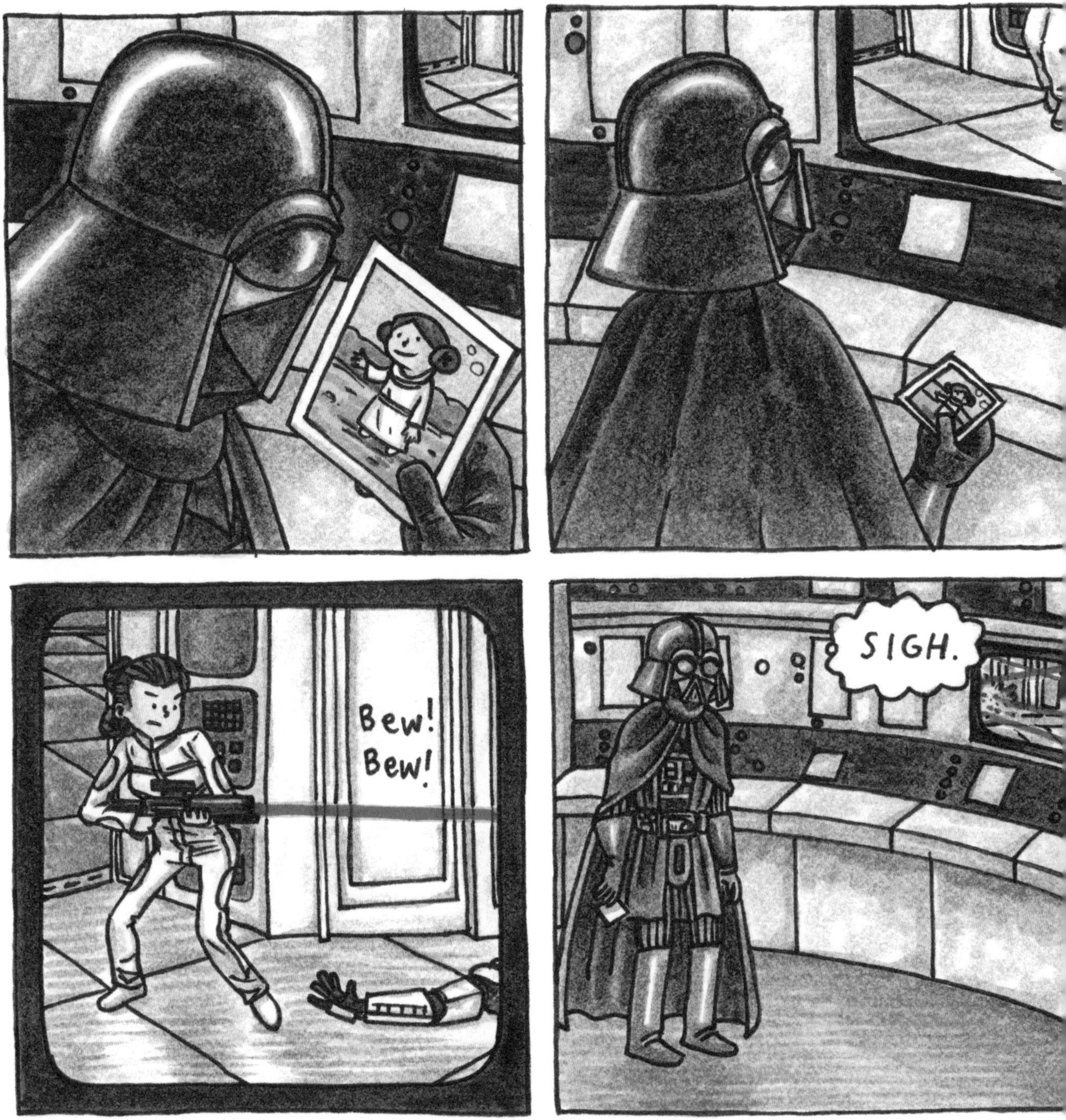
Bew!
Bew!
SIGH.

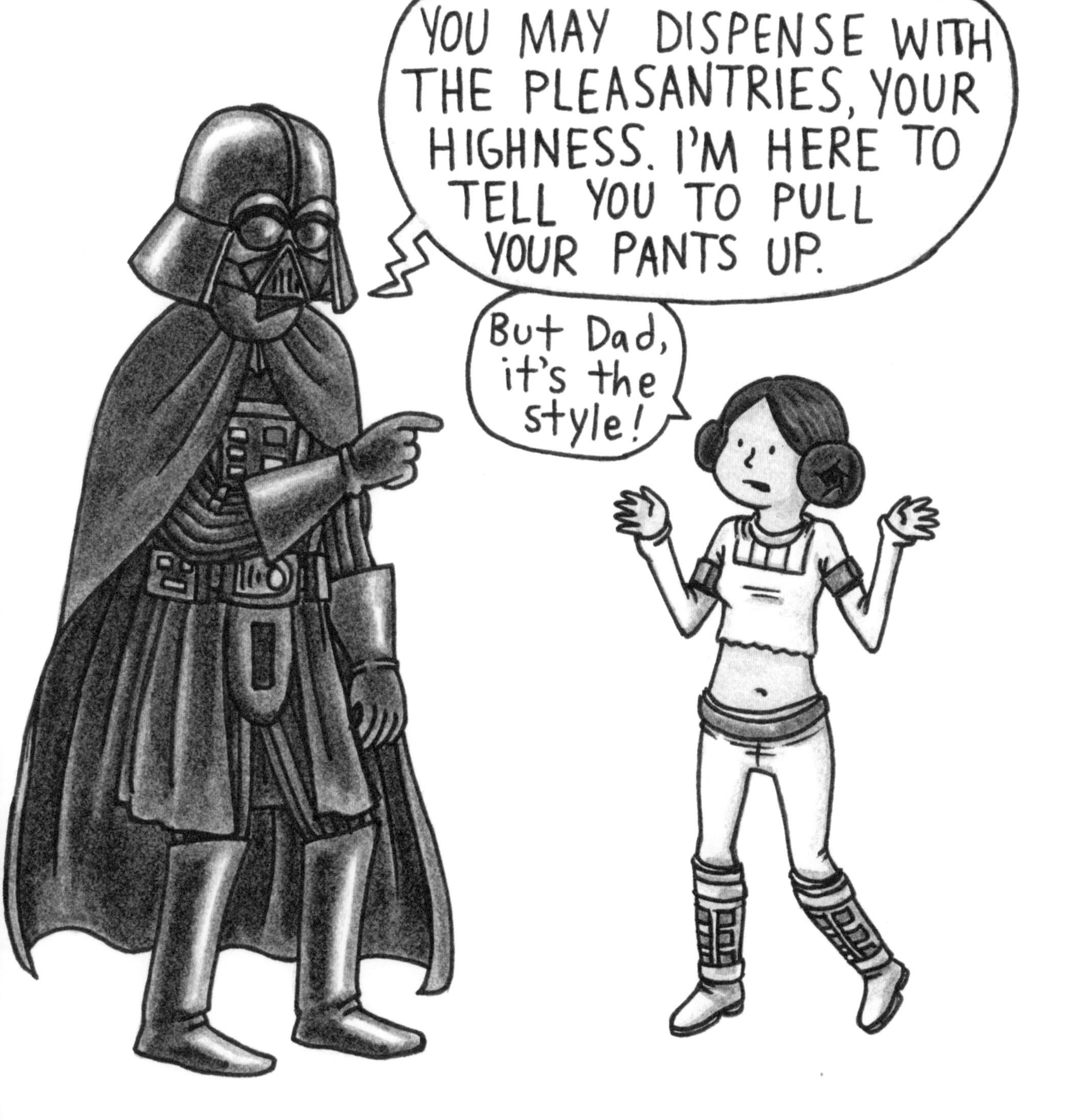
YOU MAY DISPENSE WITH THE PLEASANTRIES, YOUR HIGHNESS. I'M HERE TO TELL YOU TO PULL YOUR PANTS UP.
But Dad, it's the style!

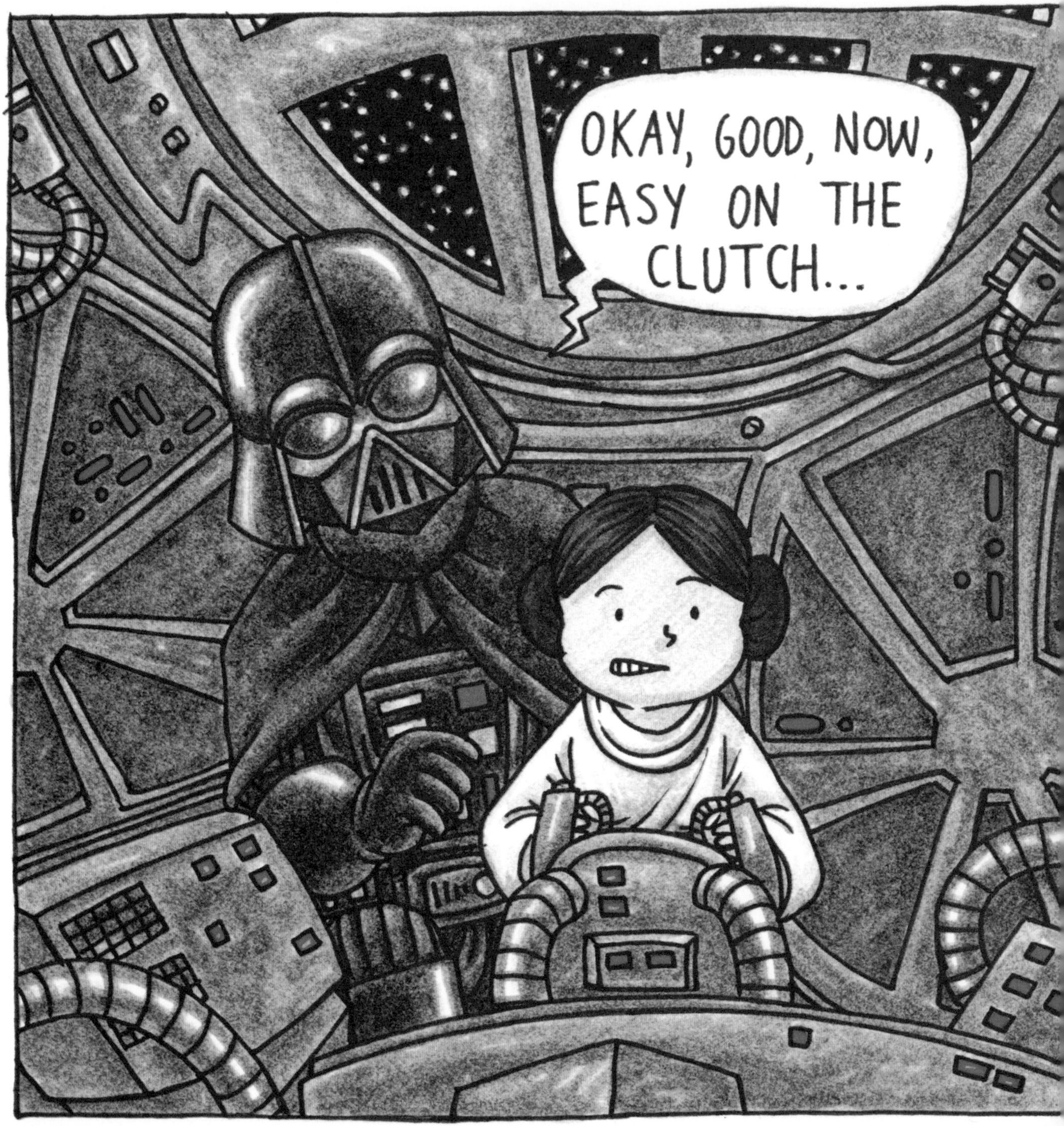
OKAY, GOOD, NOW, EASY ON THE CLUTCH...

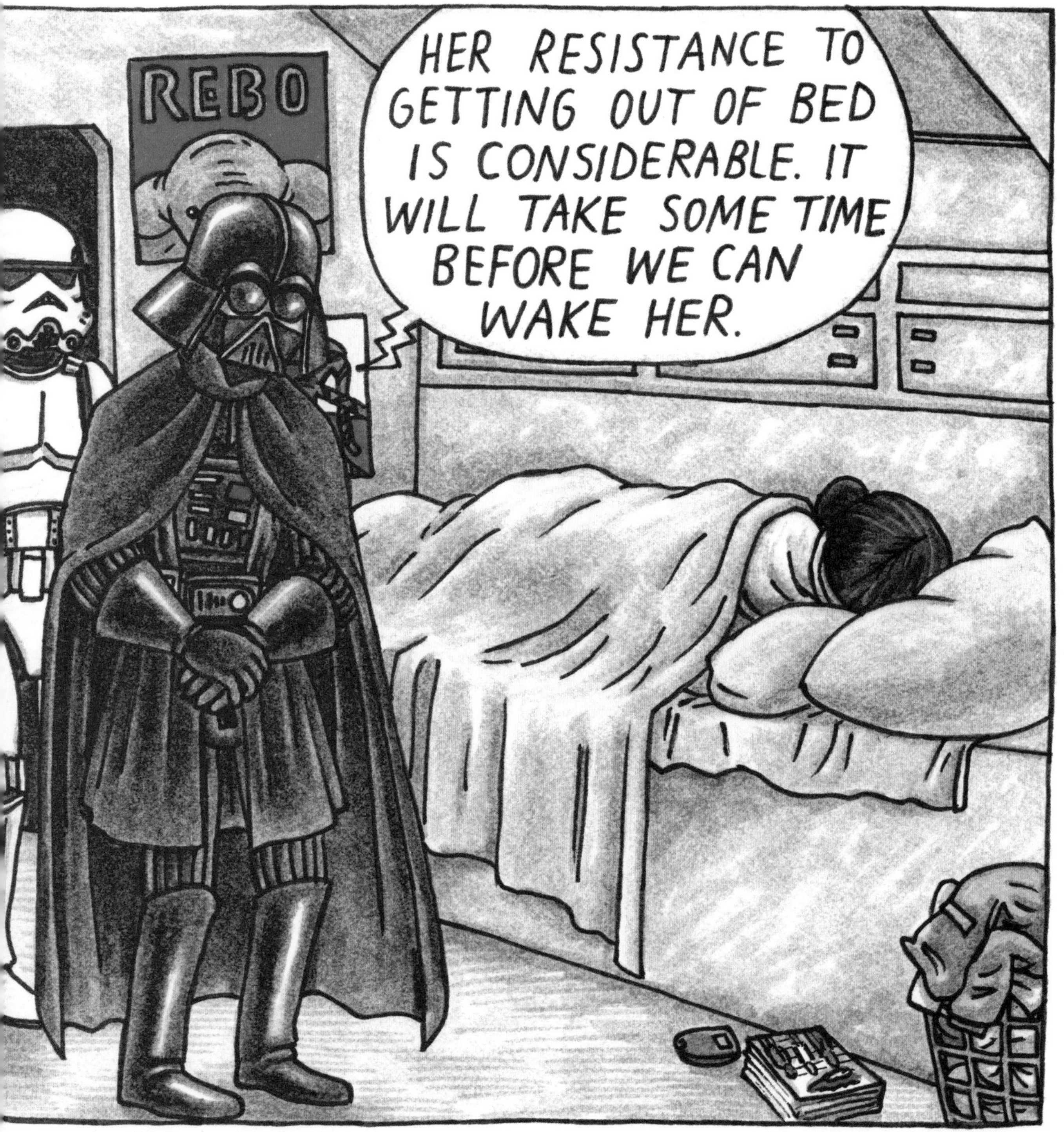
REBO
HER RESISTANCE TO GETTING OUT OF BED IS CONSIDERABLE. IT WILL TAKE SOME TIME BEFORE WE CAN WAKE HER.

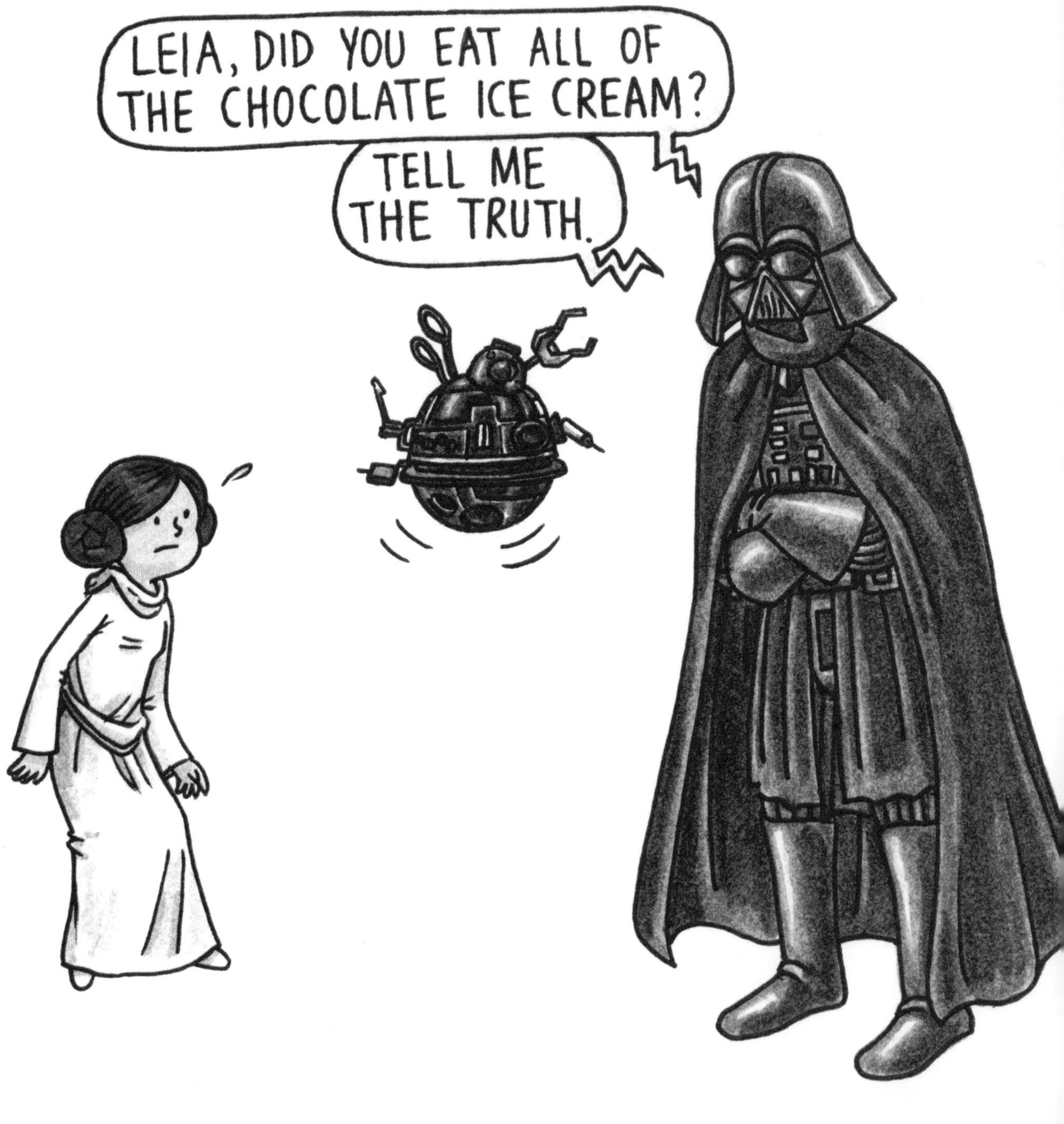
LEIA, DID YOU EAT ALL OF THE CHOCOLATE ICE CREAM?
TELL ME THE TRUTH.

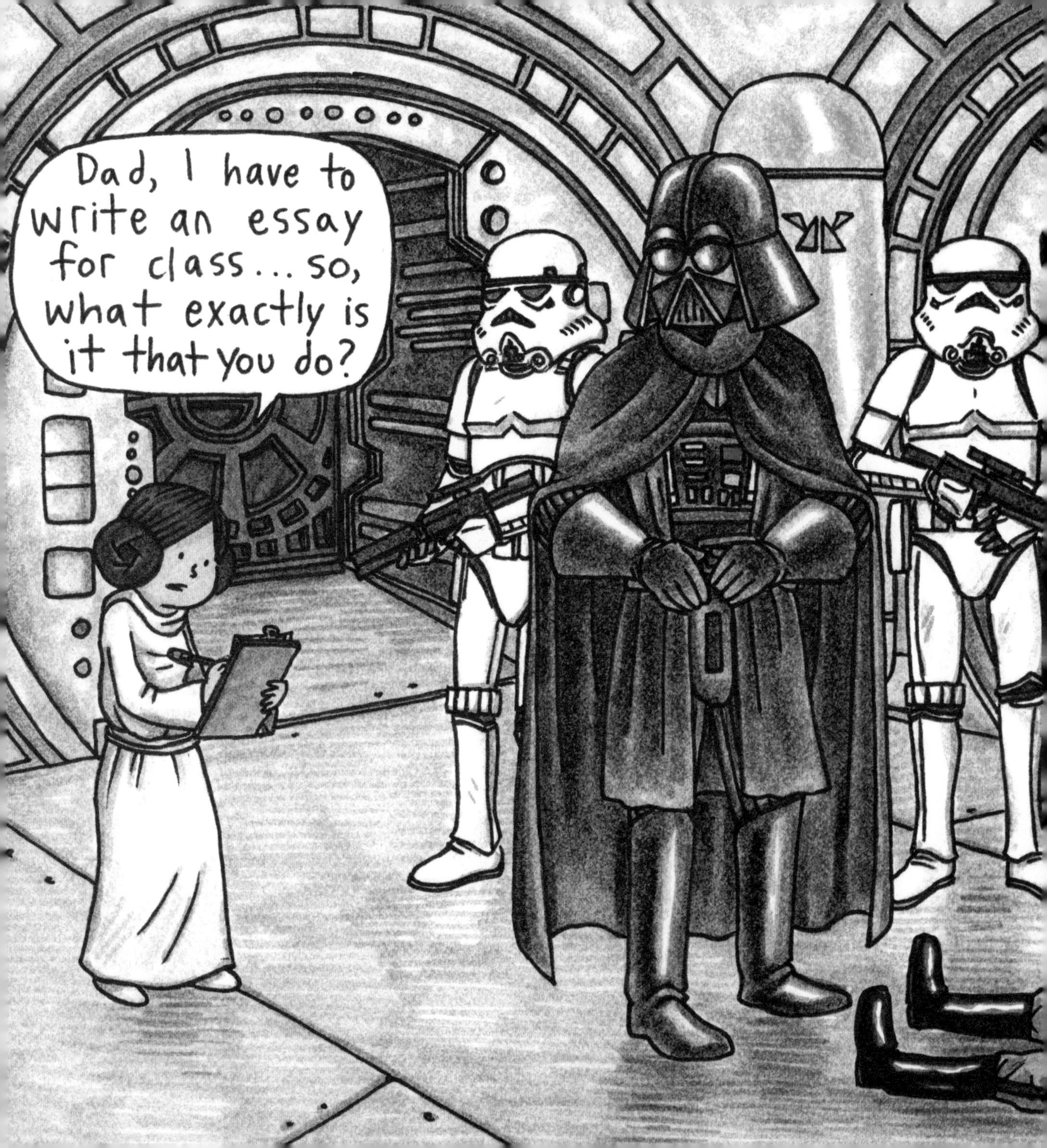
Dad, I have to write an essay for class... so, what exactly is it that you do?

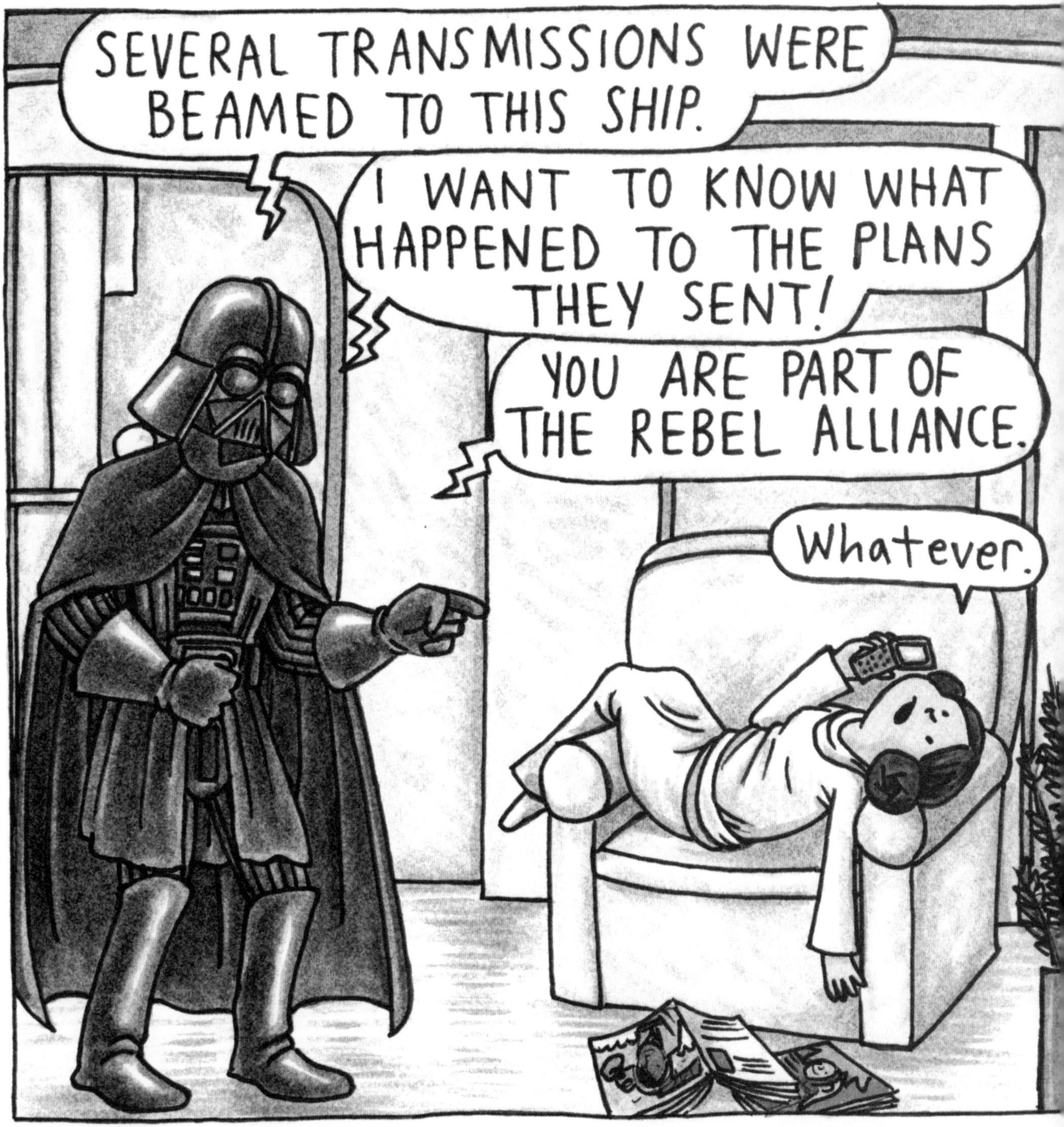
SEVERAL TRANSMISSIONS WERE BEAMED TO THIS SHIP.
I WANT TO KNOW WHAT HAPPENED TO THE PLANS THEY SENT!
YOU ARE PART OF THE REBEL ALLIANCE.
Whatever.

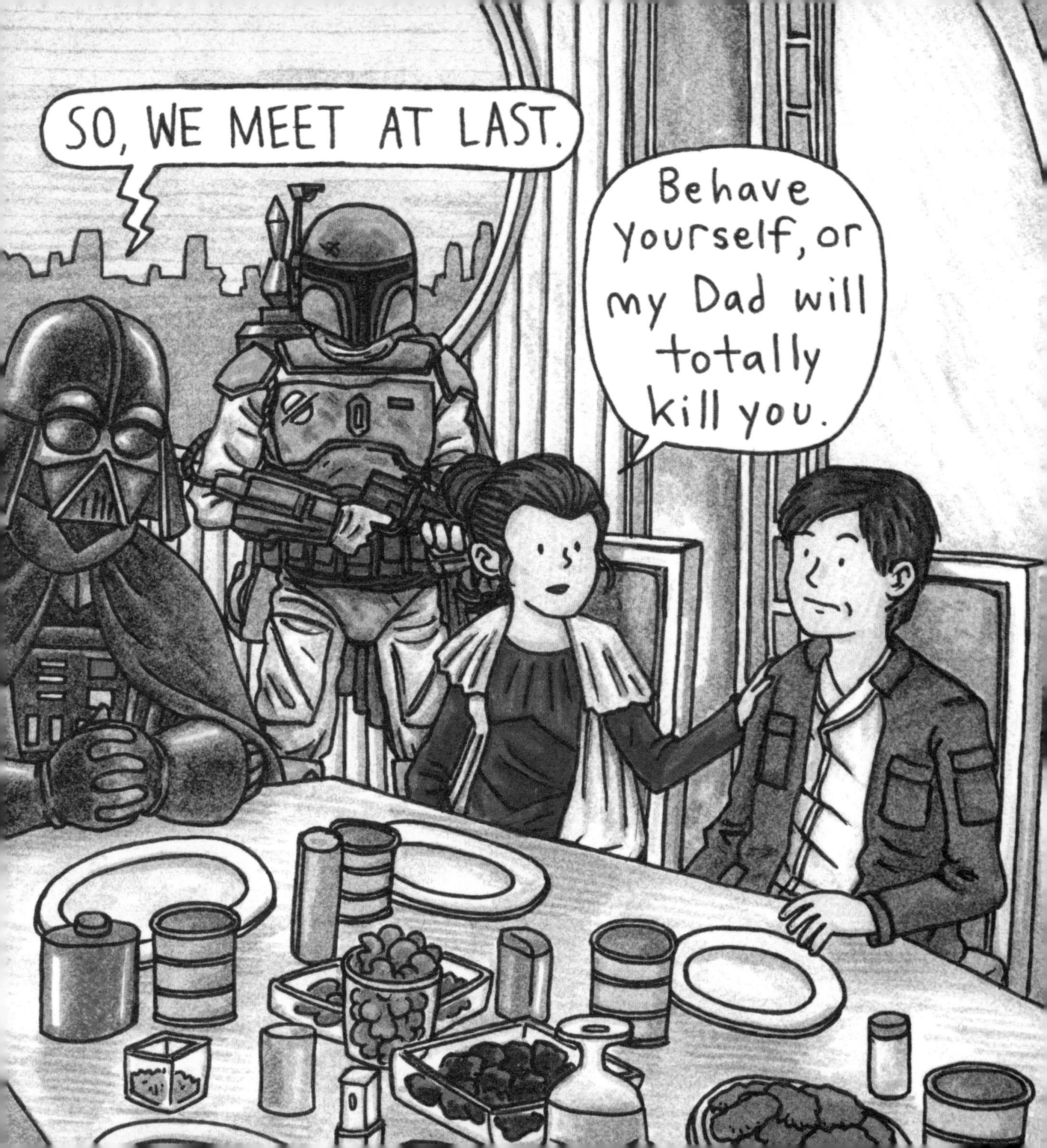
SO, WE MEET AT LAST.
Behave yourself, or my Dad will totally kill you.

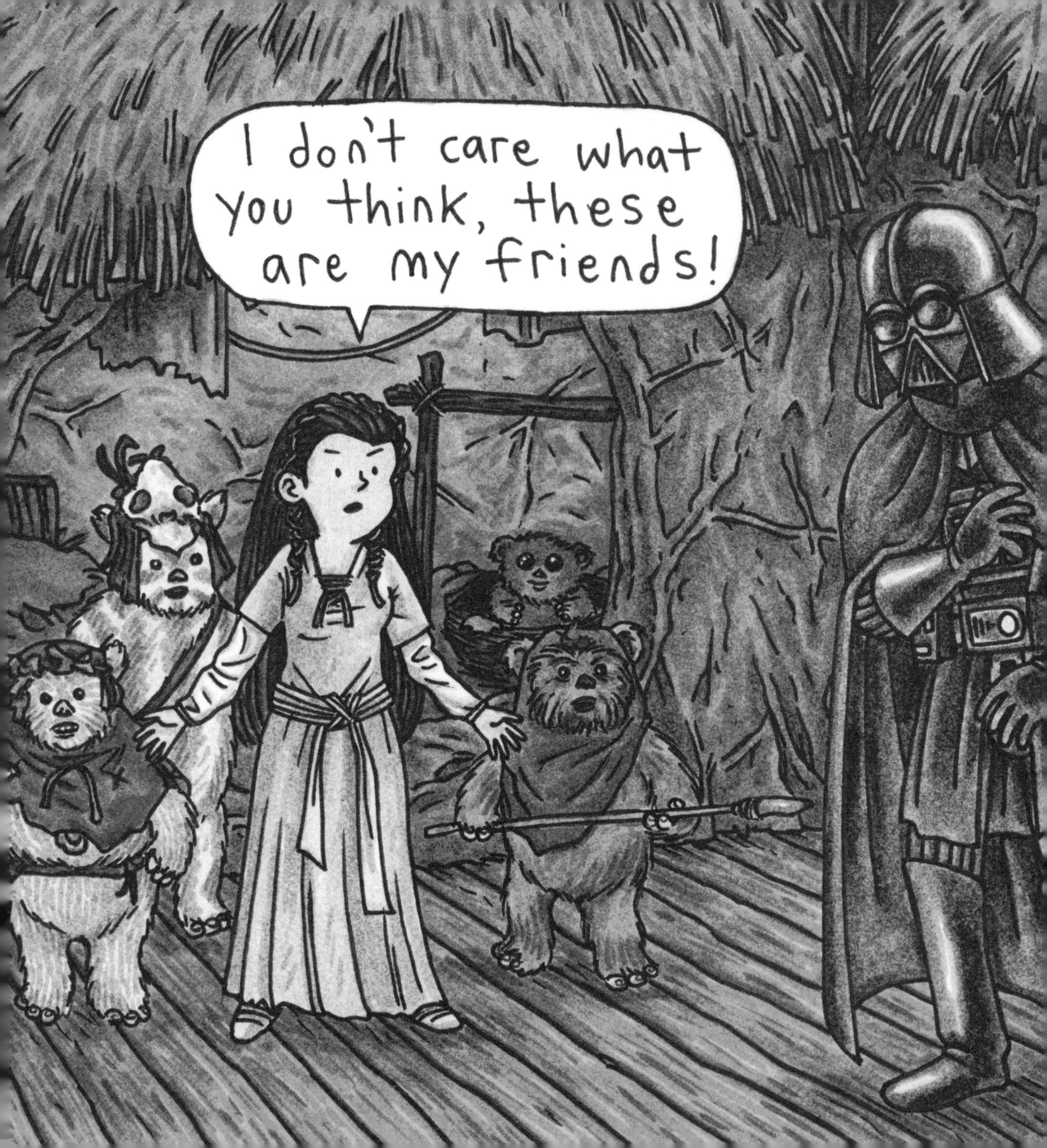
I don't care what you think, these are my friends!

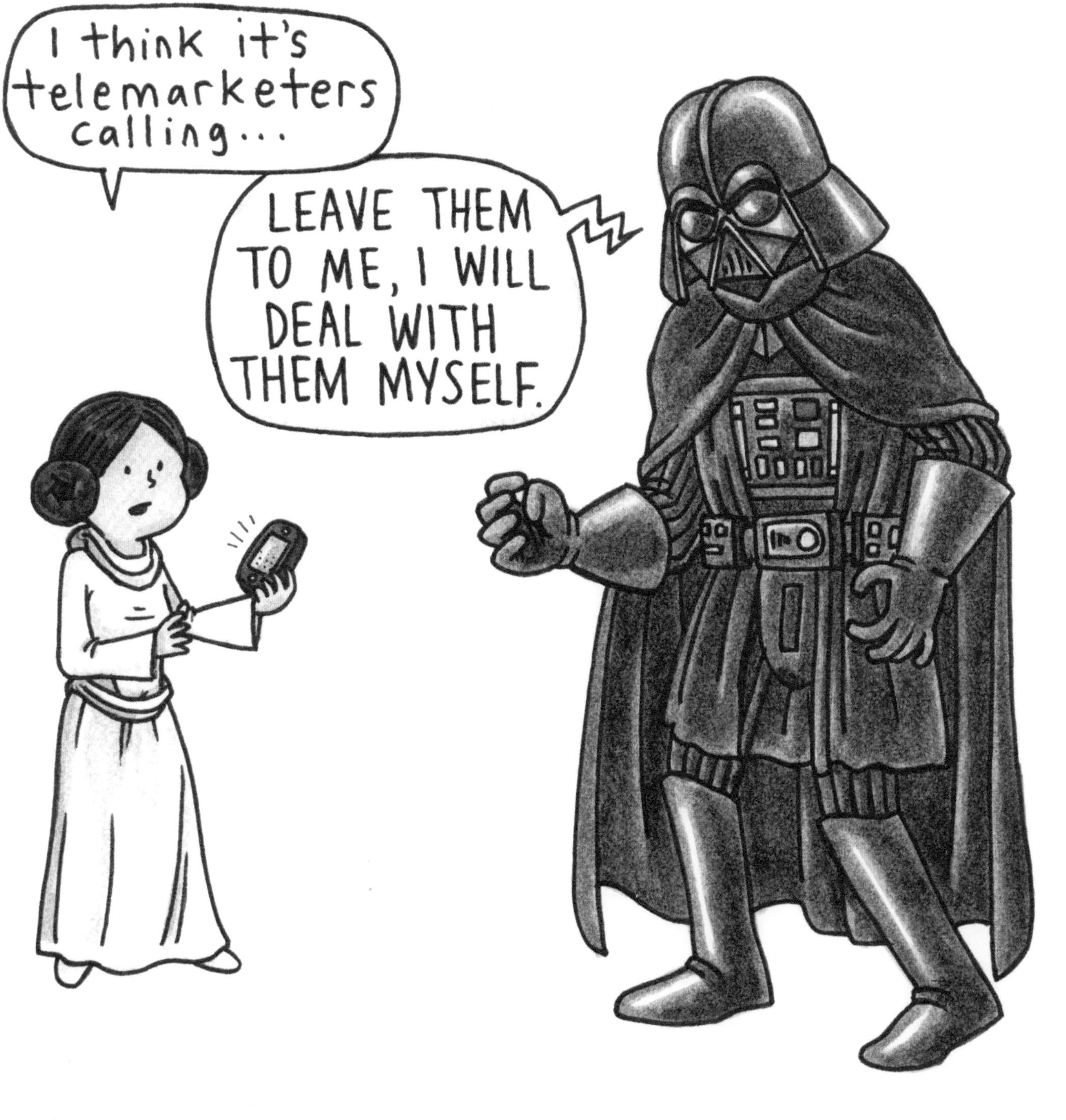
I think it's telemarketers calling...
LEAVE THEM TO ME, I WILL DEAL WITH THEM MYSELF.

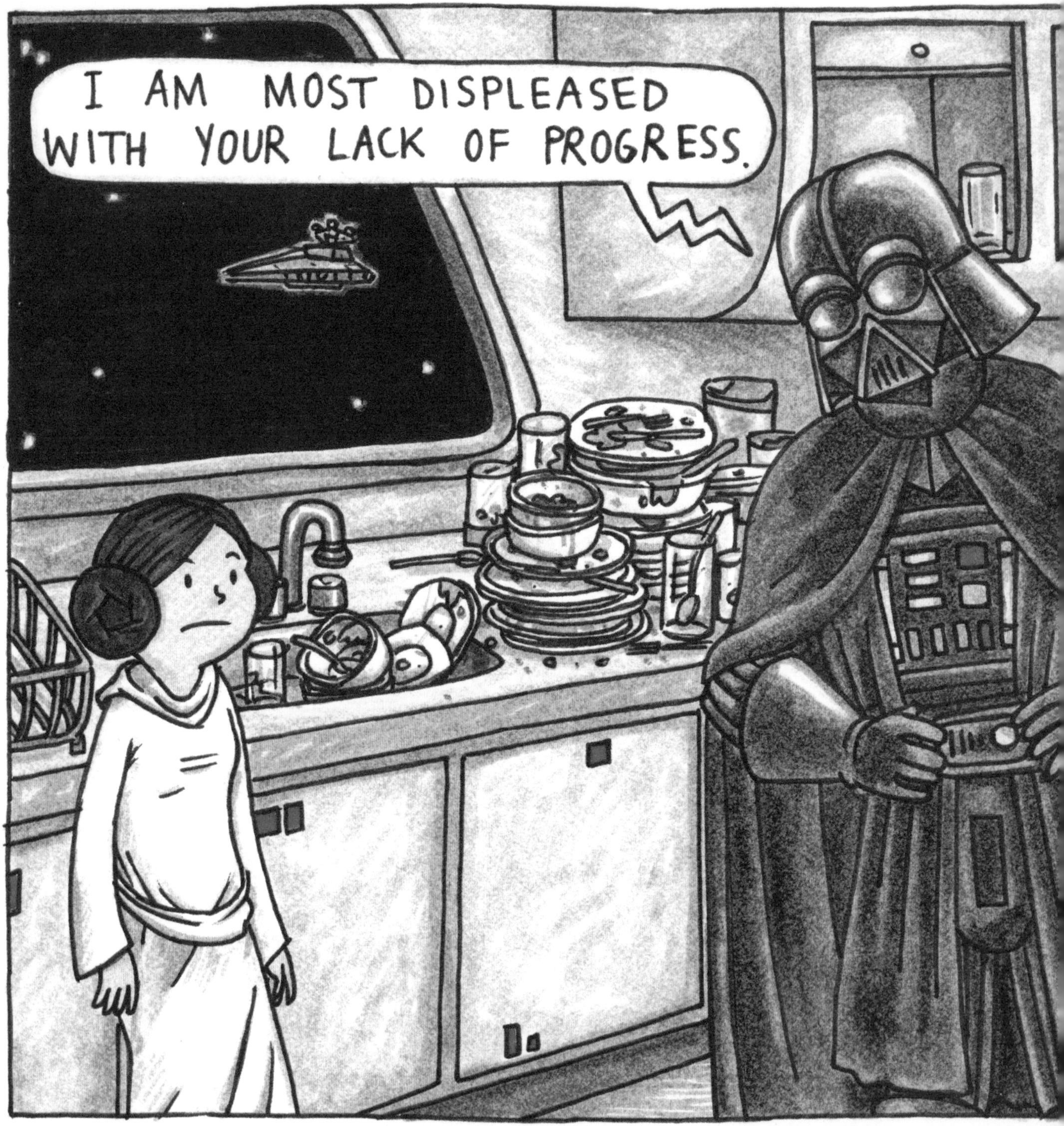
I AM MOST DISPLEASED WITH YOUR LACK OF PROGRESS.

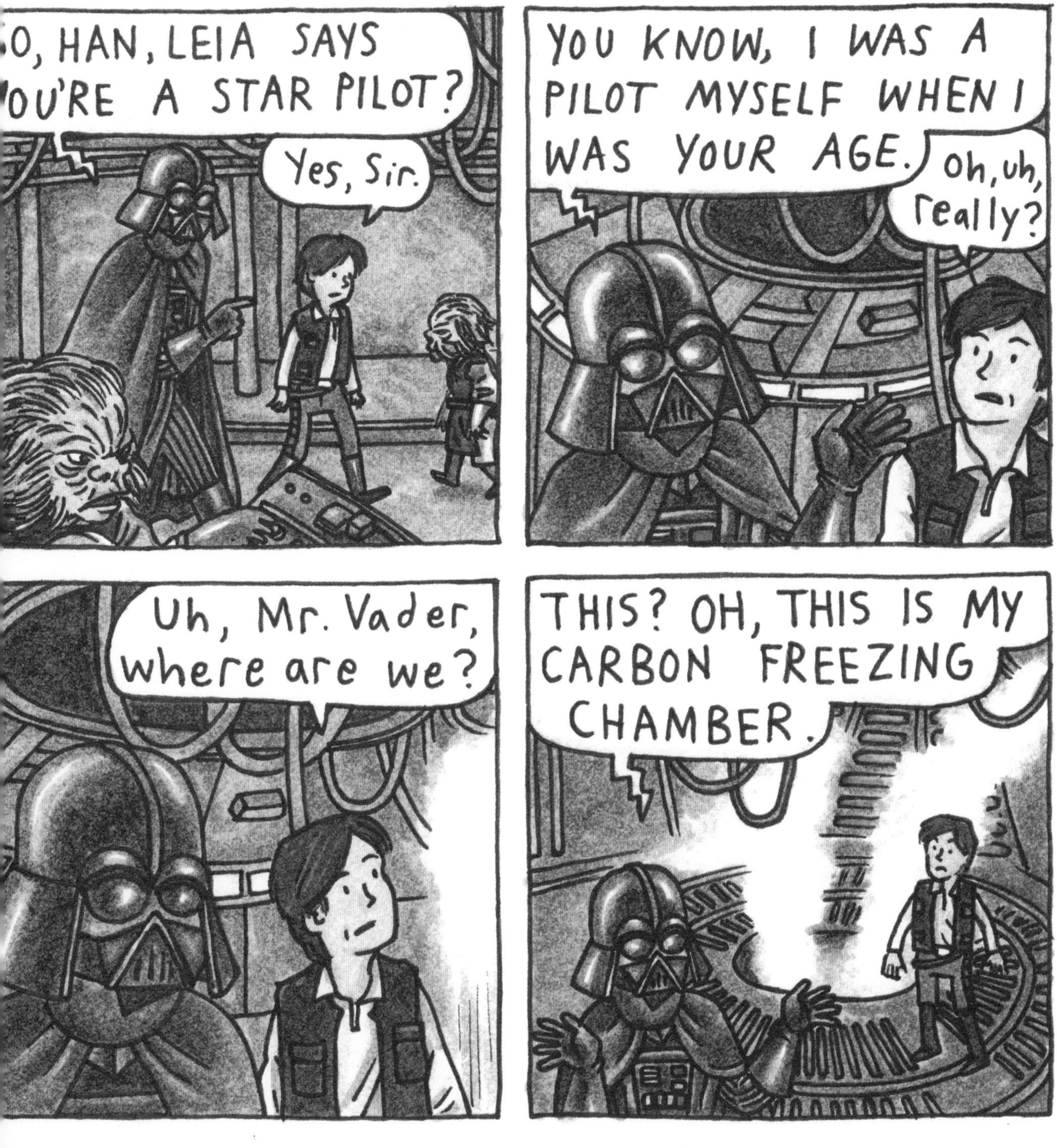
O, HAN, LEIA SAYS OU'RE A STAR PILOT?
Yes, Sir.
YOU KNOW, I WAS A PILOT MYSELF WHEN I WAS YOUR AGE.
Oh, uh, really?
Uh, Mr. Vader, where are we?
THIS? OH, THIS IS MY CARBON FREEZING CHAMBER.

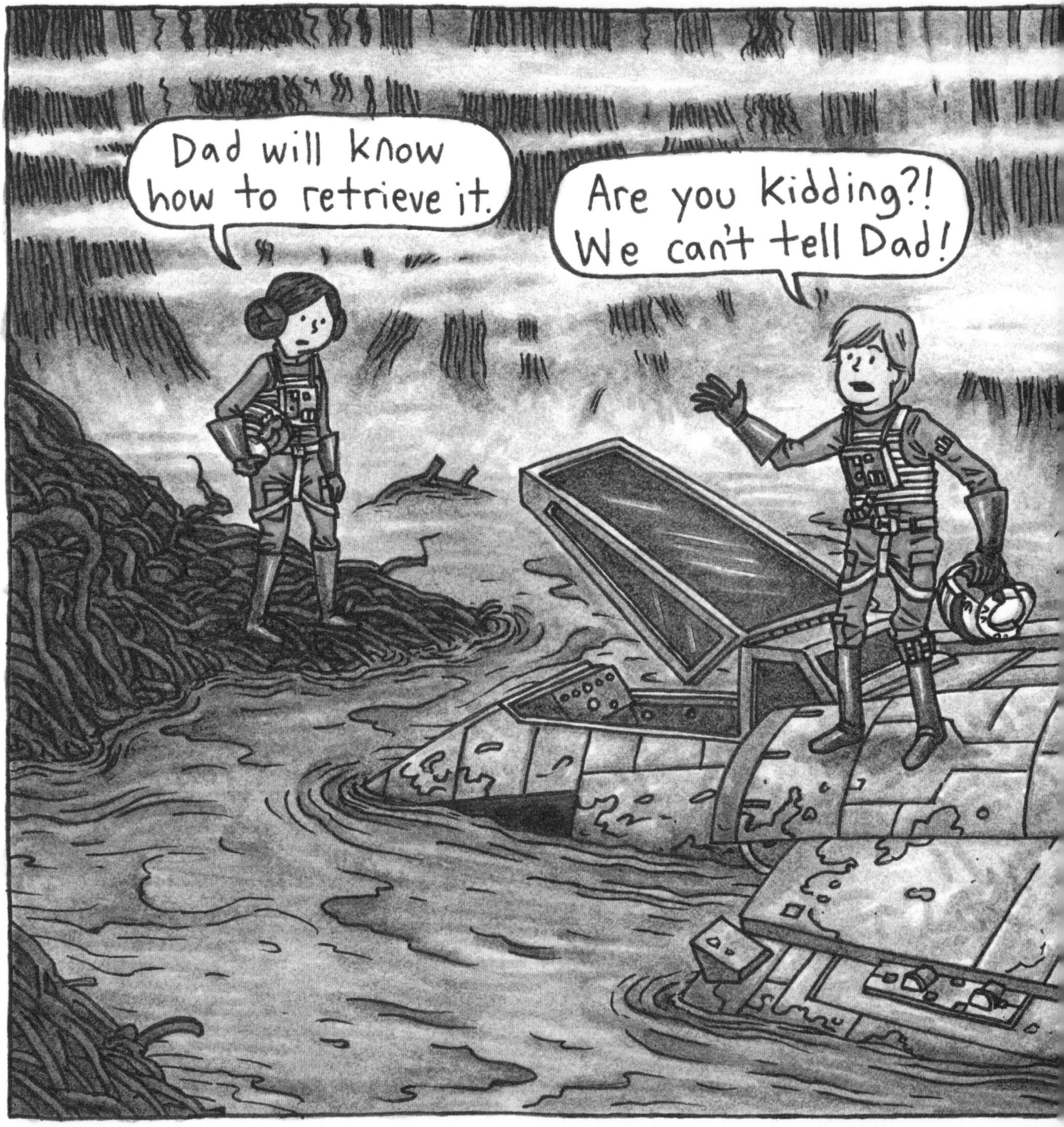
Dad will know how to retrieve it.
Are you kidding?! We can't tell Dad!

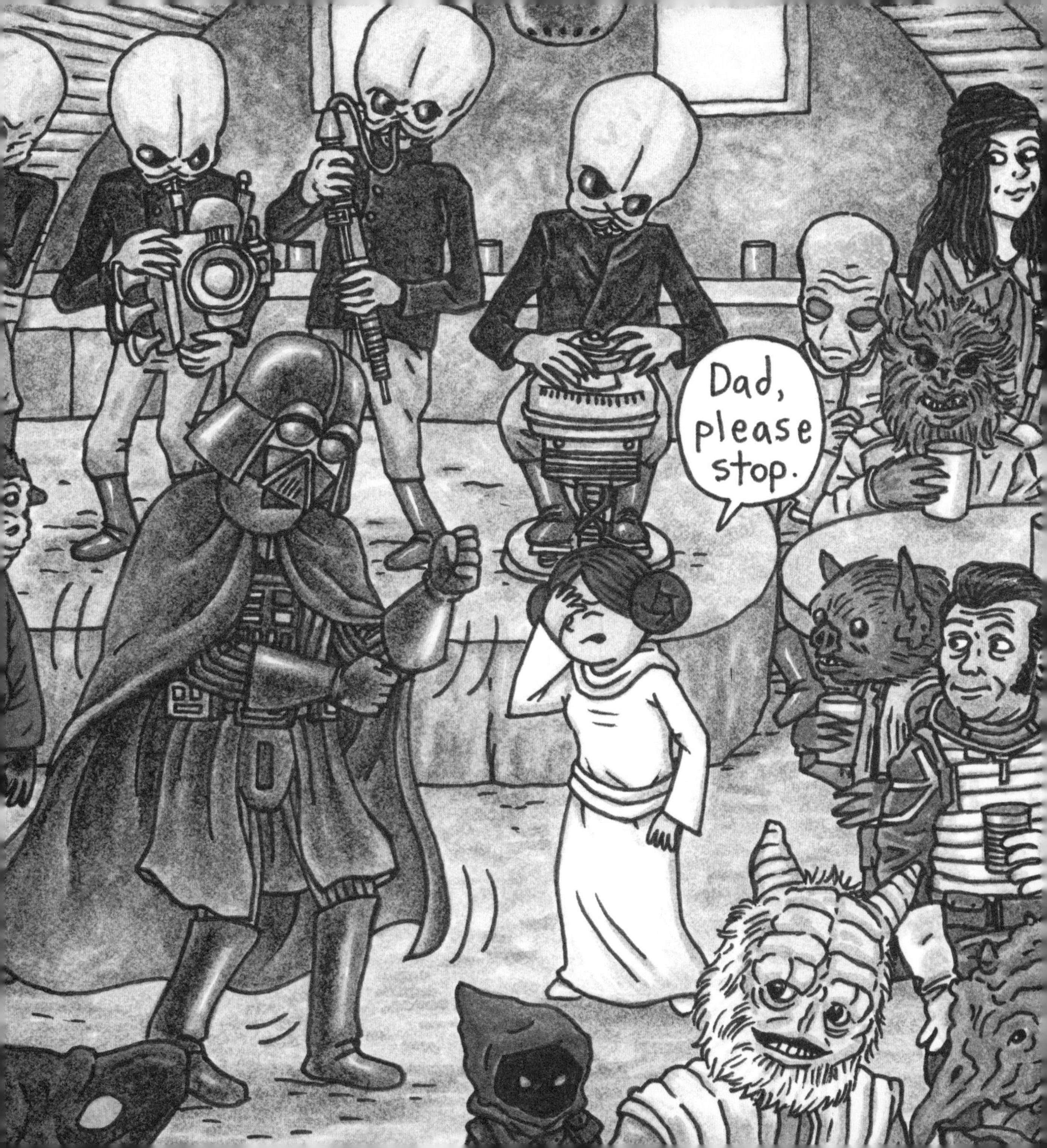
Dad, please stop.

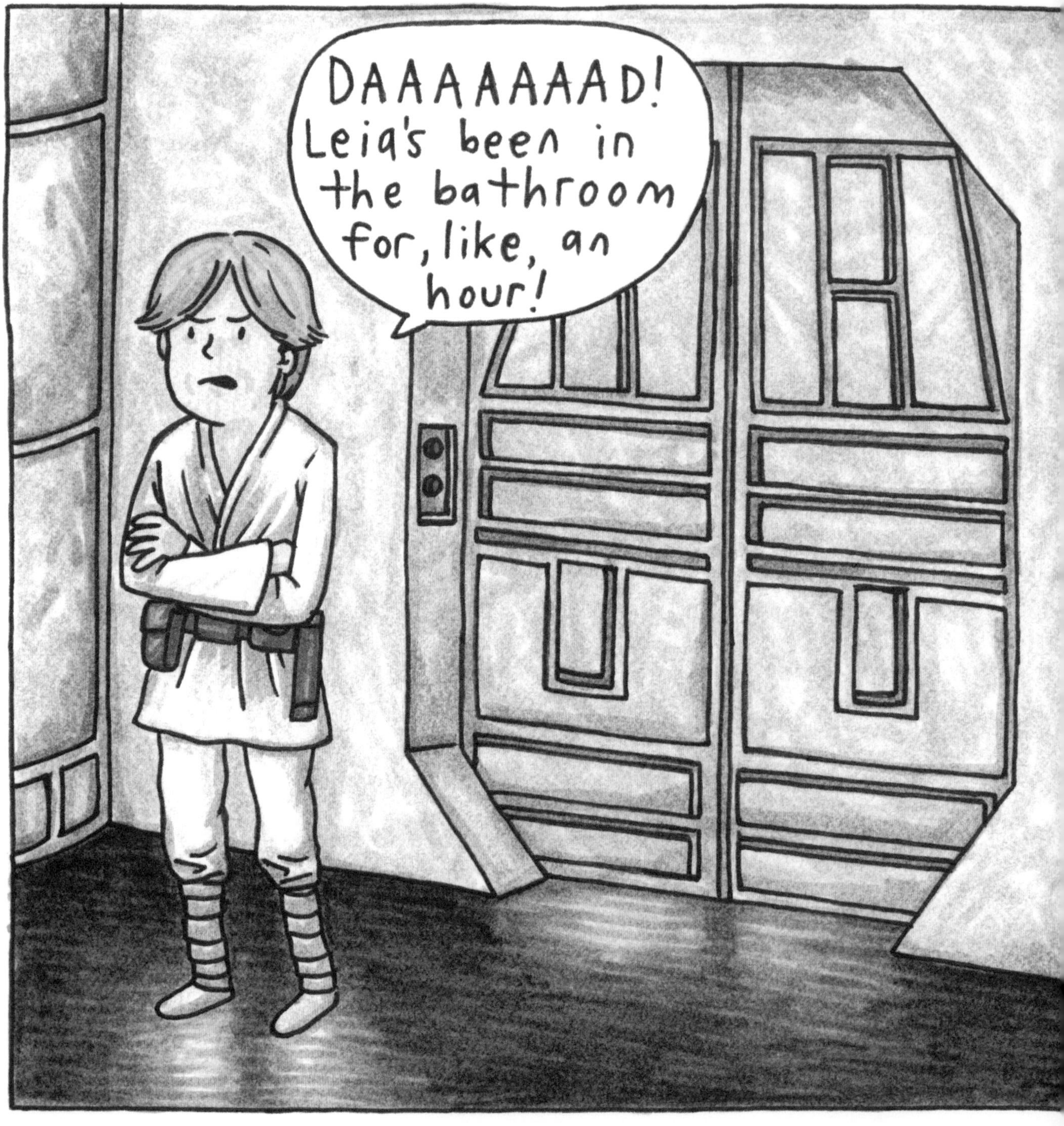
DAAAAAAAD! Leia's been in the bathroom for, like, an hour!

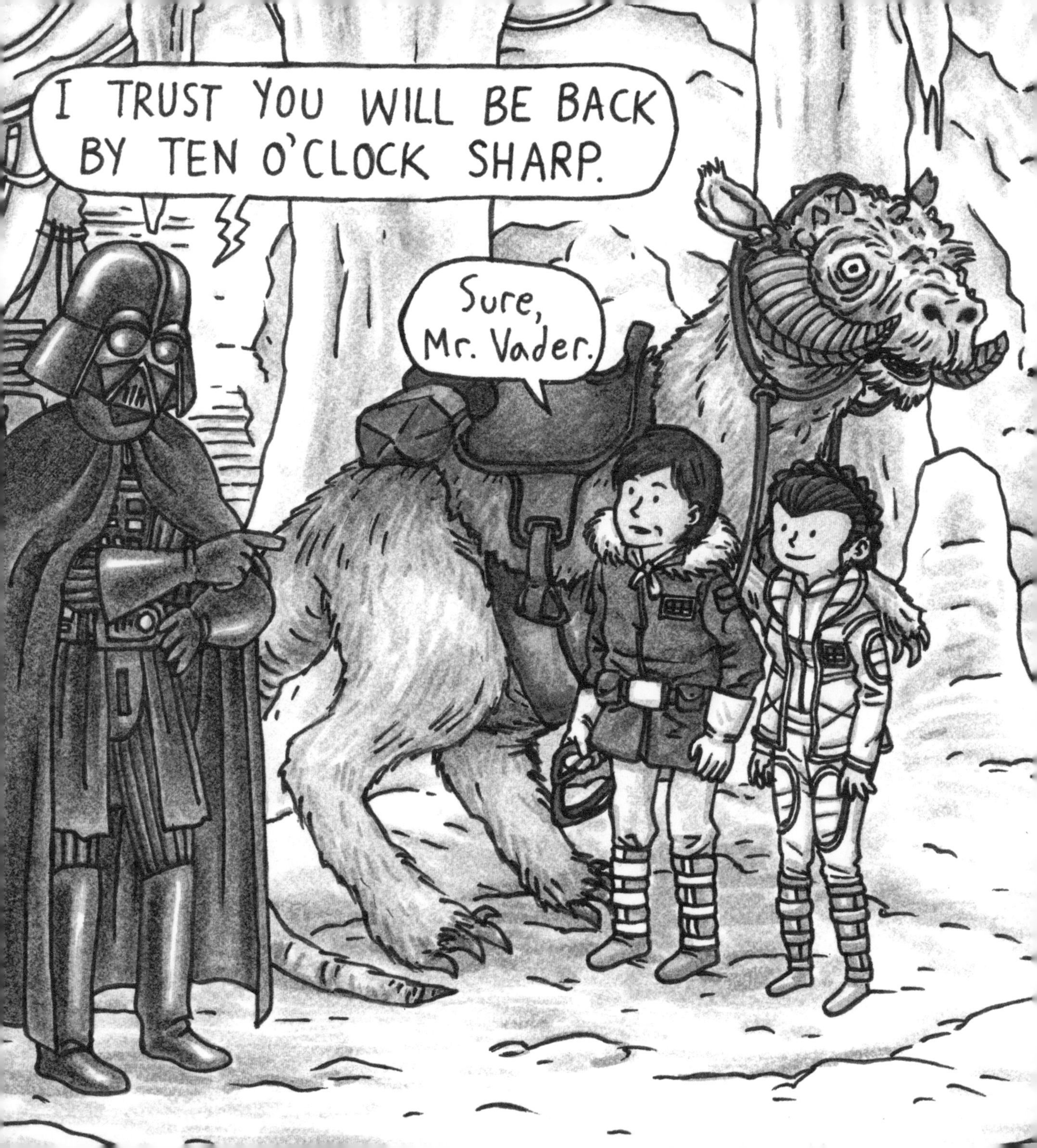
I TRUST YOU WILL BE BACK BY TEN O'CLOCK SHARP.
Sure, Mr. Vader.

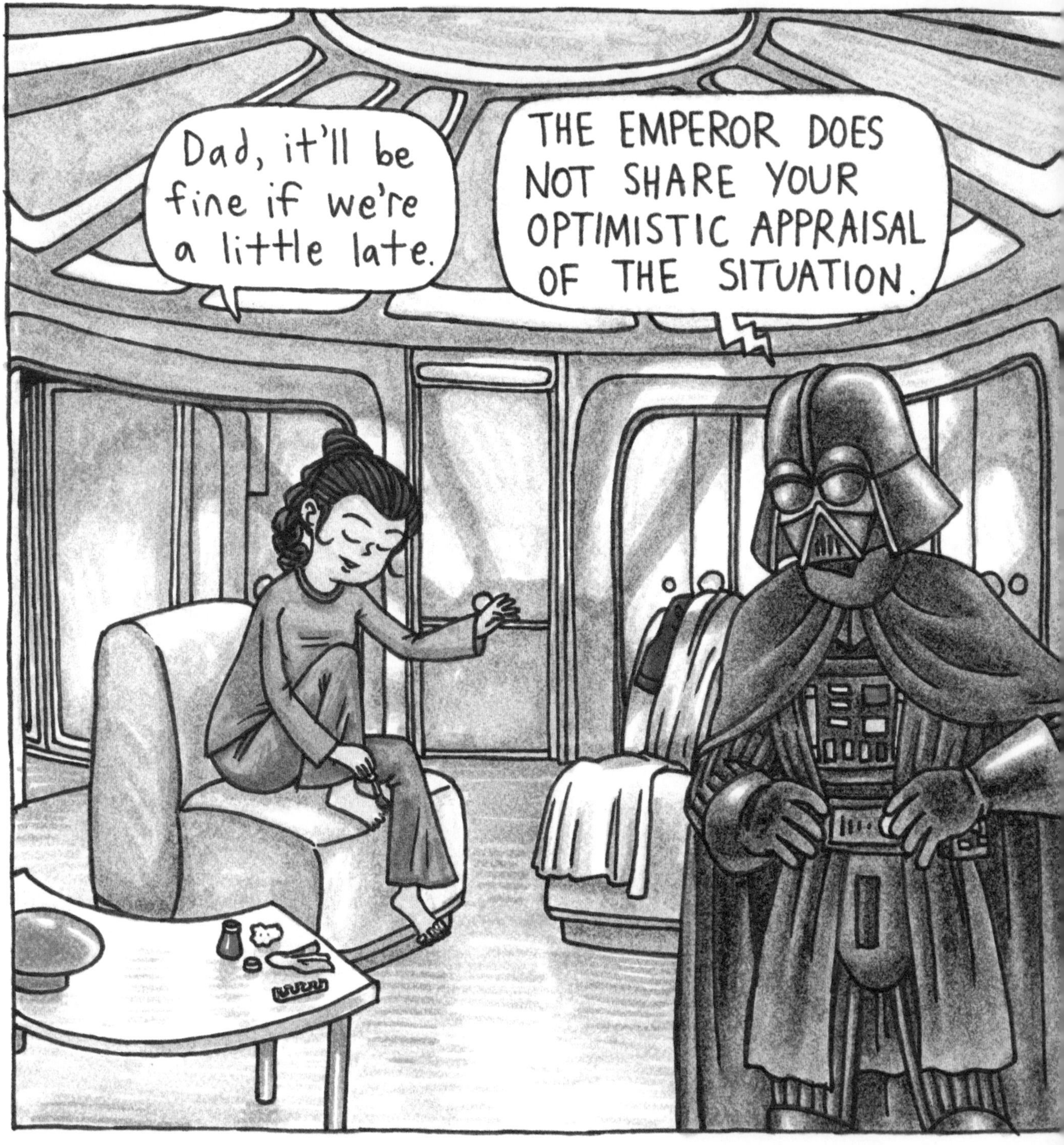
Dad, it'll be fine if we're a little late.
THE EMPEROR DOES NOT SHARE YOUR OPTIMISTIC APPRAISAL OF THE SITUATION.

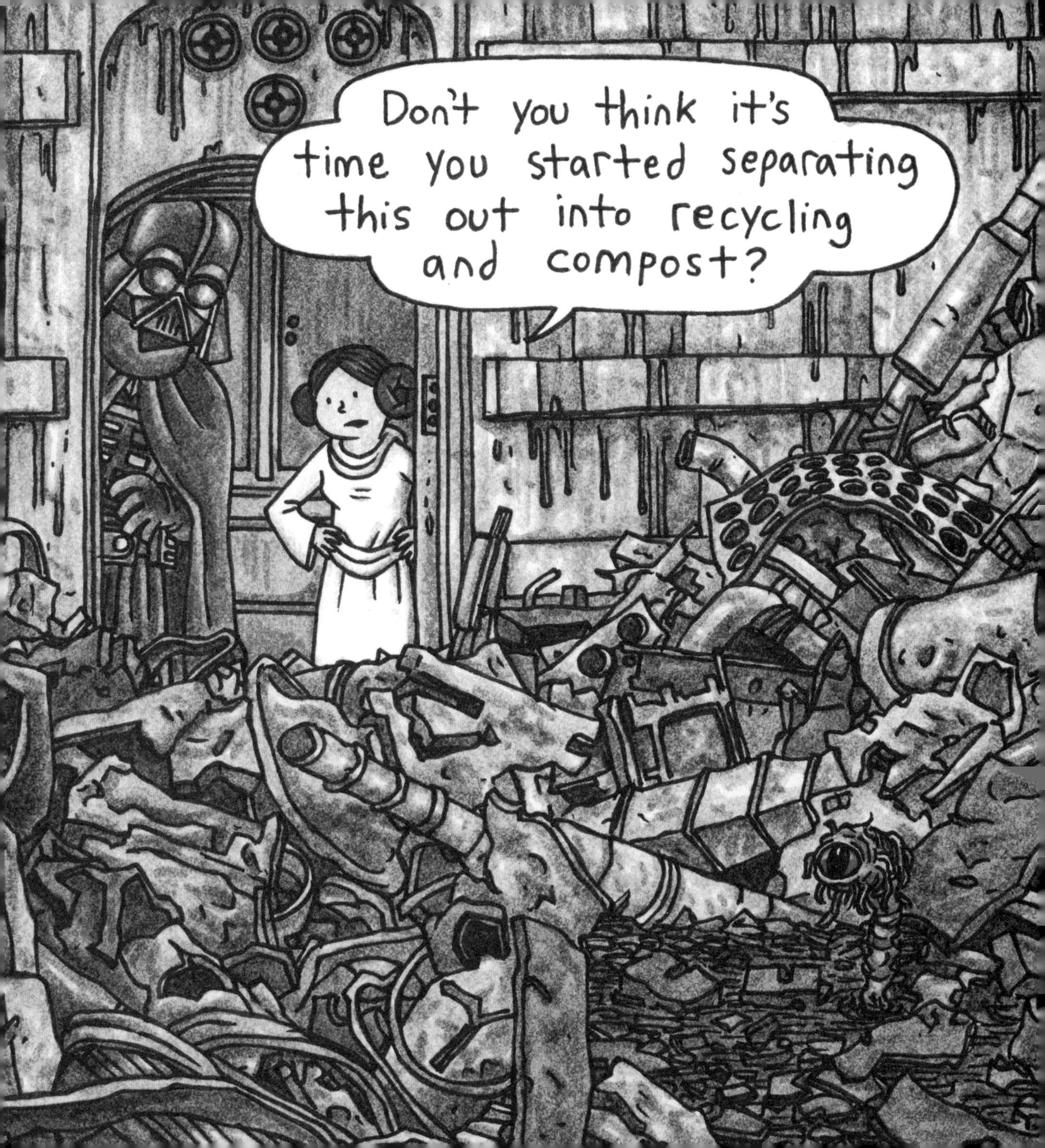
Don't you think it's time you started separating this out into recycling and compost?

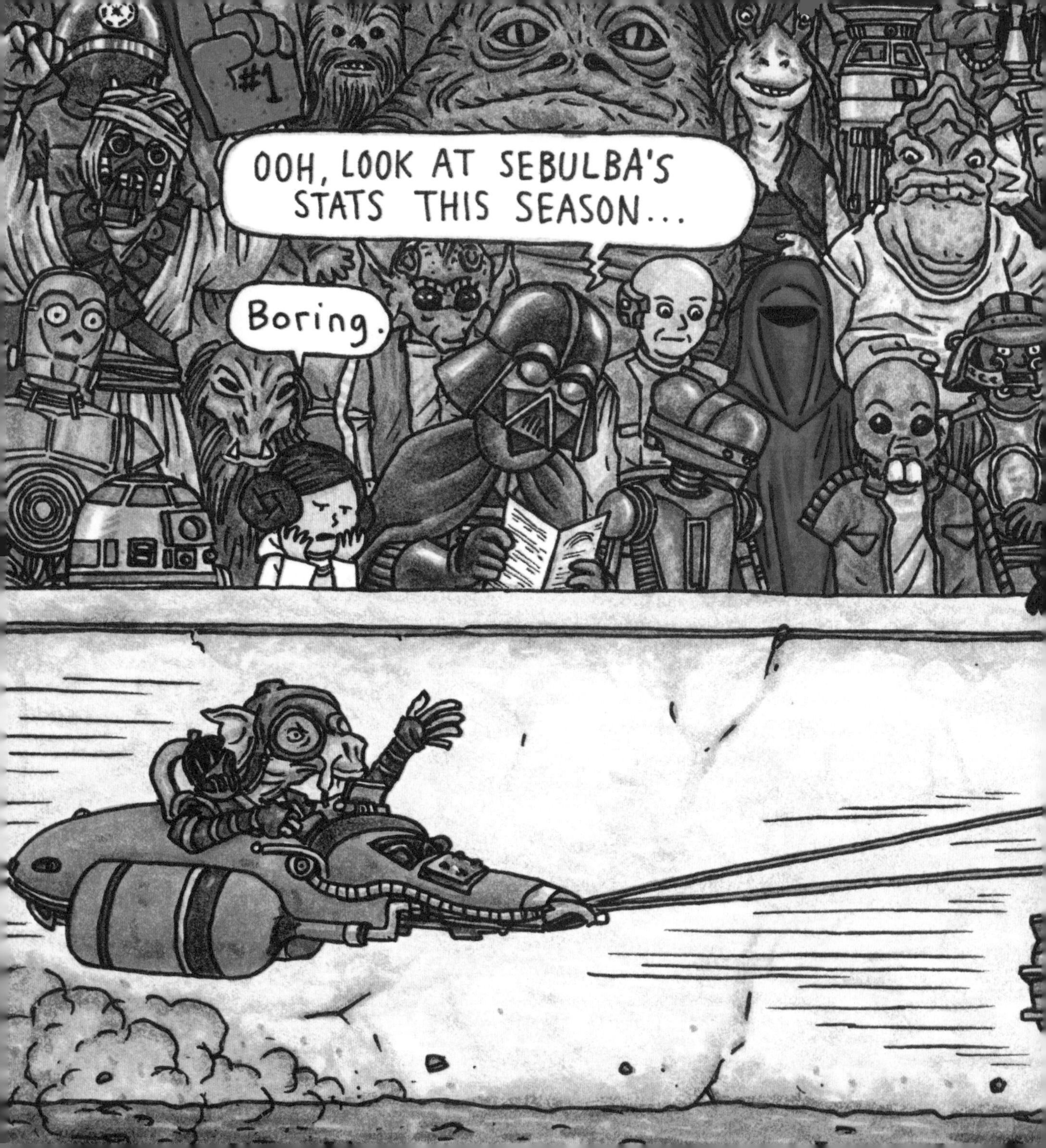
OOH, LOOK AT SEBULBA'S STATS THIS SEASON...
Boring.
#1

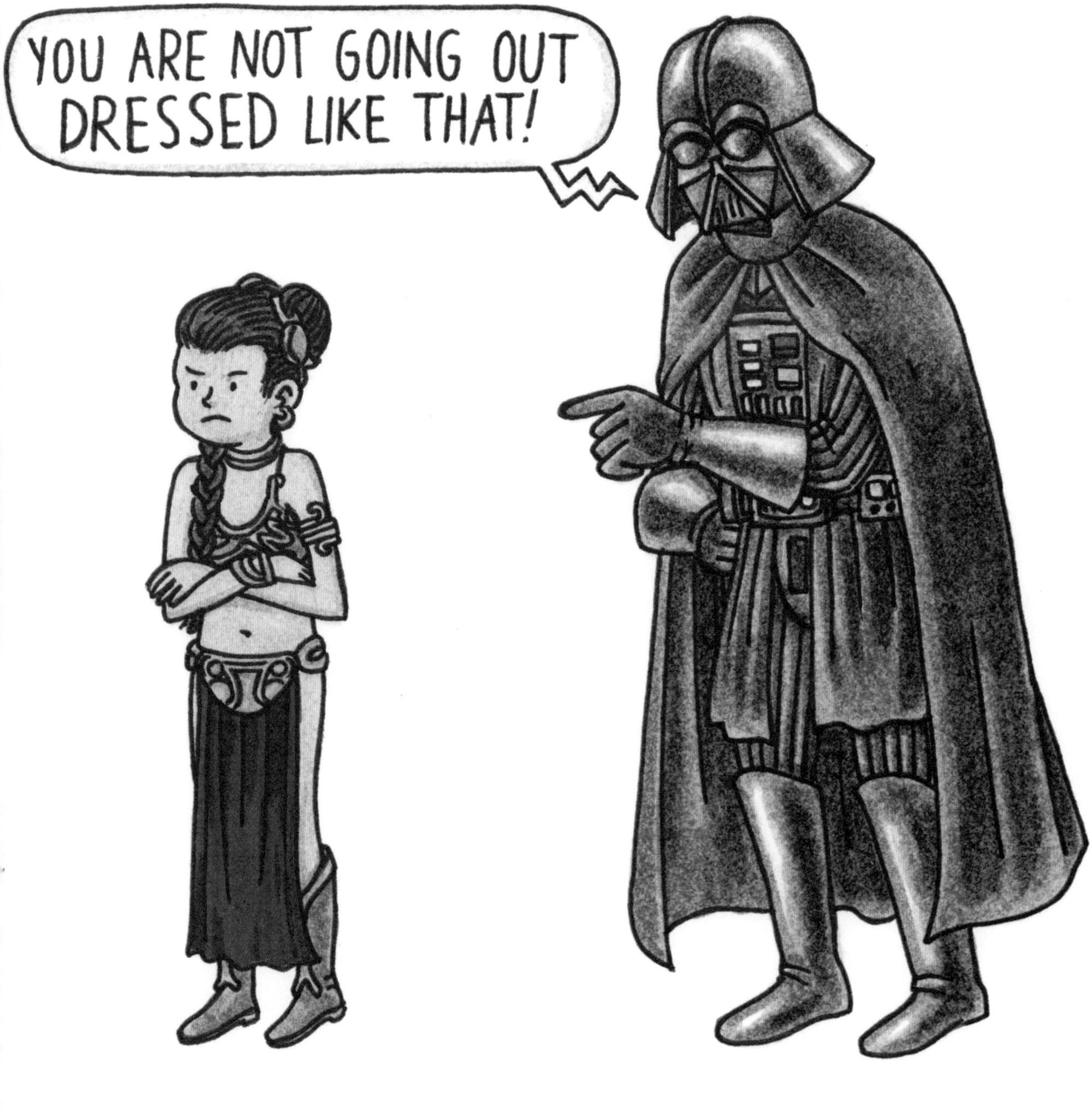
YOU ARE NOT GOING OUT DRESSED LIKE THAT!

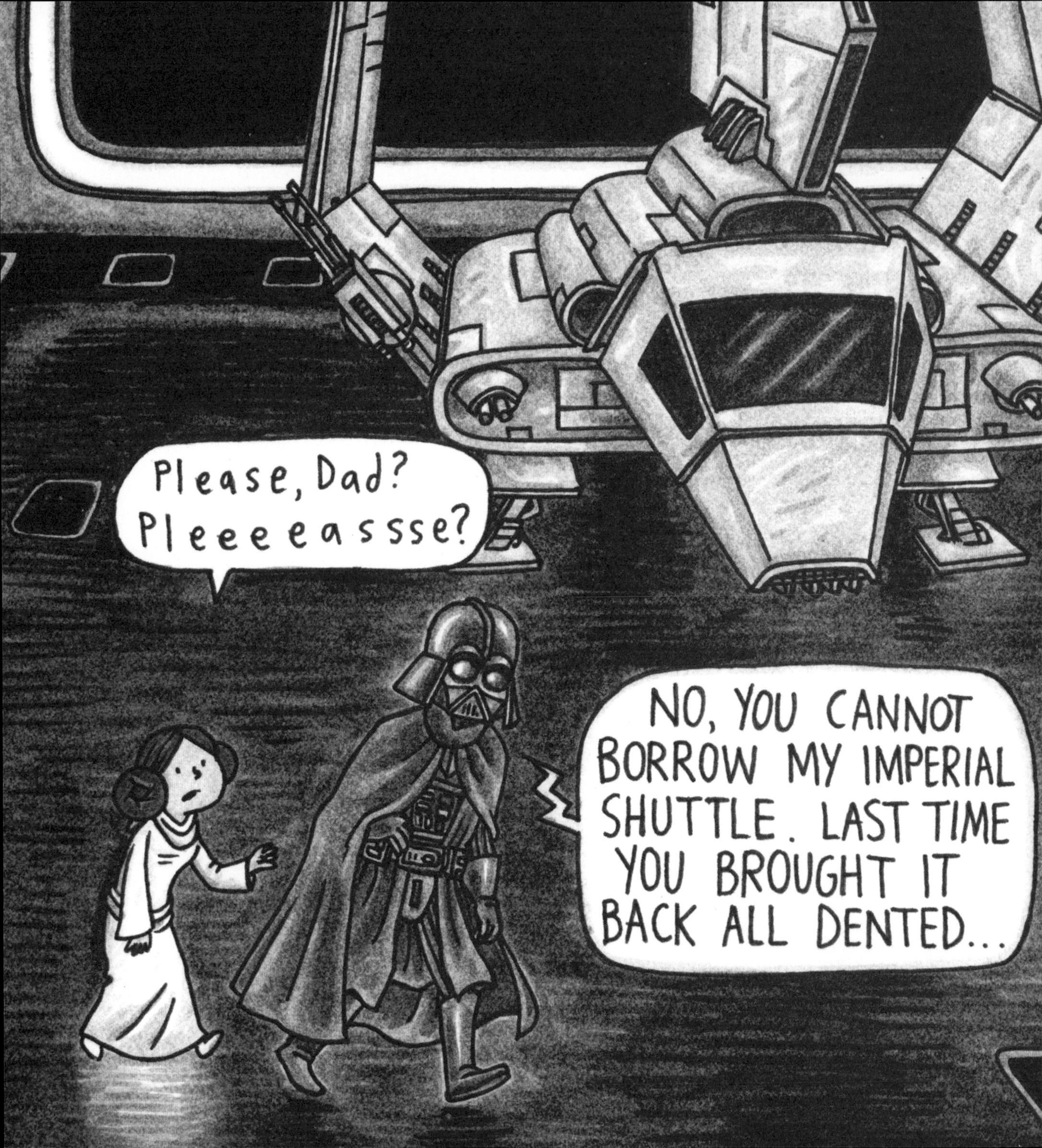
Please, Dad? Pleeeeeassse?
NO, YOU CANNOT BORROW MY IMPERIAL SHUTTLE. LAST TIME YOU BROUGHT IT BACK ALL DENTED...

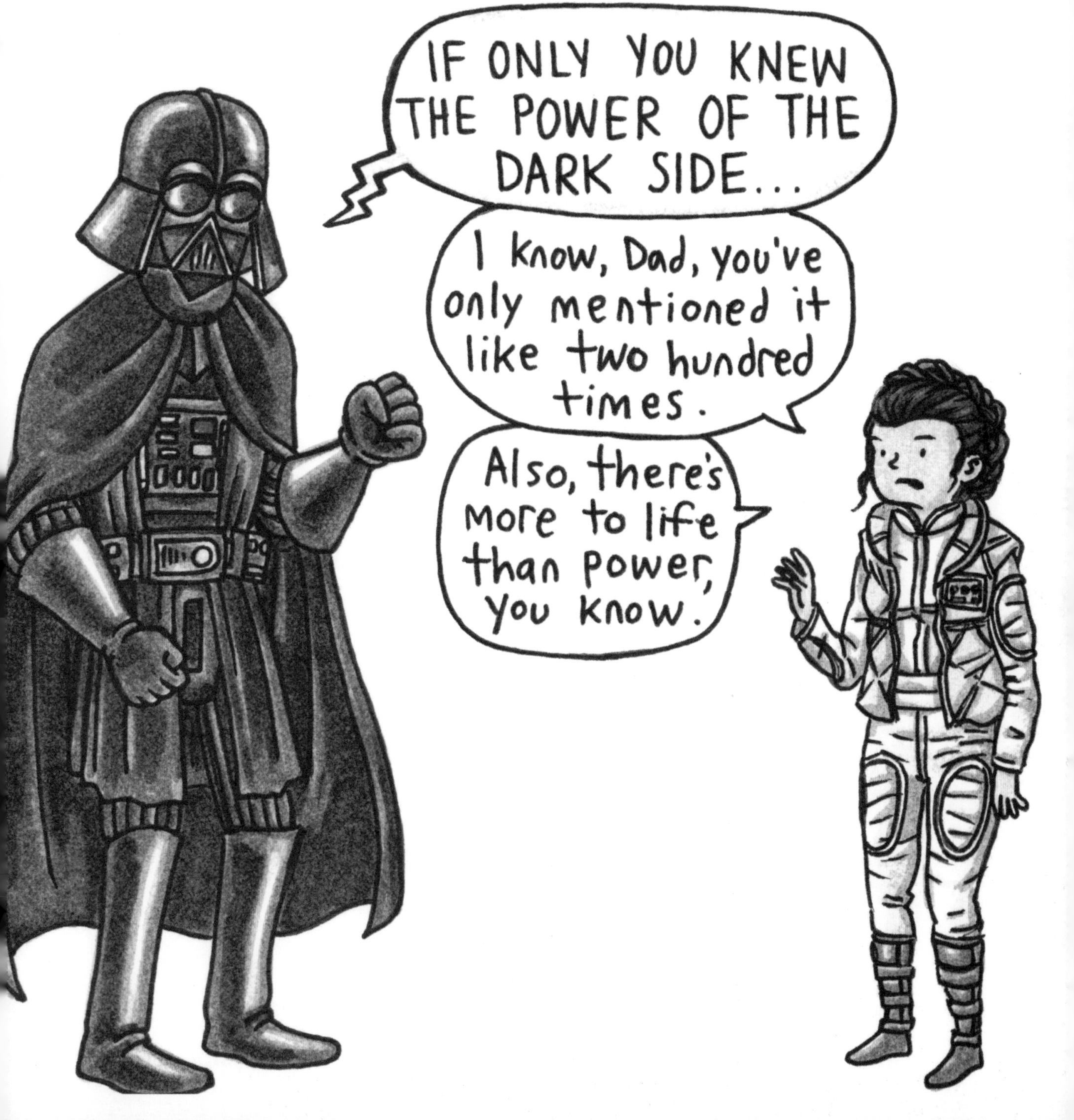
IF ONLY YOU KNEW THE POWER OF THE DARK SIDE...
I know, Dad, you've only mentioned it like two hundred times.
Also, there's more to life than power, you know.

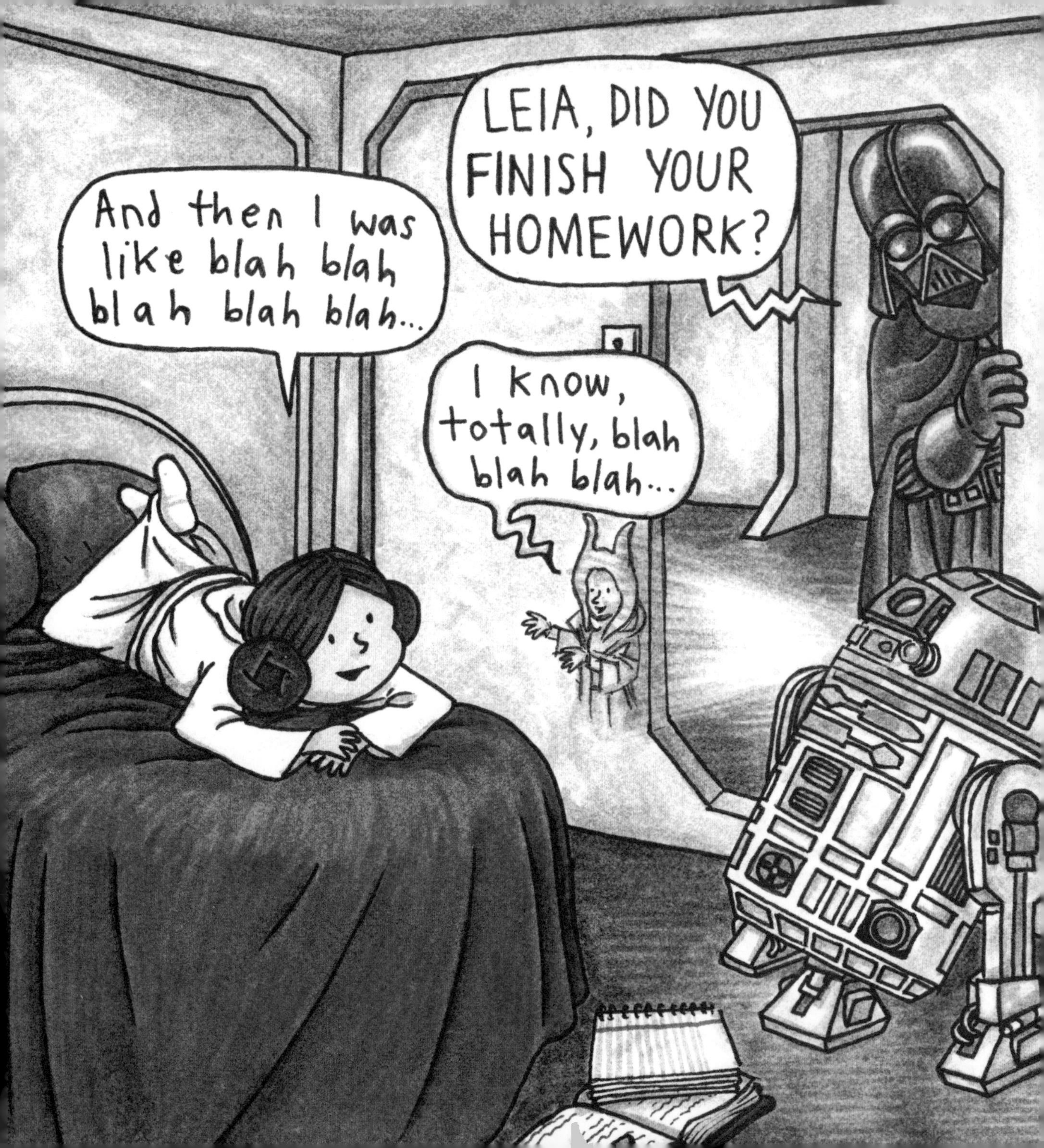
And then I was like blah blah blah blah blah...
I know, totally, blah blah blah...
LEIA, DID YOU FINISH YOUR HOMEWORK?

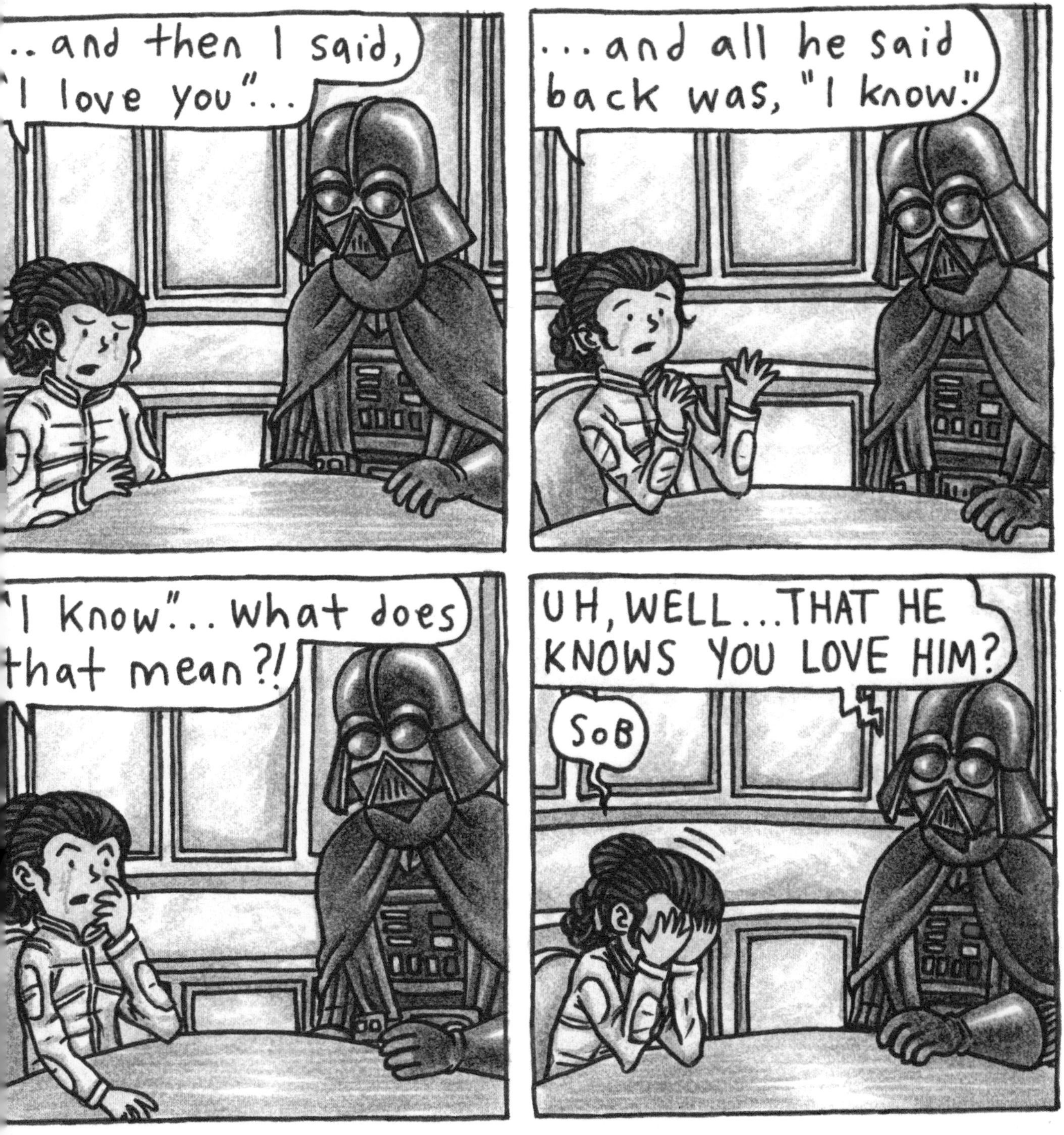
..and then I said, "I love you"...
...and all he said back was, "I know."
"I know"...what does that mean?!
UH, WELL...THAT HE KNOWS YOU LOVE HIM?
SoB

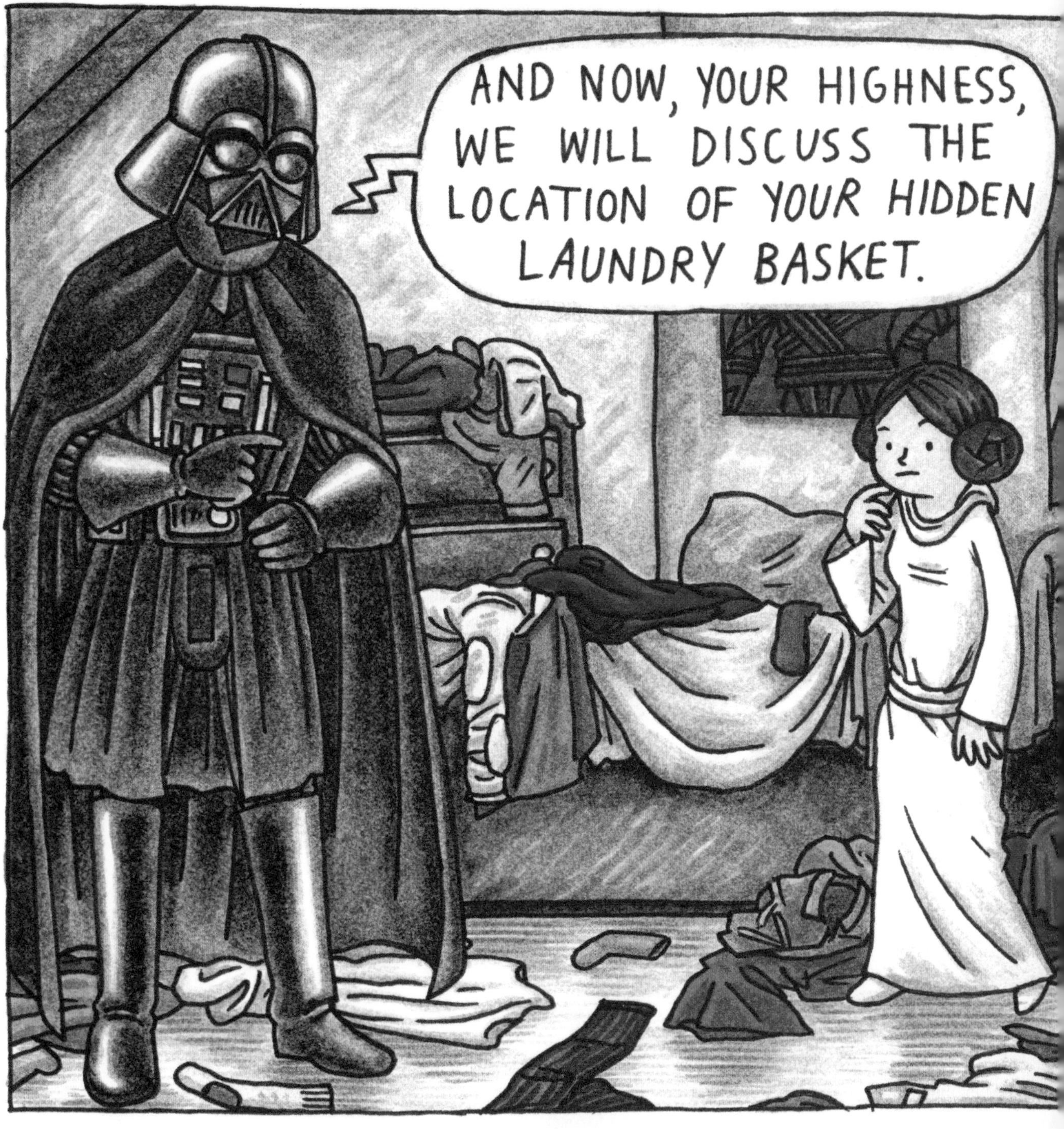
AND NOW, YOUR HIGHNESS, WE WILL DISCUSS THE LOCATION OF YOUR HIDDEN LAUNDRY BASKET.

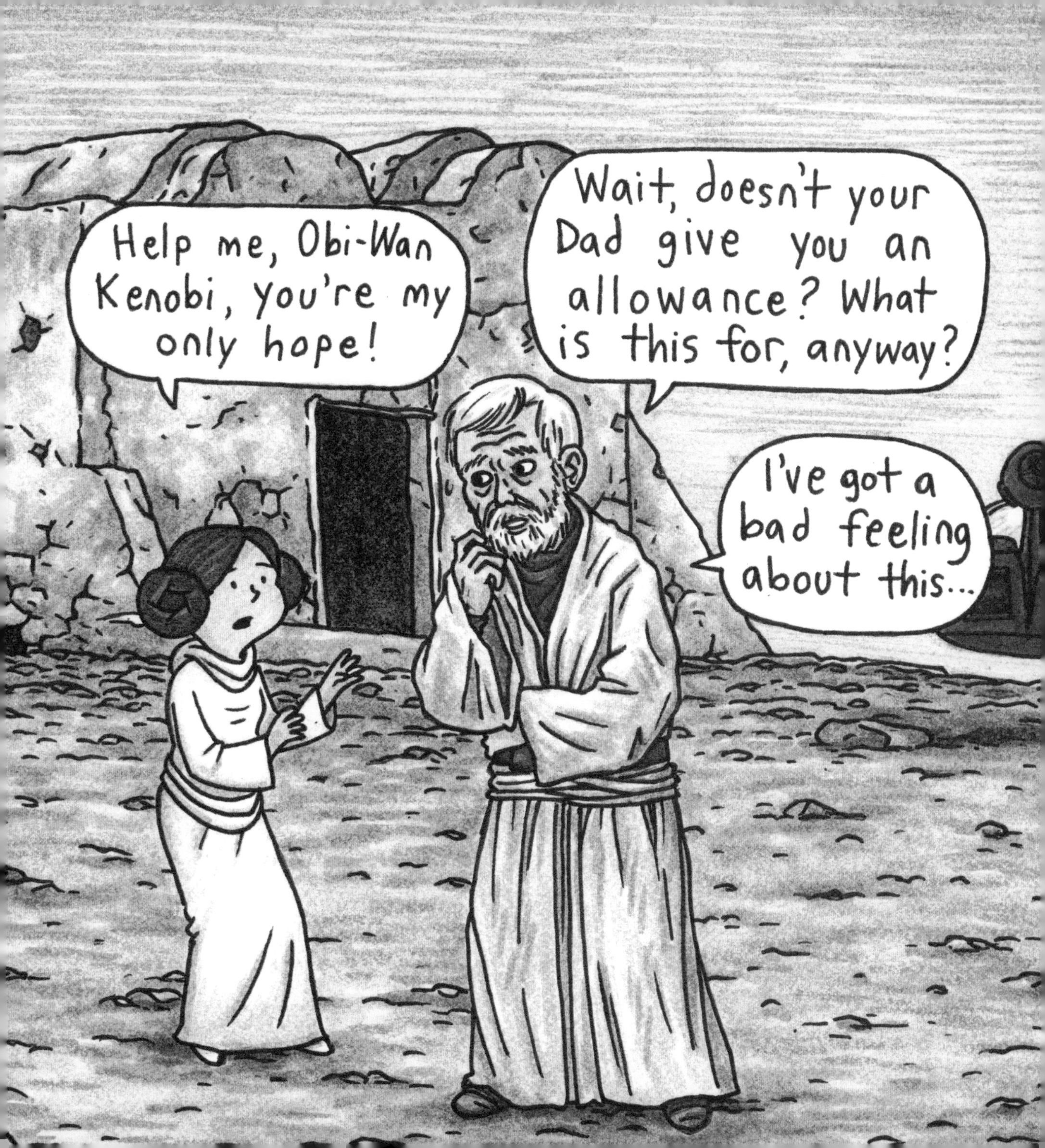

Help me, Obi-Wan Kenobi, you're my only hope!
Wait, doesn't your Dad give you an allowance? What is this for, anyway?
I've got a bad feeling about this...

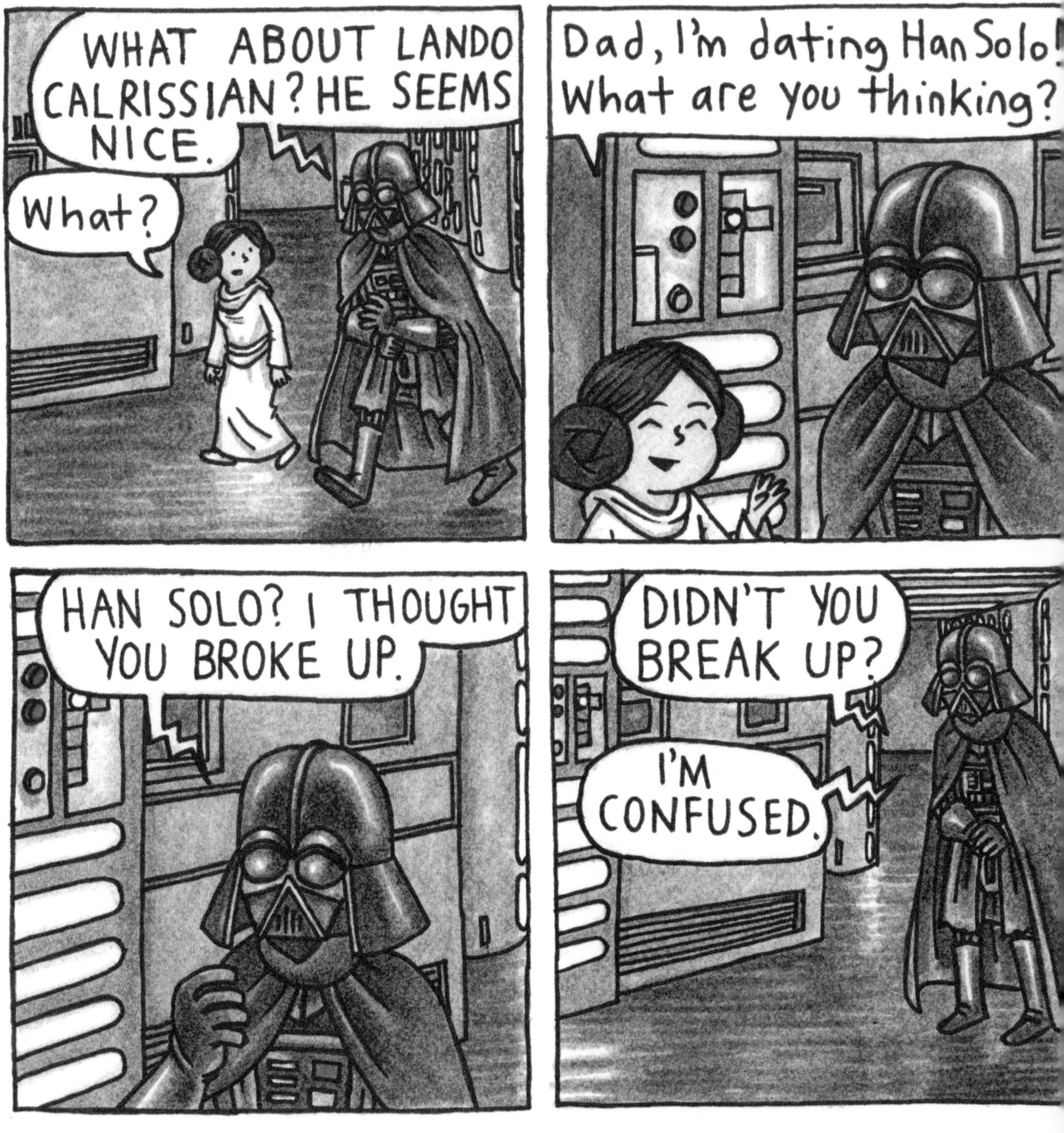
WHAT ABOUT LANDO CALRISSIAN? HE SEEMS NICE.
What?
Dad, I'm dating Han Solo! What are you thinking?
HAN SOLO? I THOUGHT YOU BROKE UP.
DIDN'T YOU BREAK UP?
I'M CONFUSED.

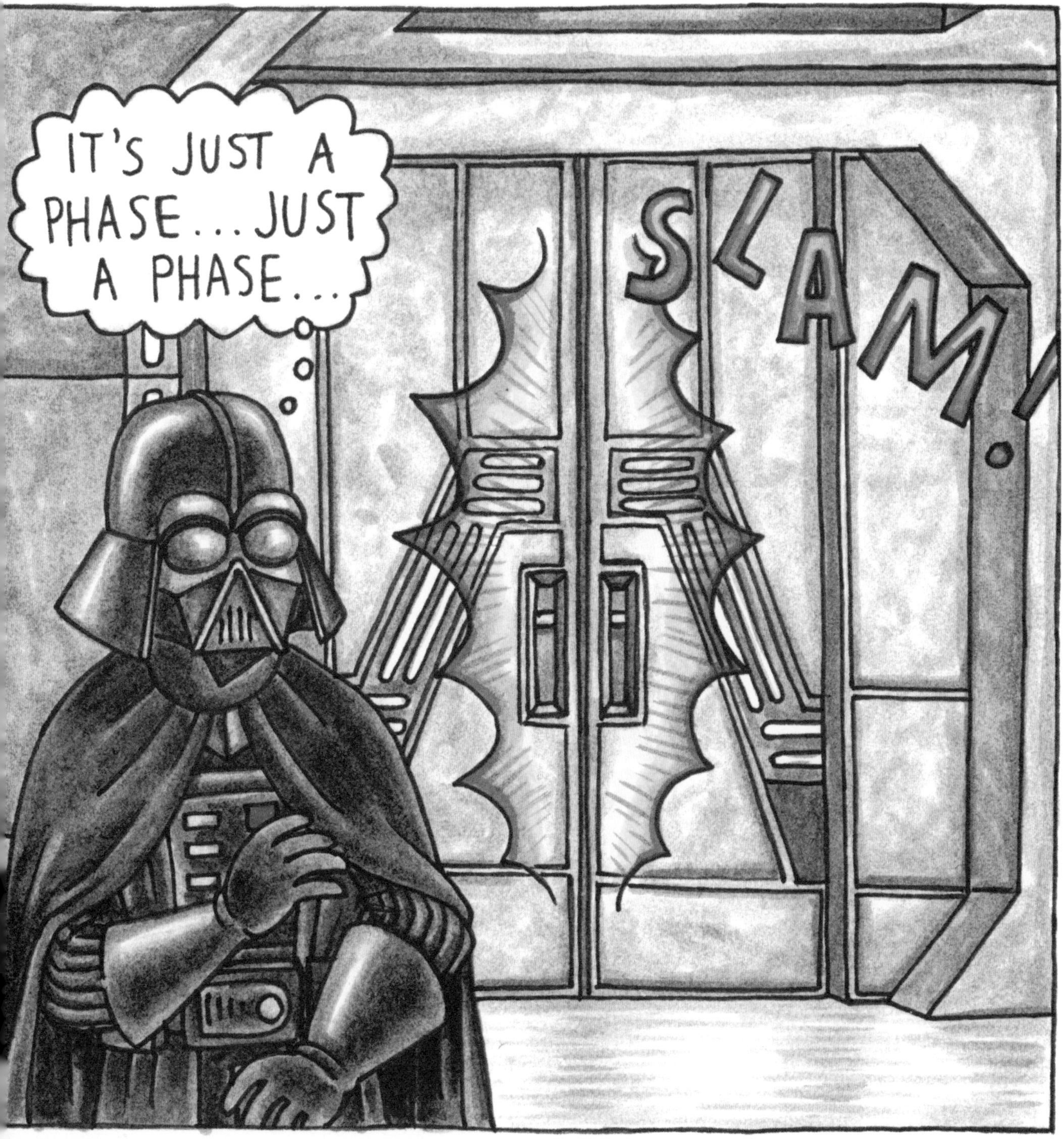
IT'S JUST A PHASE... JUST A PHASE...
SLAM!

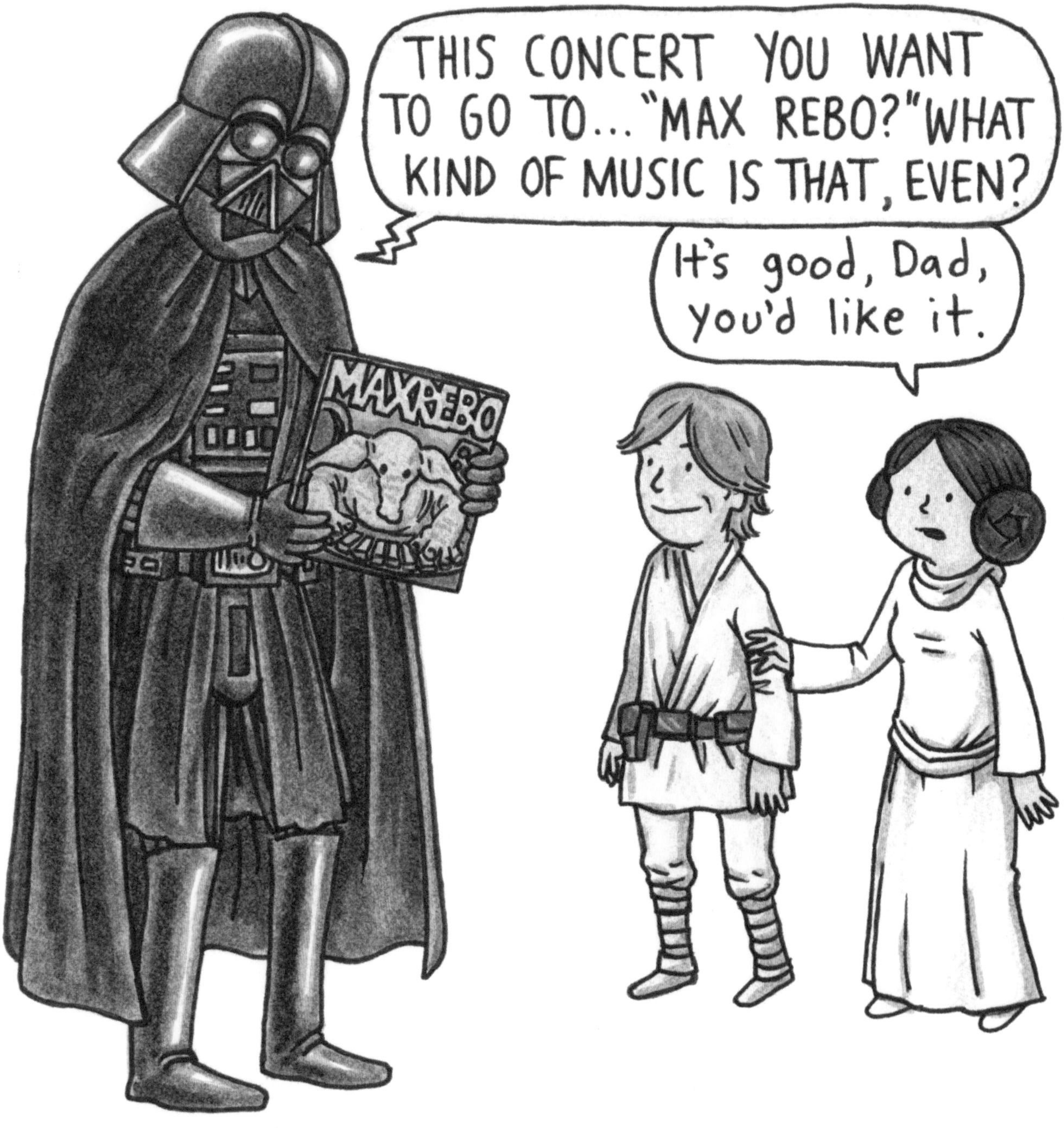
THIS CONCERT YOU WANT TO GO TO... "MAX REBO?" WHAT KIND OF MUSIC IS THAT, EVEN?
It's good, Dad, you'd like it.
MAX REBO

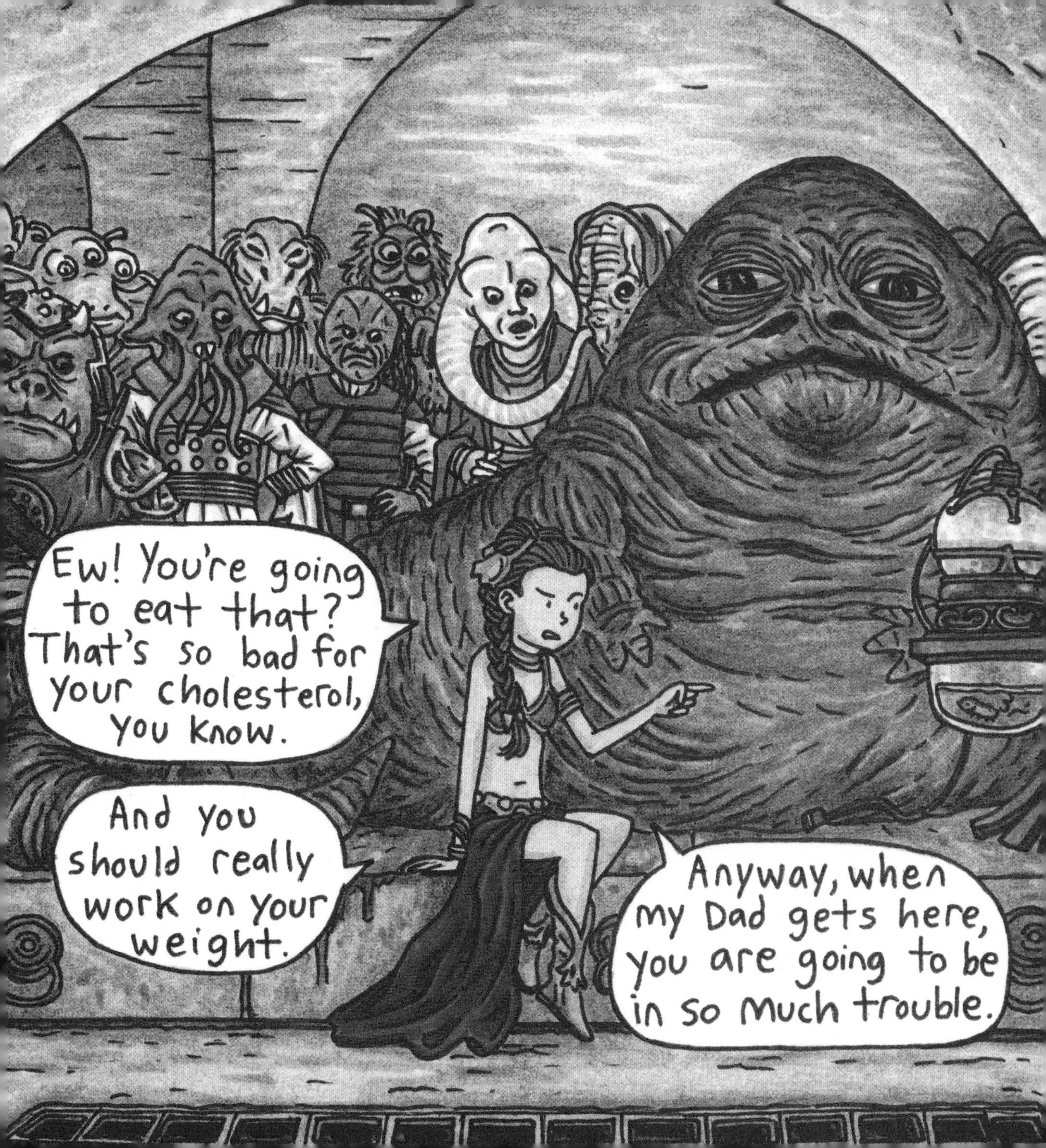
Ew! You're going to eat that? That's so bad for your cholesterol, you know.
And you should really work on your weight.
Anyway, when my Dad gets here, you are going to be in so much trouble.

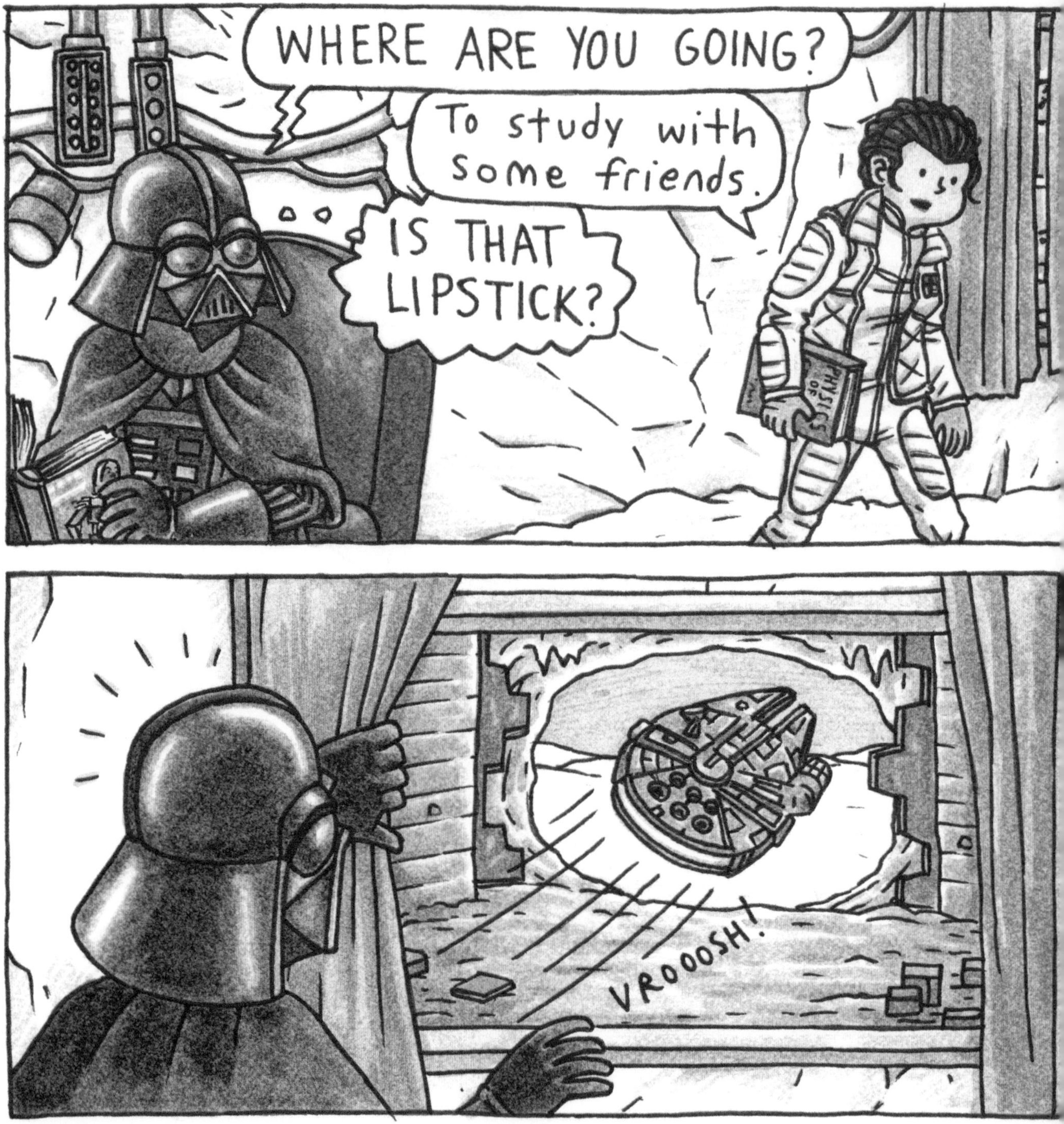
WHERE ARE YOU GOING?
To study with some friends.
IS THAT LIPSTICK?
PHYSICS OF
VROOOSH!

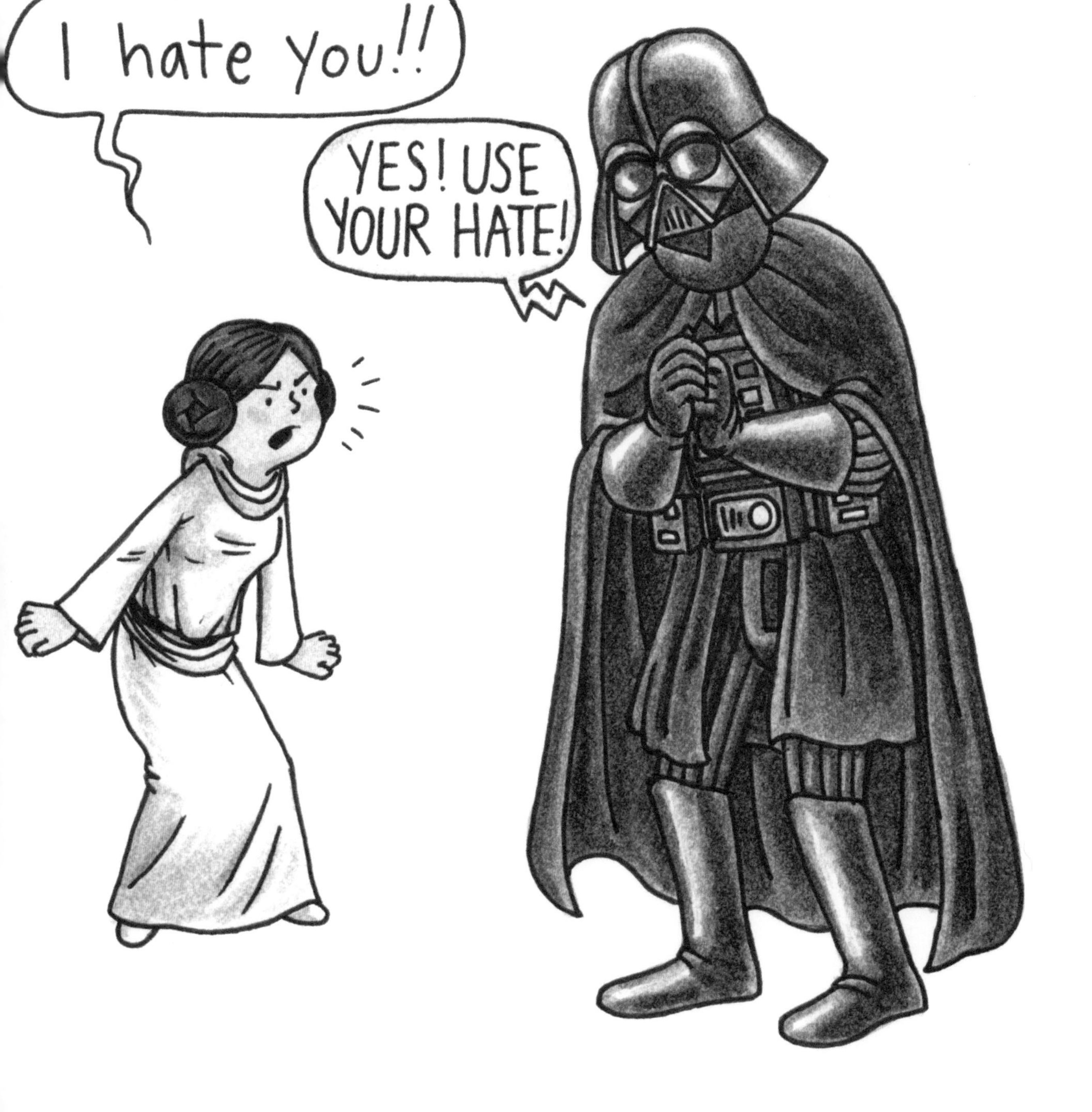
I hate you!!
YES! USE YOUR HATE!

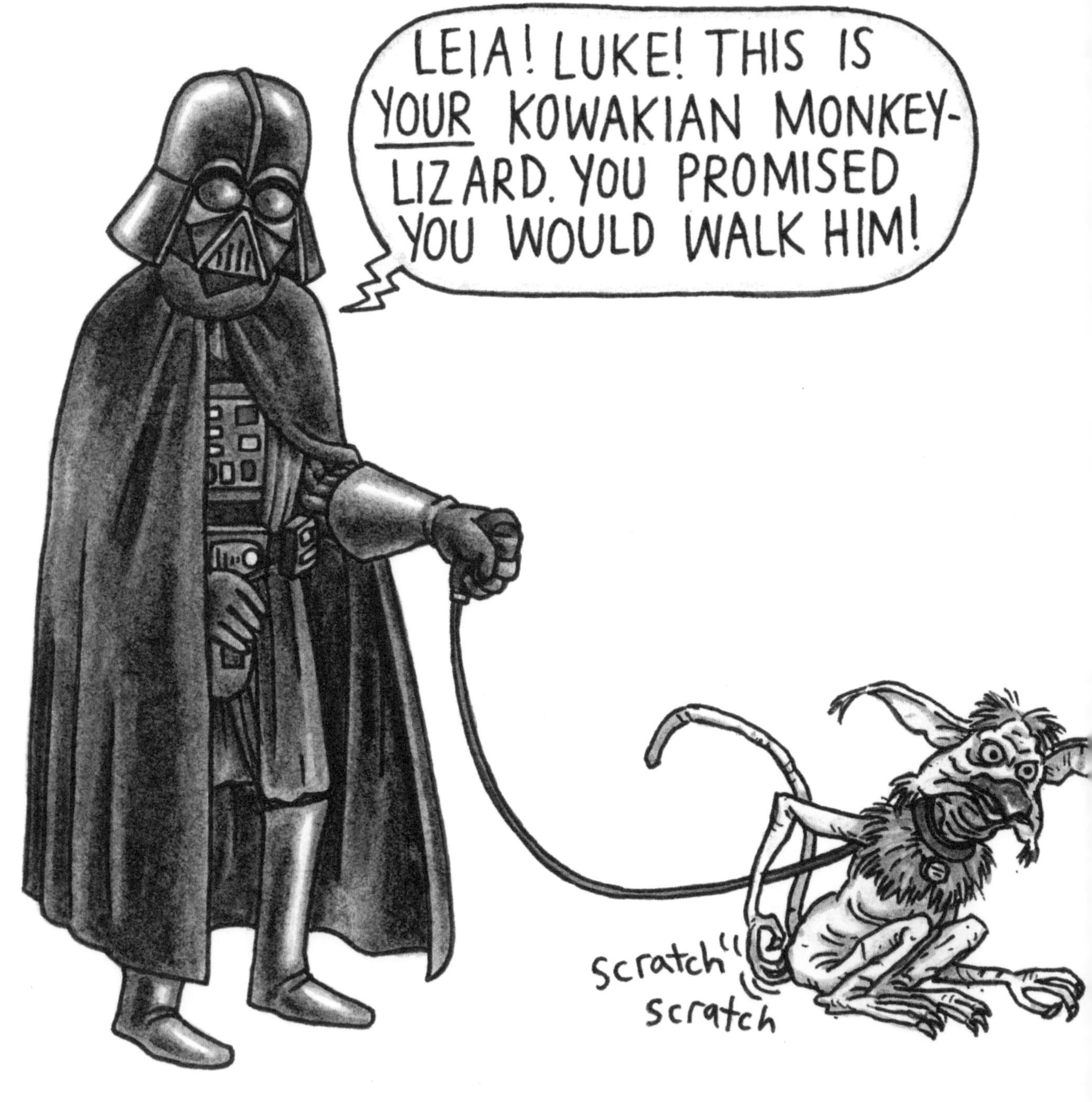
LEIA! LUKE! THIS IS YOUR KOWAKIAN MONKEY-LIZARD. YOU PROMISED YOU WOULD WALK HIM!
scratch
scratch

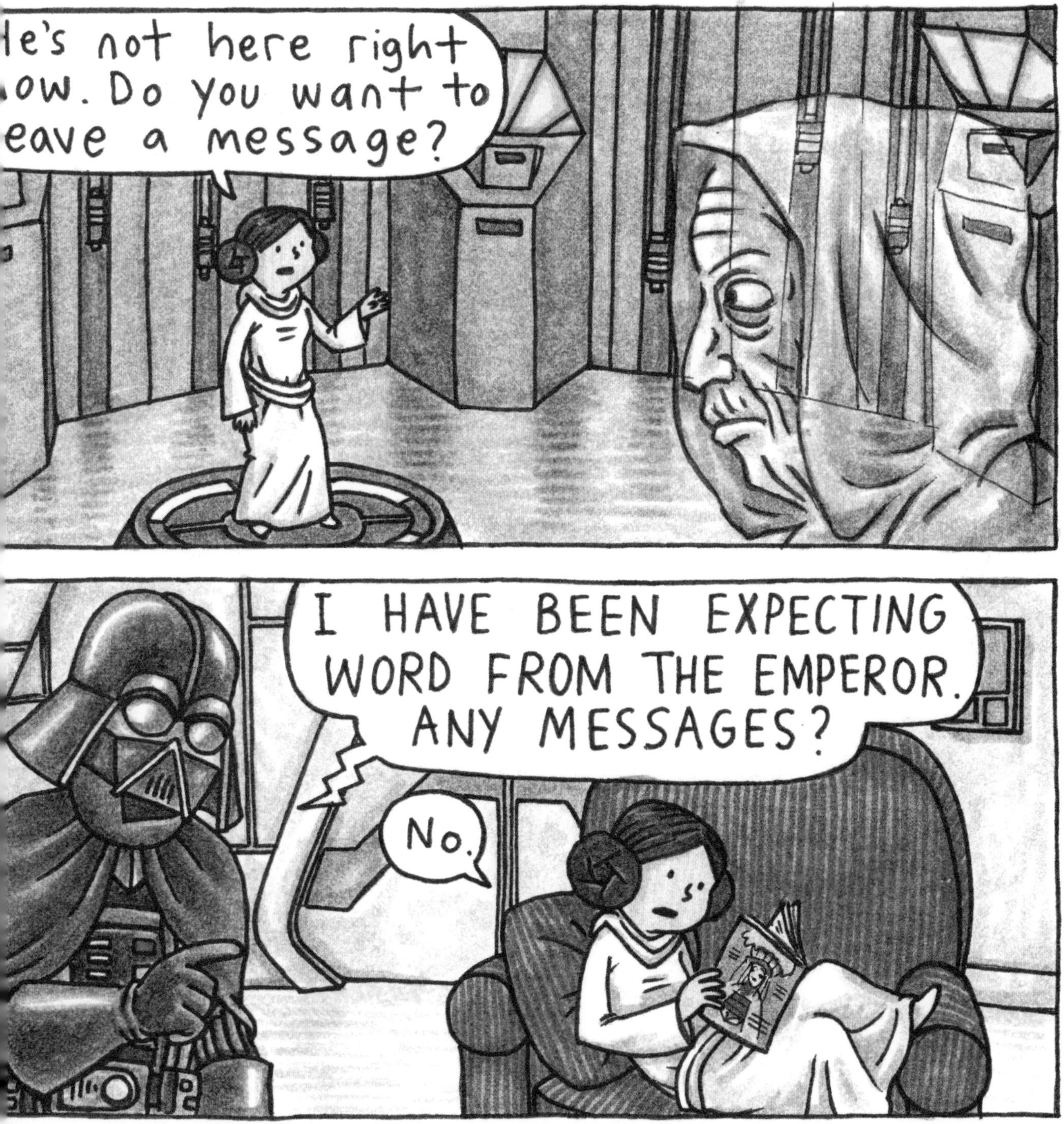
le's not here right ow. Do you want to eave a message?
I HAVE BEEN EXPECTING WORD FROM THE EMPEROR. ANY MESSAGES?
No.

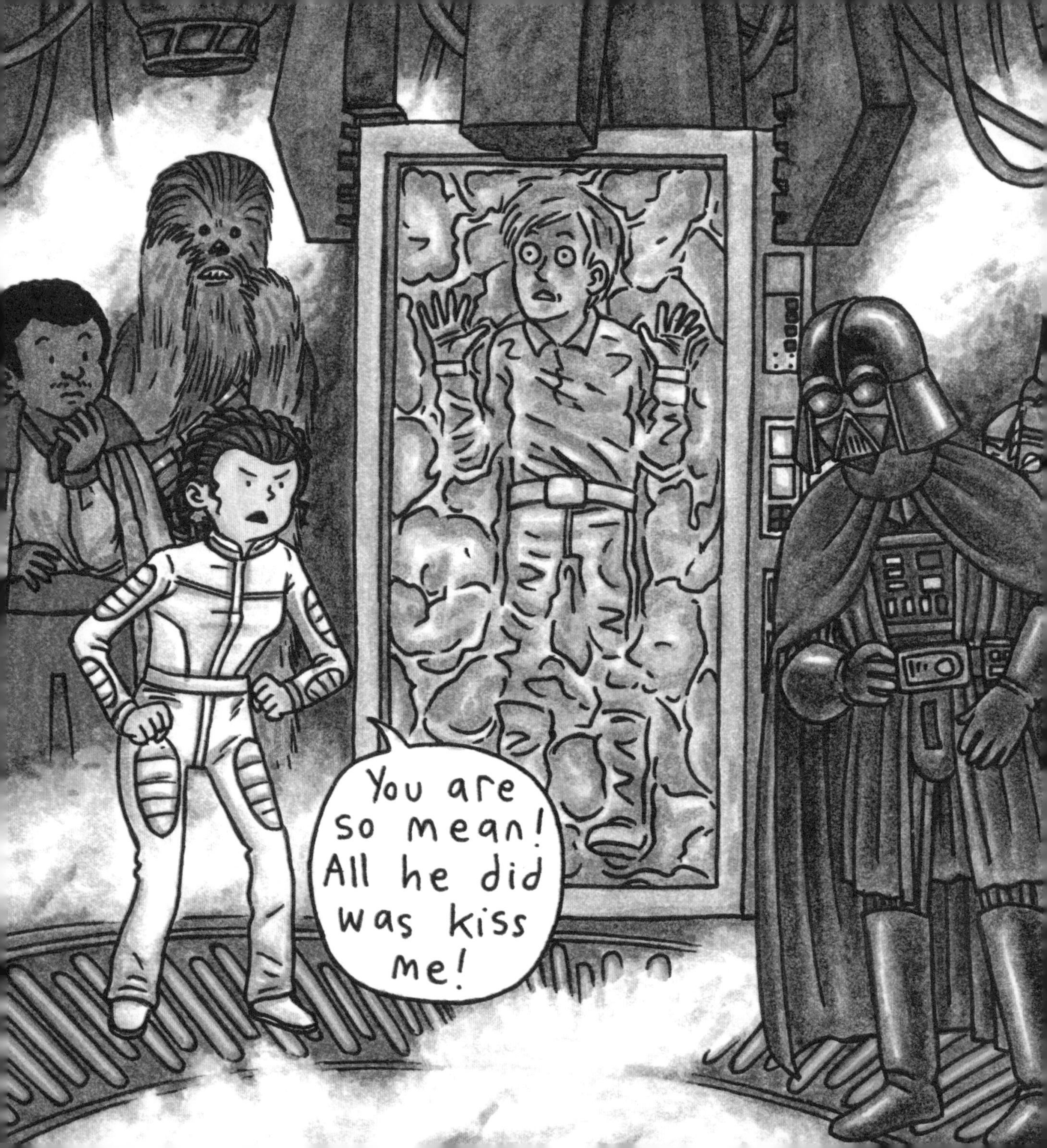
You are so mean! All he did was kiss me!

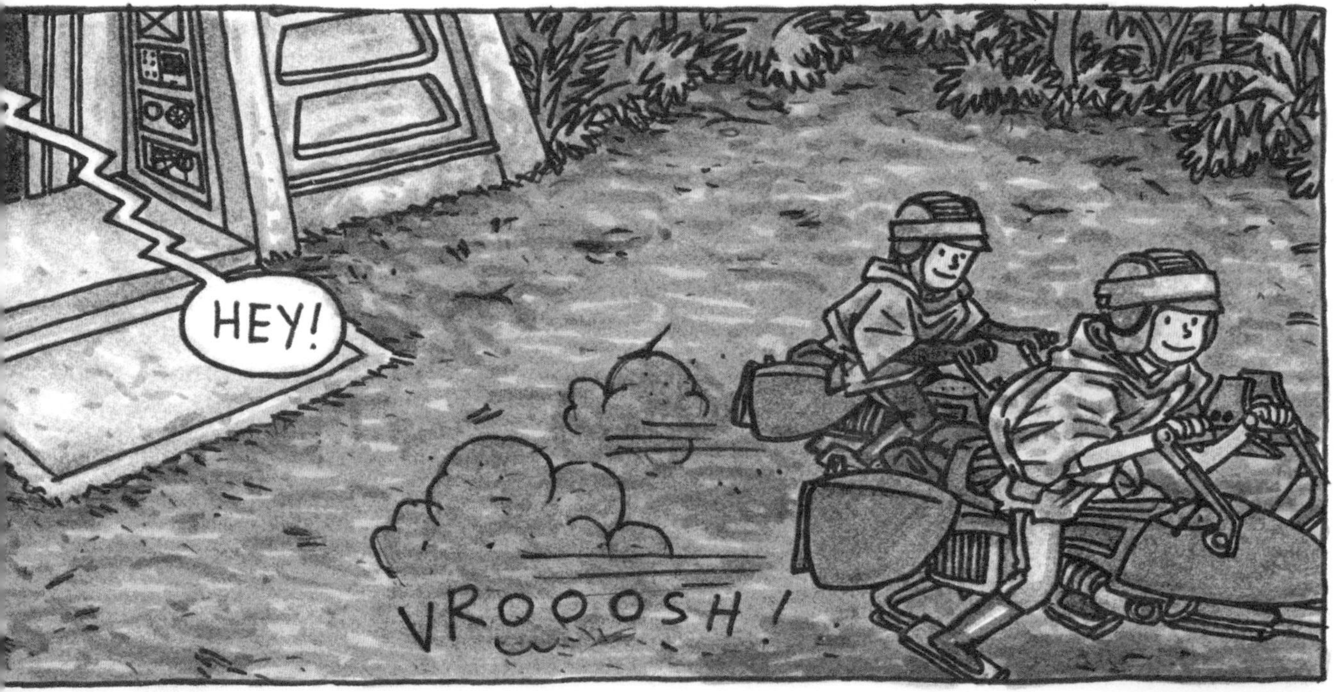
HEY!
VROOOSH!

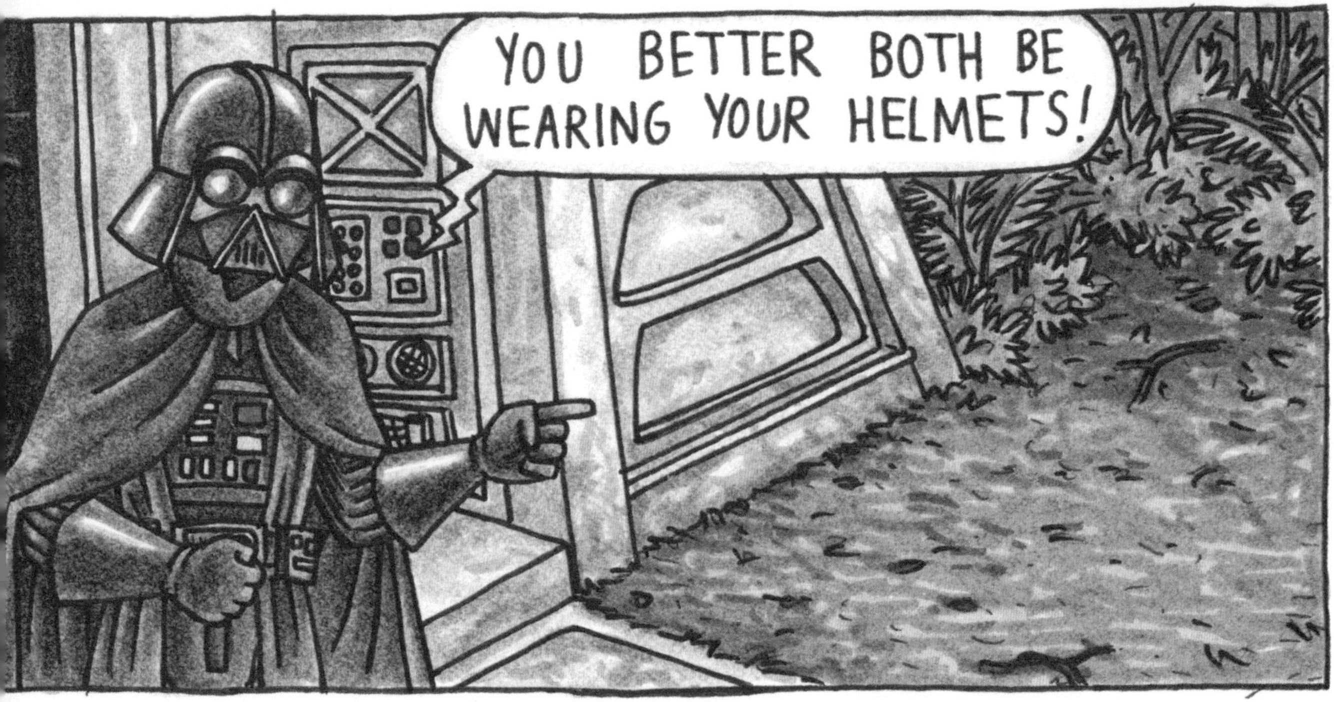
YOU BETTER BOTH BE WEARING YOUR HELMETS!

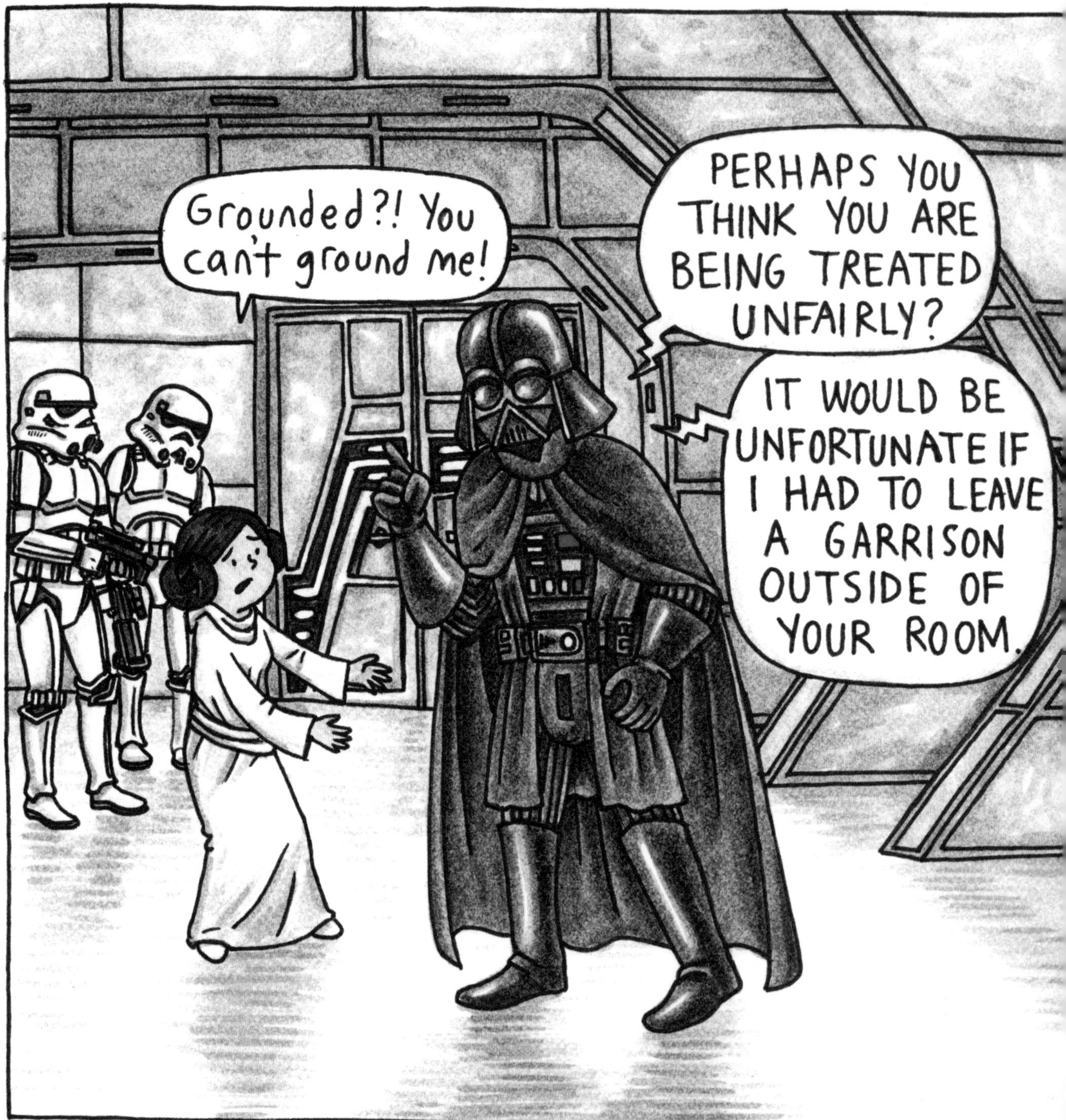
Grounded?! You can't ground me!
PERHAPS YOU THINK YOU ARE BEING TREATED UNFAIRLY?
IT WOULD BE UNFORTUNATE IF I HAD TO LEAVE A GARRISON OUTSIDE OF YOUR ROOM.

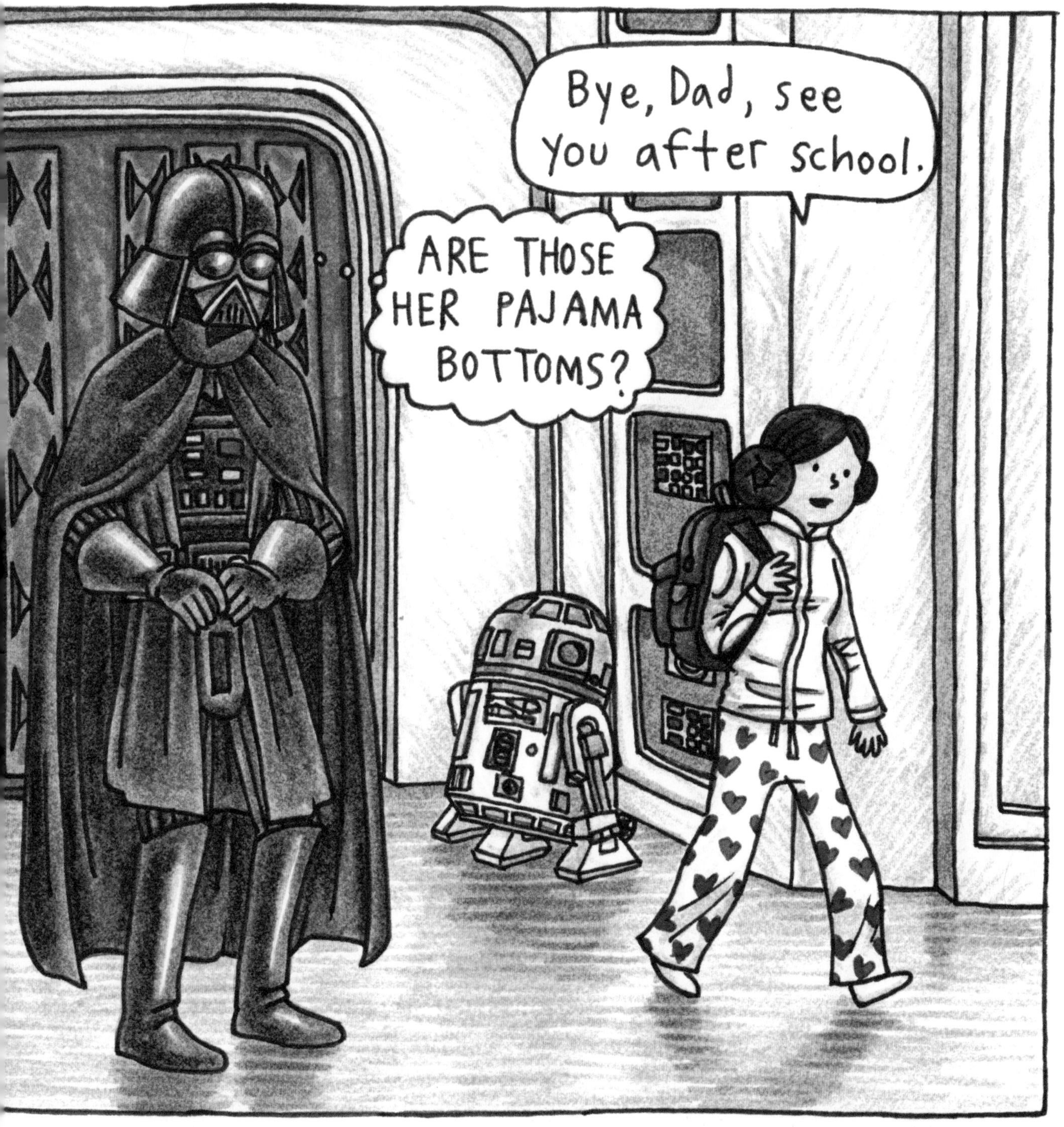
Bye, Dad, see you after school.
ARE THOSE HER PAJAMA BOTTOMS?

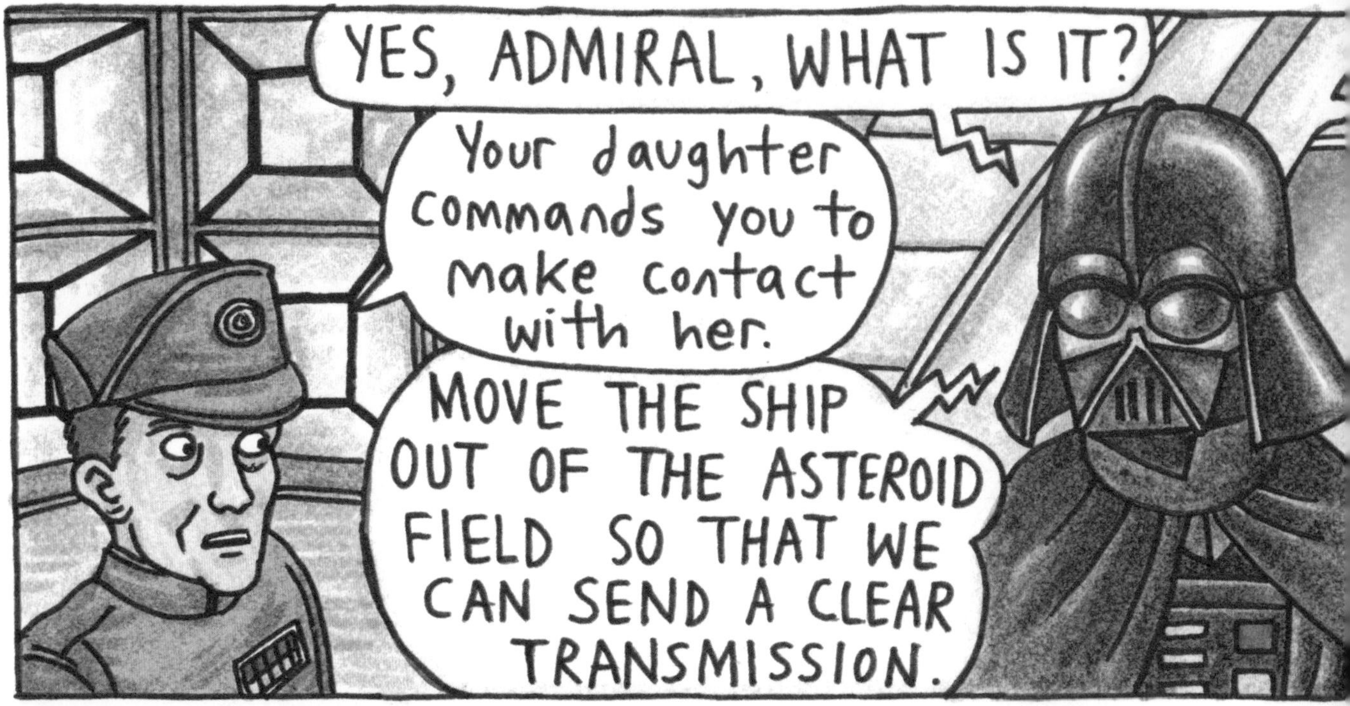
YES, ADMIRAL, WHAT IS IT?
Your daughter commands you to make contact with her.
MOVE THE SHIP OUT OF THE ASTEROID FIELD SO THAT WE CAN SEND A CLEAR TRANSMISSION.

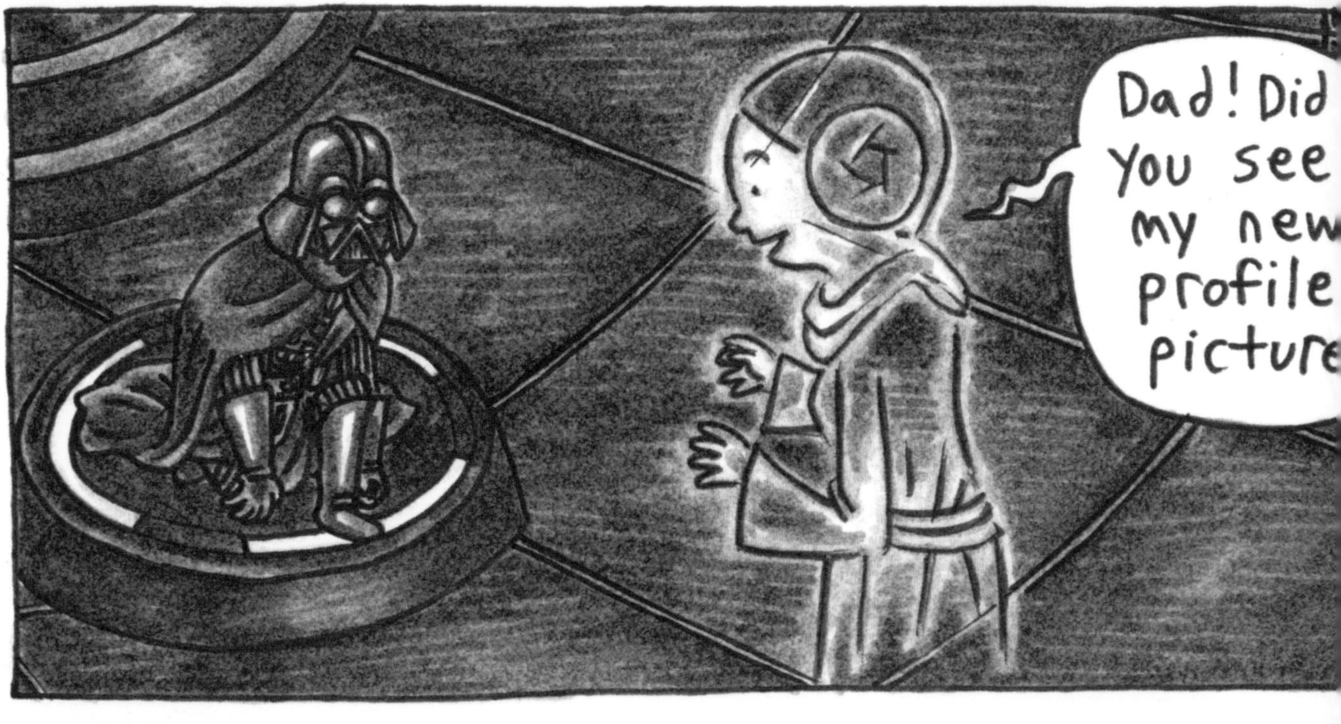
Dad! Did you see my new profile picture

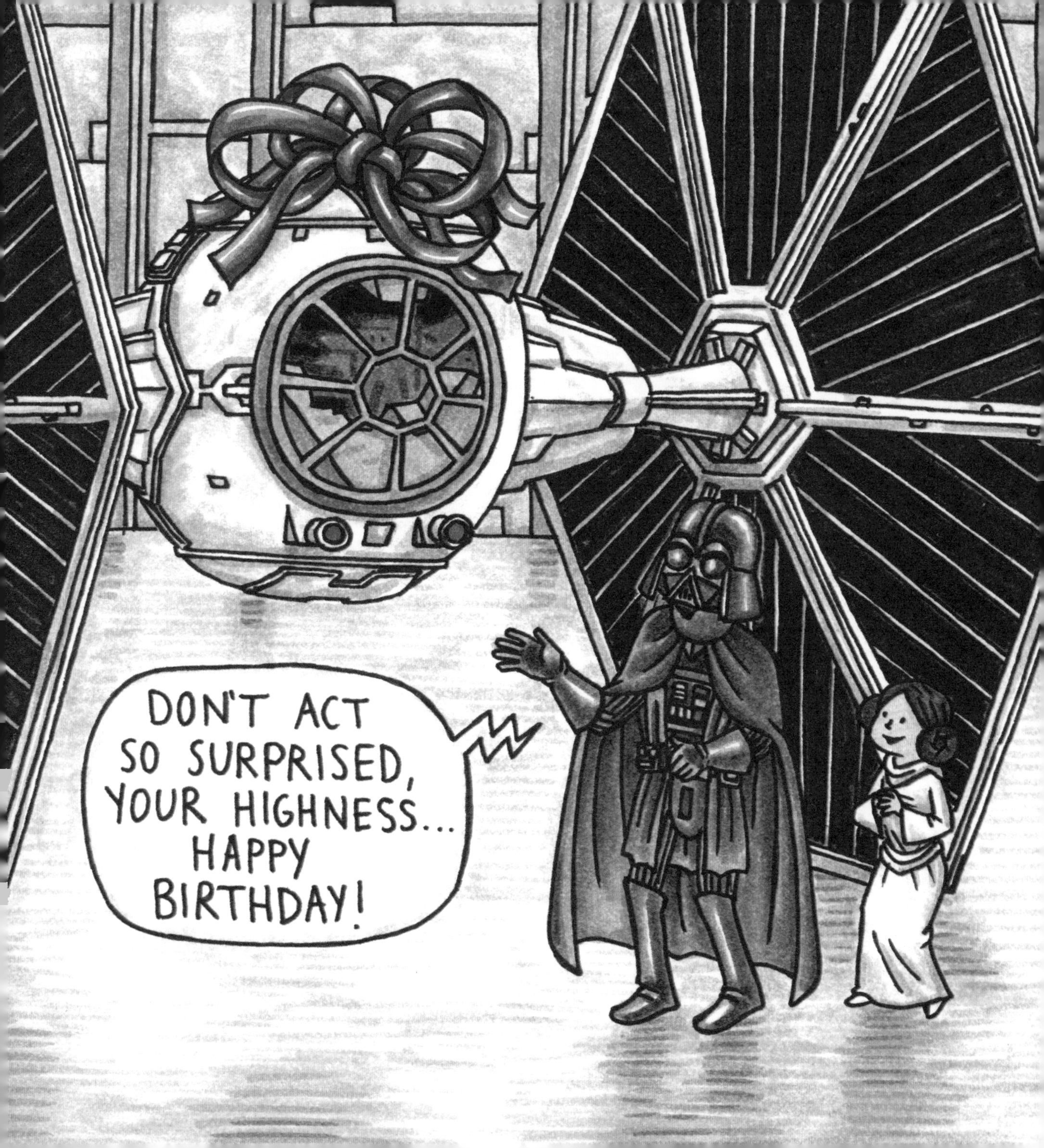
DON'T ACT SO SURPRISED, YOUR HIGHNESS... HAPPY BIRTHDAY!

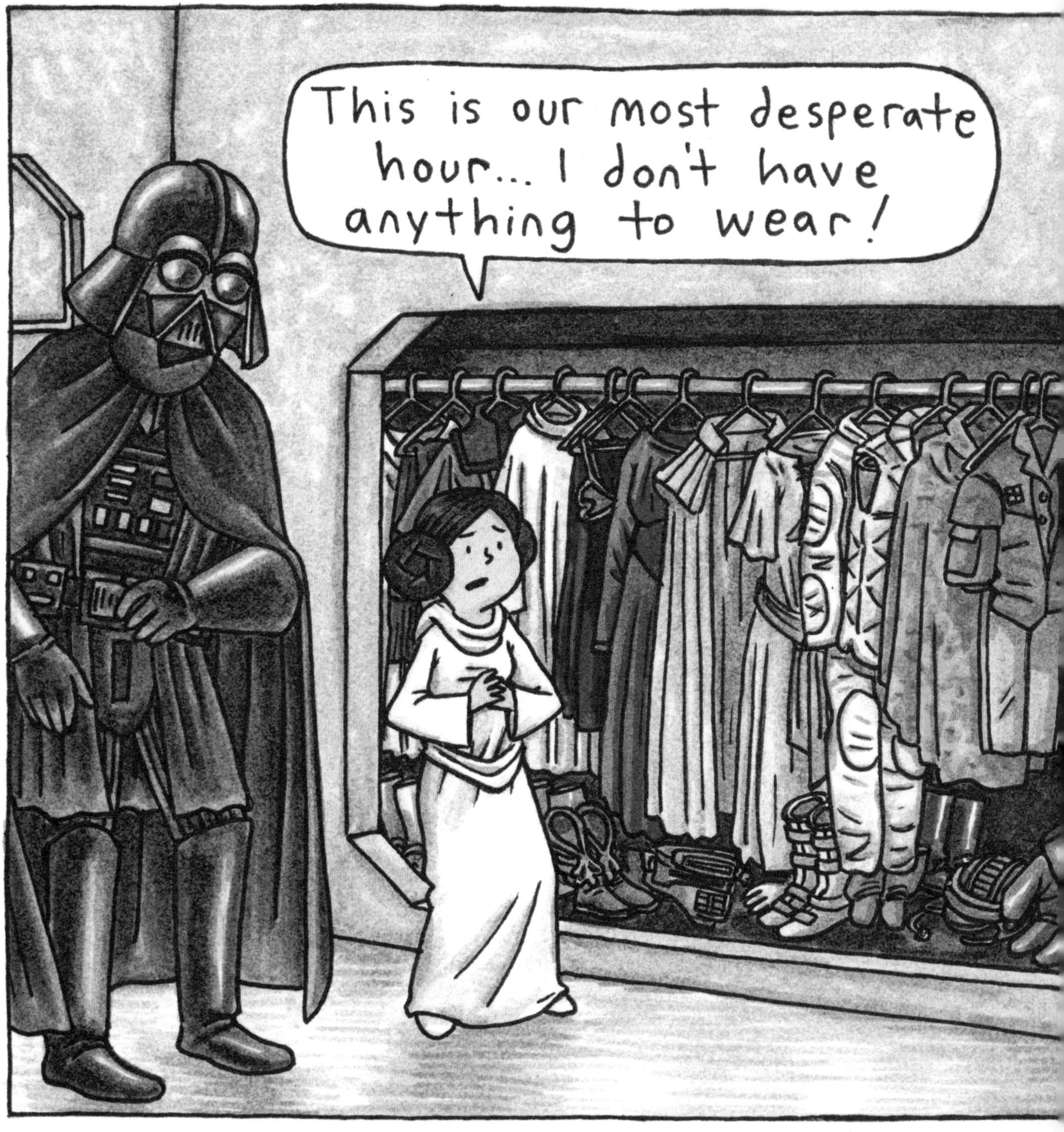
This is our most desperate hour... I don't have anything to wear!

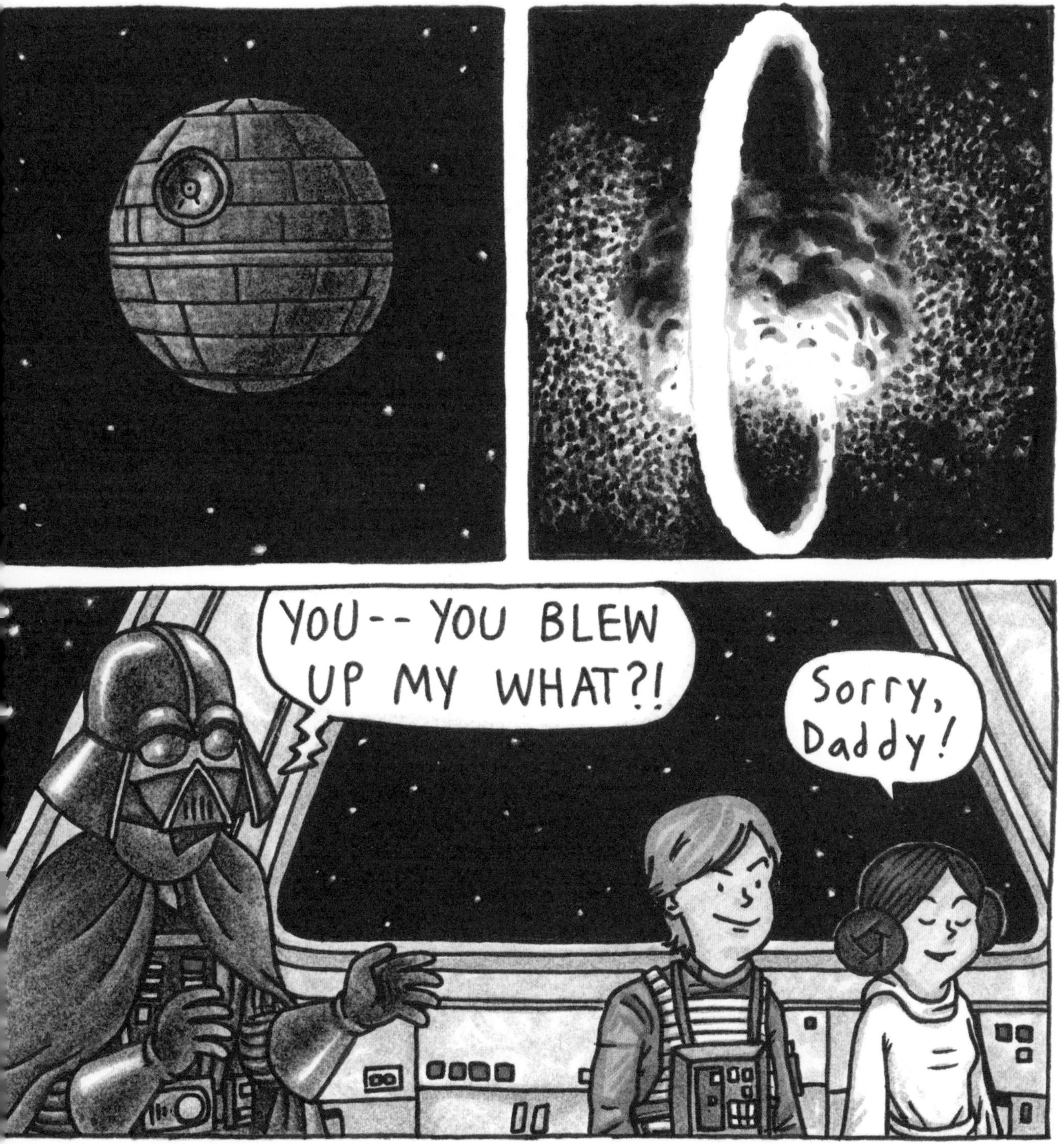
YOU-- YOU BLEW UP MY WHAT?!
Sorry, Daddy!

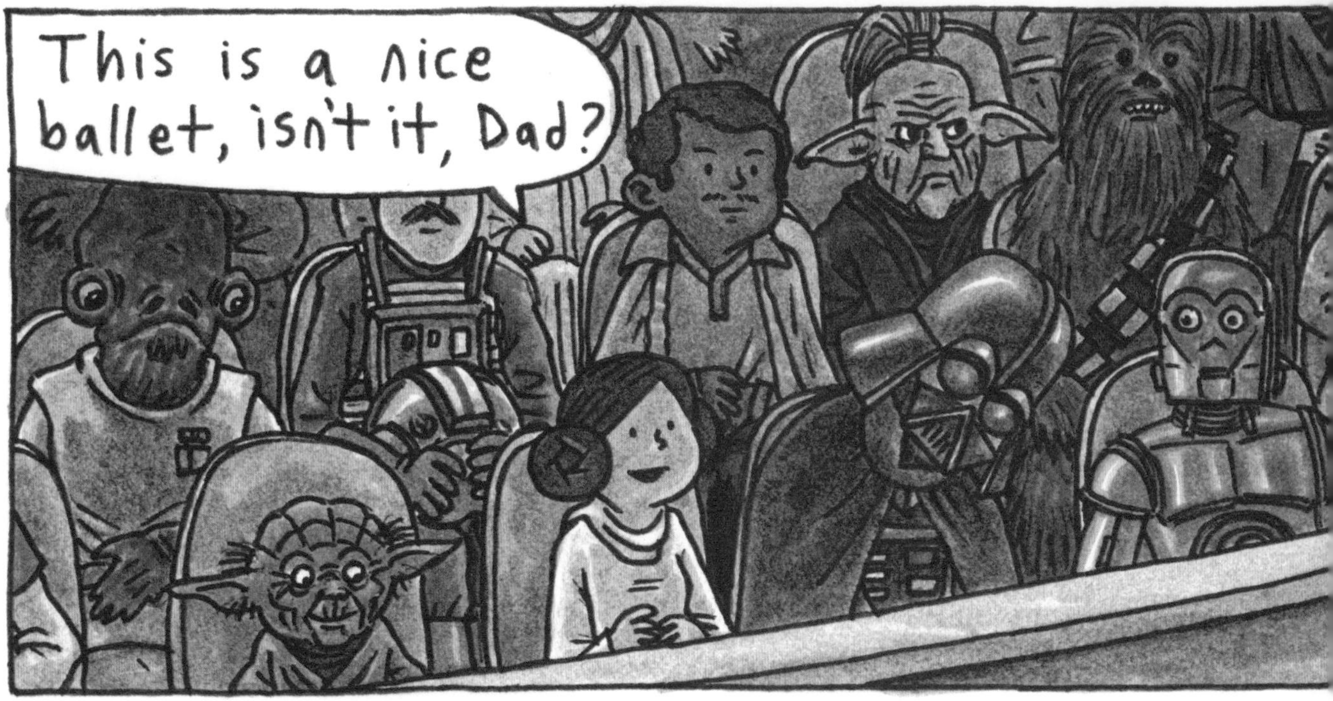
This is a nice ballet, isn't it, Dad?

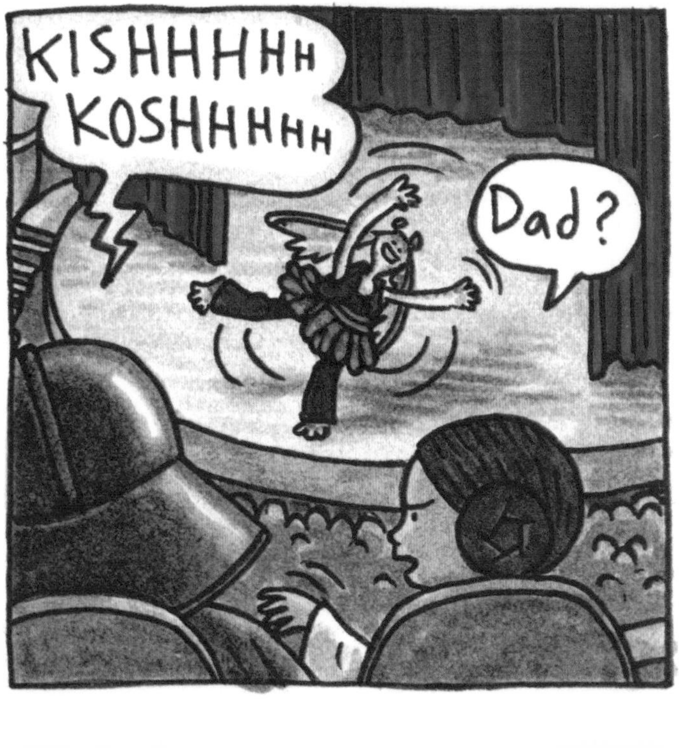
KISHHHHH
KOSHHHHH
Dad?

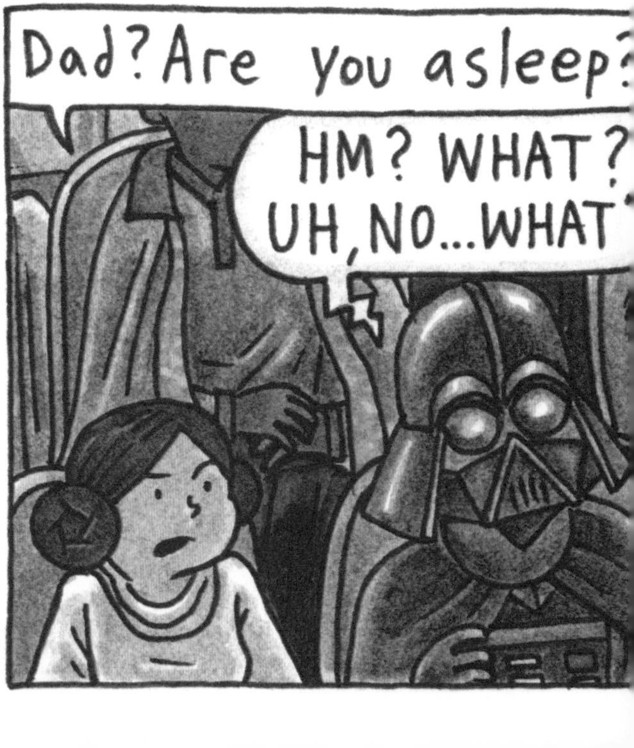
Dad? Are you asleep?
HM? WHAT?
UH, NO...WHAT

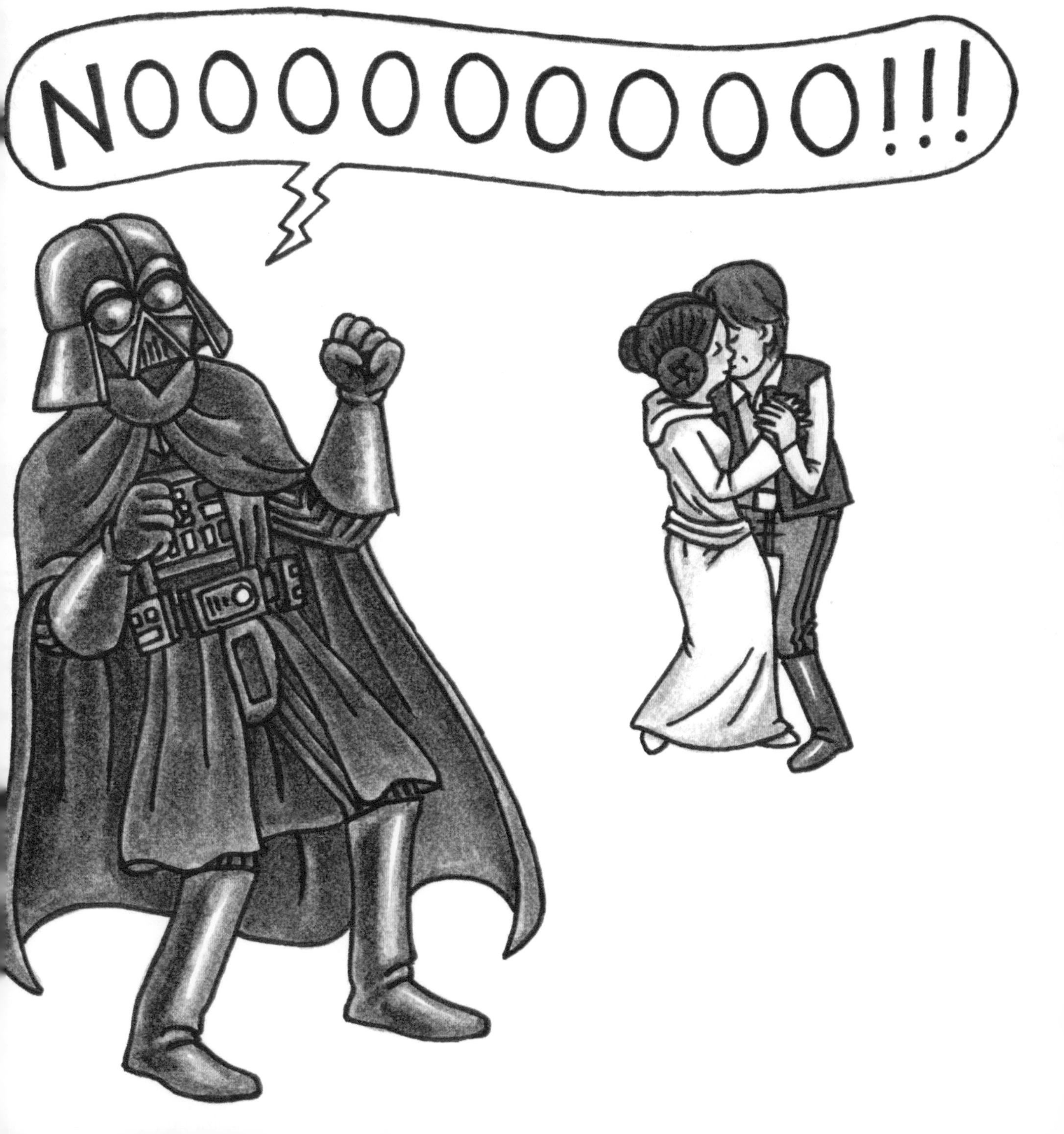
NOOOOOOOOOO!!!

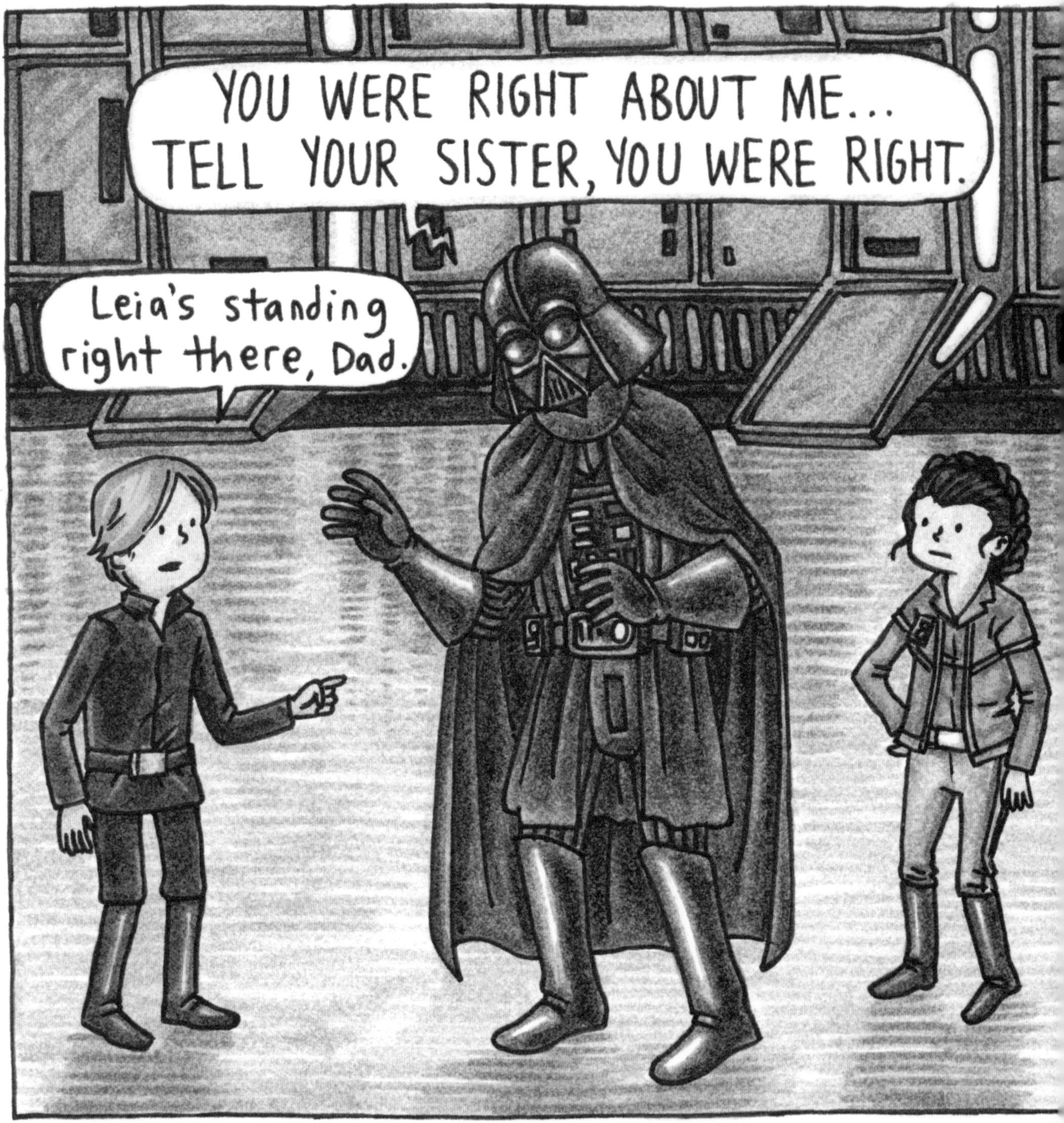
YOU WERE RIGHT ABOUT ME... TELL YOUR SISTER, YOU WERE RIGHT.
Leia's standing right there, Dad.

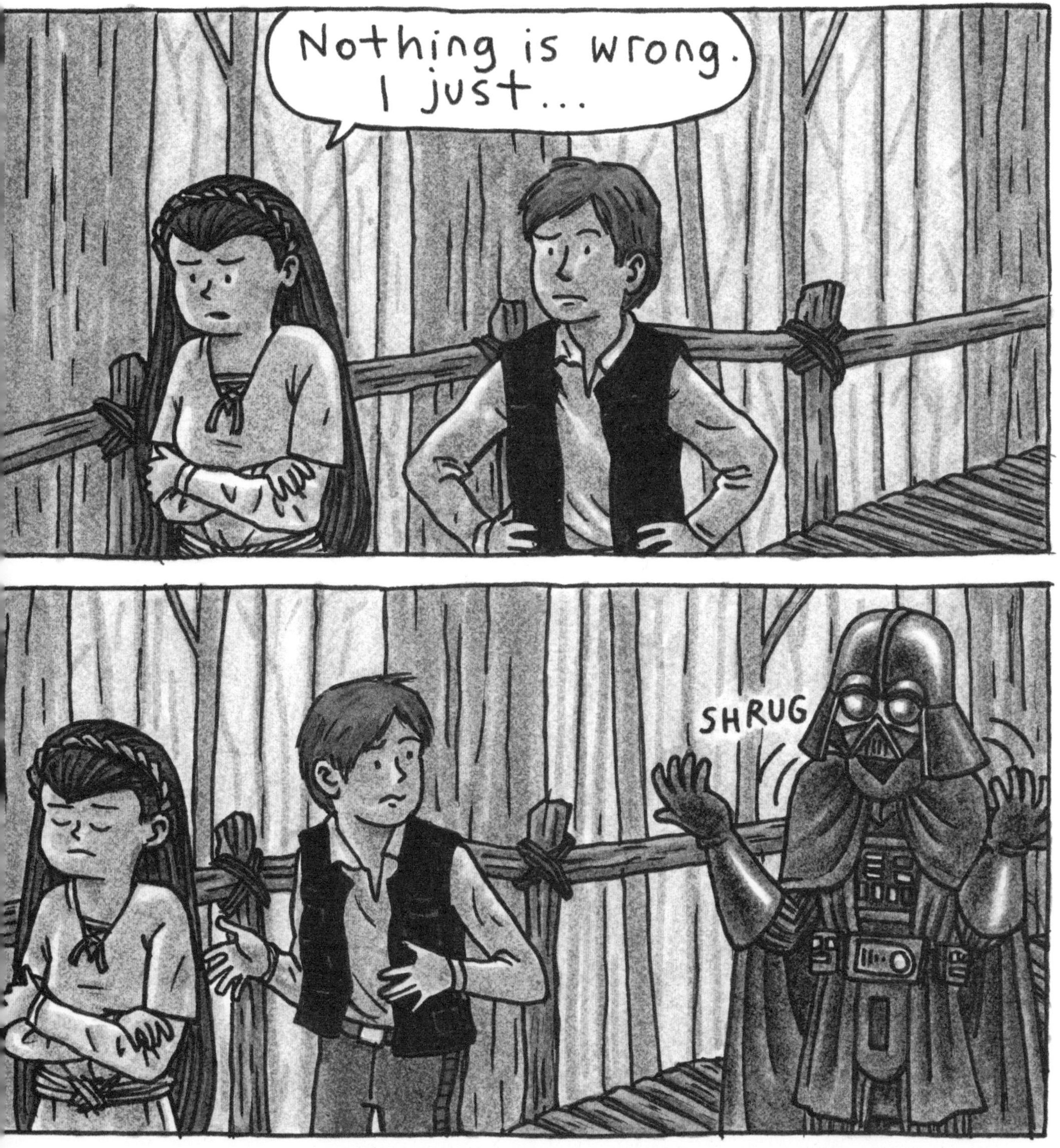
Nothing is wrong. I just...
SHRUG

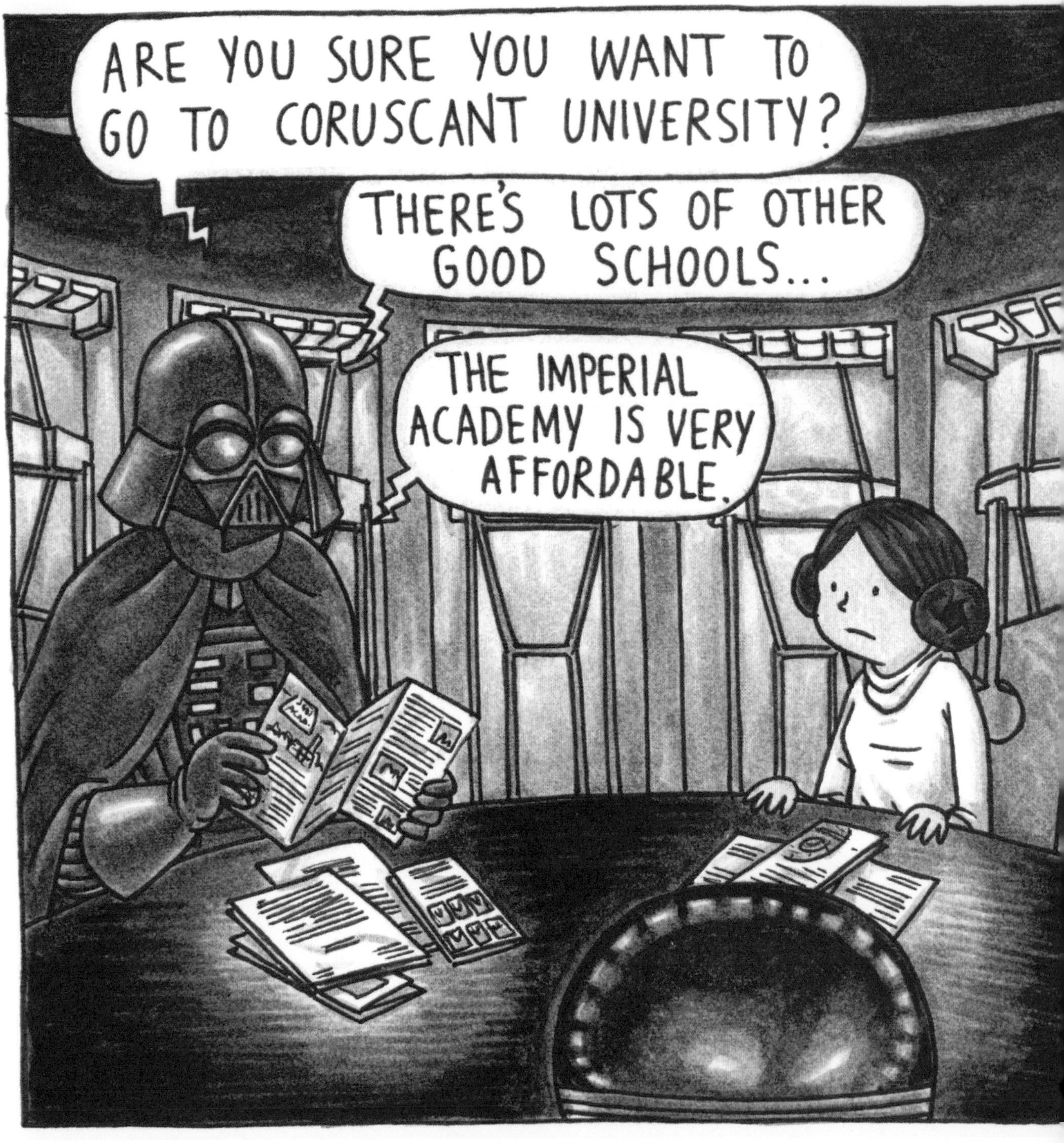
ARE YOU SURE YOU WANT TO GO TO CORUSCANT UNIVERSITY?
THERE'S LOTS OF OTHER GOOD SCHOOLS...
THE IMPERIAL ACADEMY IS VERY AFFORDABLE.

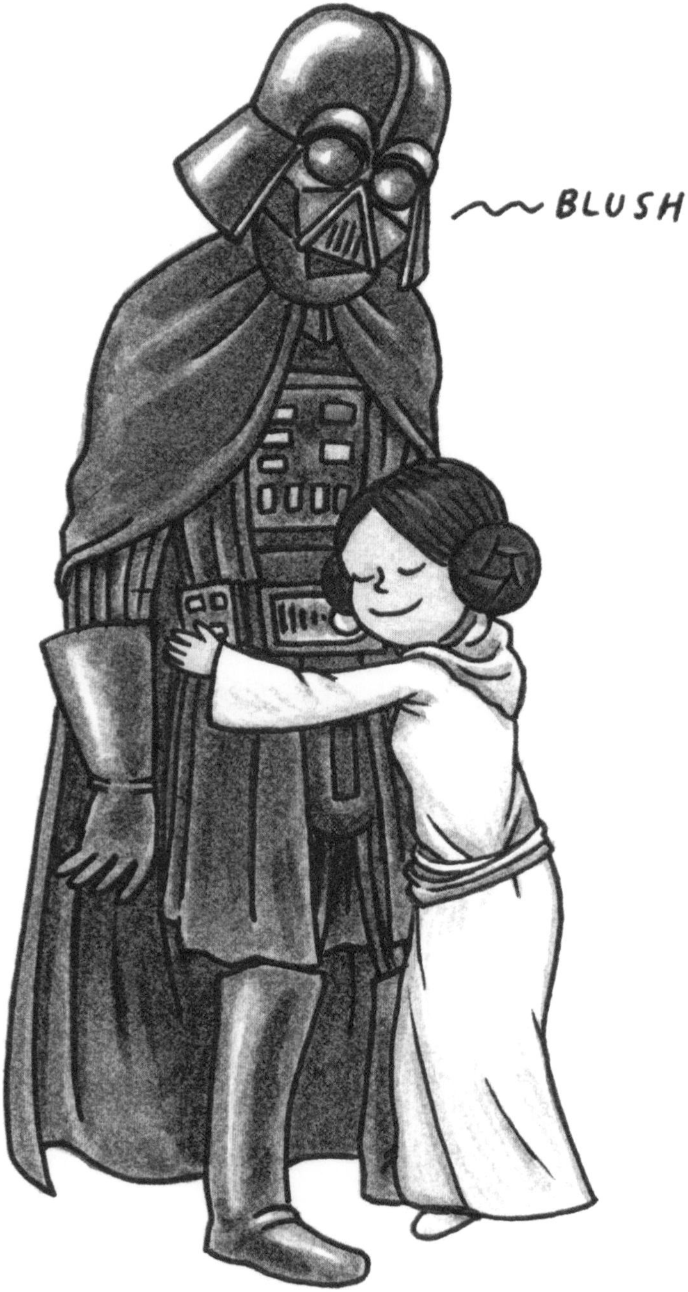
BLUSH

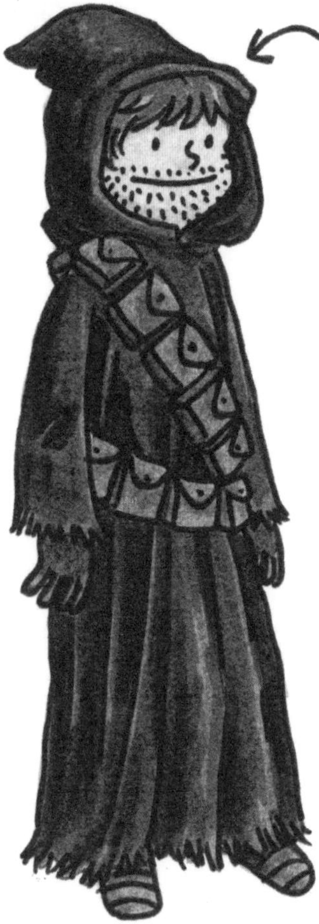

Jeffrey Brown is best known for his autobiographical comics and humorous graphic novels. He grew up watching Star Wars, playing with Star Wars action figures, and collecting Star Wars trading cards. He lives in Chicago with his wife and two sons.

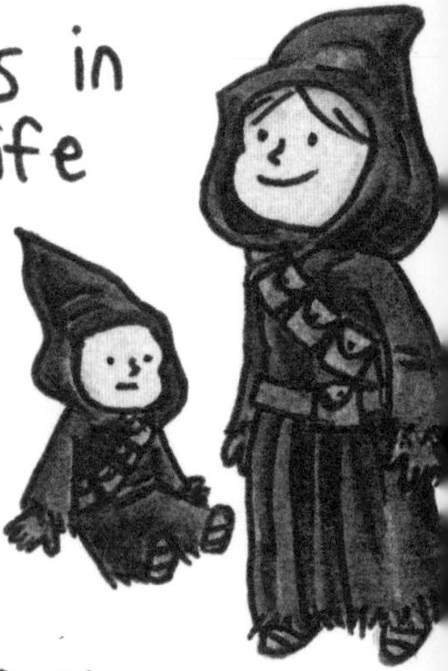

P.O. Box 120
DEERFIELD IL
60015-0120
USA

WWW.JEFFREYBROWNCOMICS.COM

MORE BOOKS BY JEFFREY BROWN

From Chronicle (WWW.CHRONICLEBOOKS.COM)

Cat Getting Out Of A Bag
Cats Are Weird
Darth Vader and Son

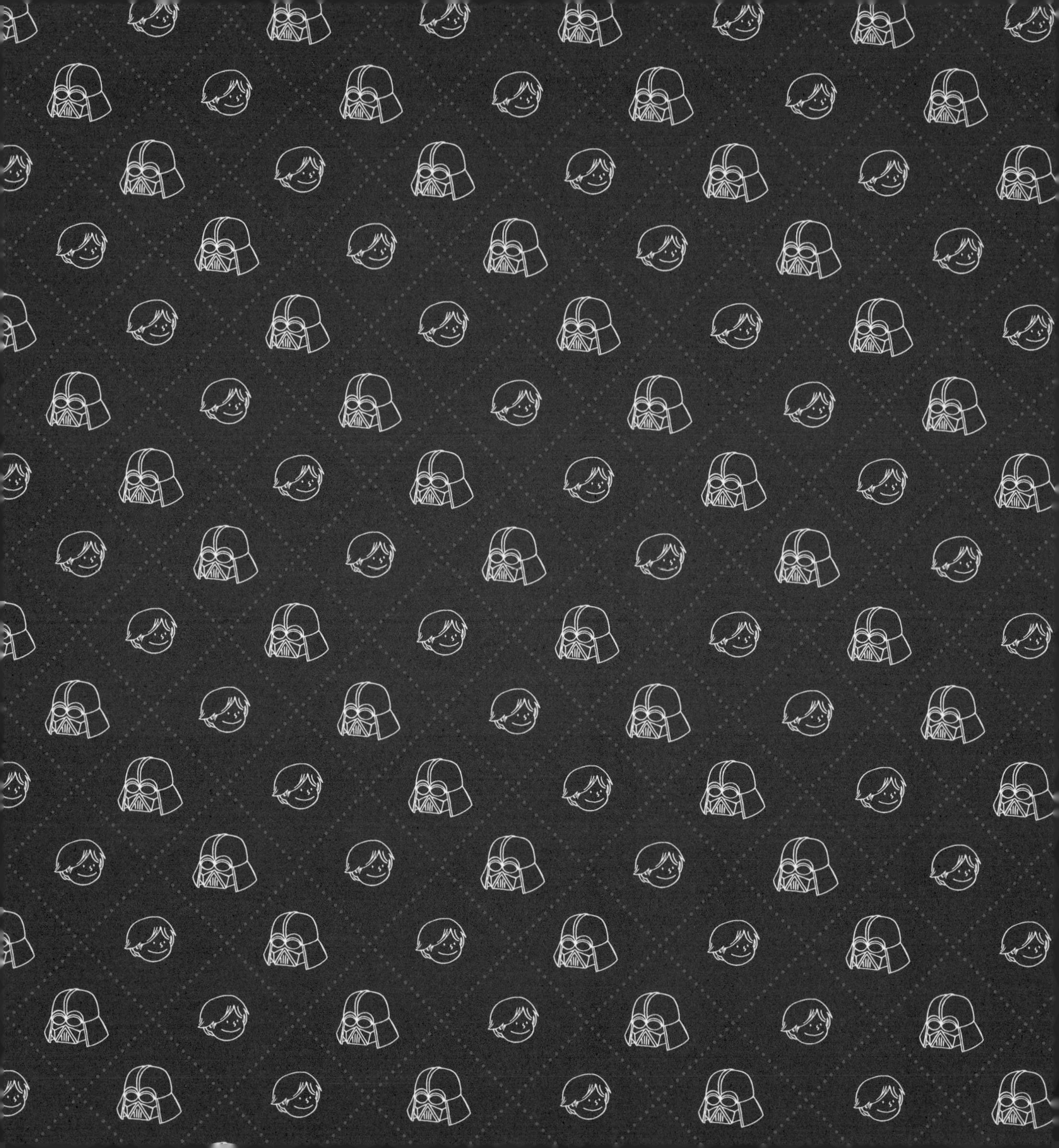

LIKE THIS

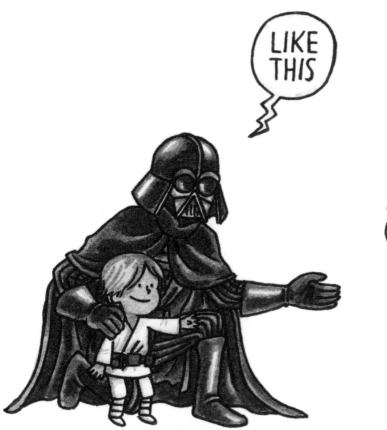

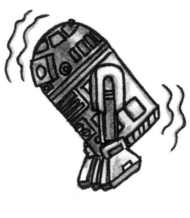

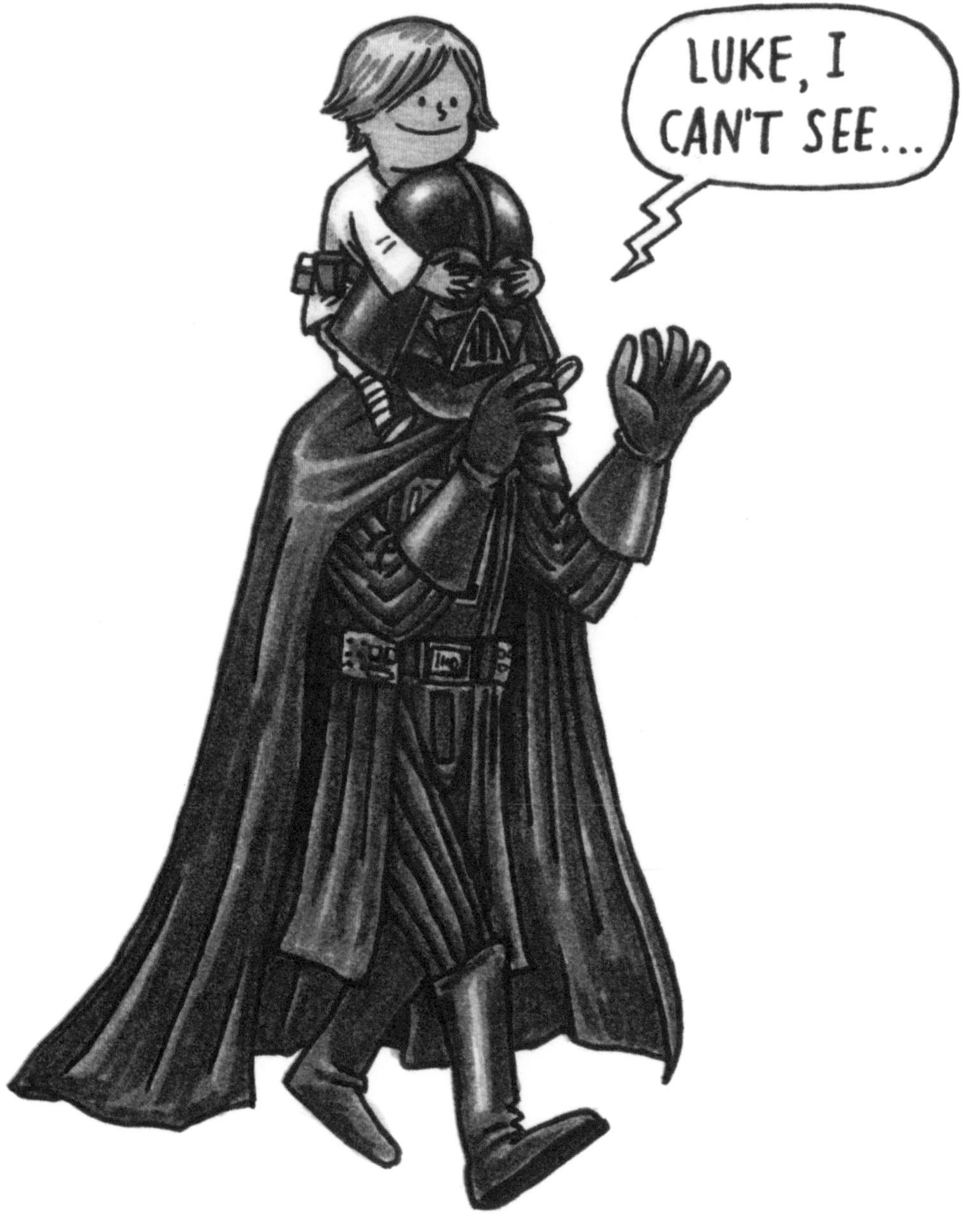
LUKE, I CAN'T SEE...

DARTH VADER™
and son

JEFFREY BROWN

CHRONICLE BOOKS
SAN FRANCISCO

THIS BOOK IS PART OF THE DARTH VADER AND SON / VADER'S LITTLE PRINCESS
BOX SET. NOT FOR INDIVIDUAL SALE.

BOX ISBN 978-1-4521-4487-0

THE LIBRARY OF CONGRESS CATALOGED THE ORIGINAL
EDITION OF THIS BOOK AS FOLLOWS:
BROWN, JEFFREY, 1975-
    DARTH VADER AND SON/BY JEFFREY BROWN.
       P.CM.
    ISBN 978-1-4521-0655-7
1. STAR WARS-COMIC BOOKS, STRIPS, ETC. 2. VADER, DARTH (FICTITIOUS
CHARACTER)-COMIC BOOKS, STRIPS, ETC. 3. FATHERS AND SONS-COMIC BOOKS,
STRIPS, ETC. 4. AMERICAN WIT AND HUMOR 5. GRAPHIC NOVELS. I. TITLE.
    PN6727.B7575D372011
    741.5'973--DC23
                    2011038954

MANUFACTURED IN CHINA

MIX
Paper from
responsible sources
FSC™ C020056

WRITTEN AND DRAWN BY JEFFREY BROWN
DESIGNED BY MICHAEL MORRIS

THANKS TO STEVE MOCKUS, J.W. RINZLER, MARC GERALD, AND
MY FAMILY. SPECIAL THANKS TO RYAN GERMICK AND MICHEAL
LOPEZ AT GOOGLE, WHO LET ME RUN WITH THEIR ORIGINAL IDEA
OF LUKE AND DARTH VADER AWKWARDLY CELEBRATING FATHER'S DAY.

10 9 8 7 6 5 4 3 2 1

CHRONICLE BOOKS LLC
680 SECOND STREET
SAN FRANCISCO, CA 94107
WWW.CHRONICLEBOOKS.COM

WWW.STAR WARS.COM

A long time ago in a galaxy far,
far away.....

Episode Three and a half:
DARTH VADER AND SON

Darth Vader, Dark Lord of
the Sith, leads the Galactic
Empire against the heroic Rebel
Alliance. Before he can take
care of the Rebels, Lord Vader
must first take care of his son—
four-year-old Luke Skywalker....

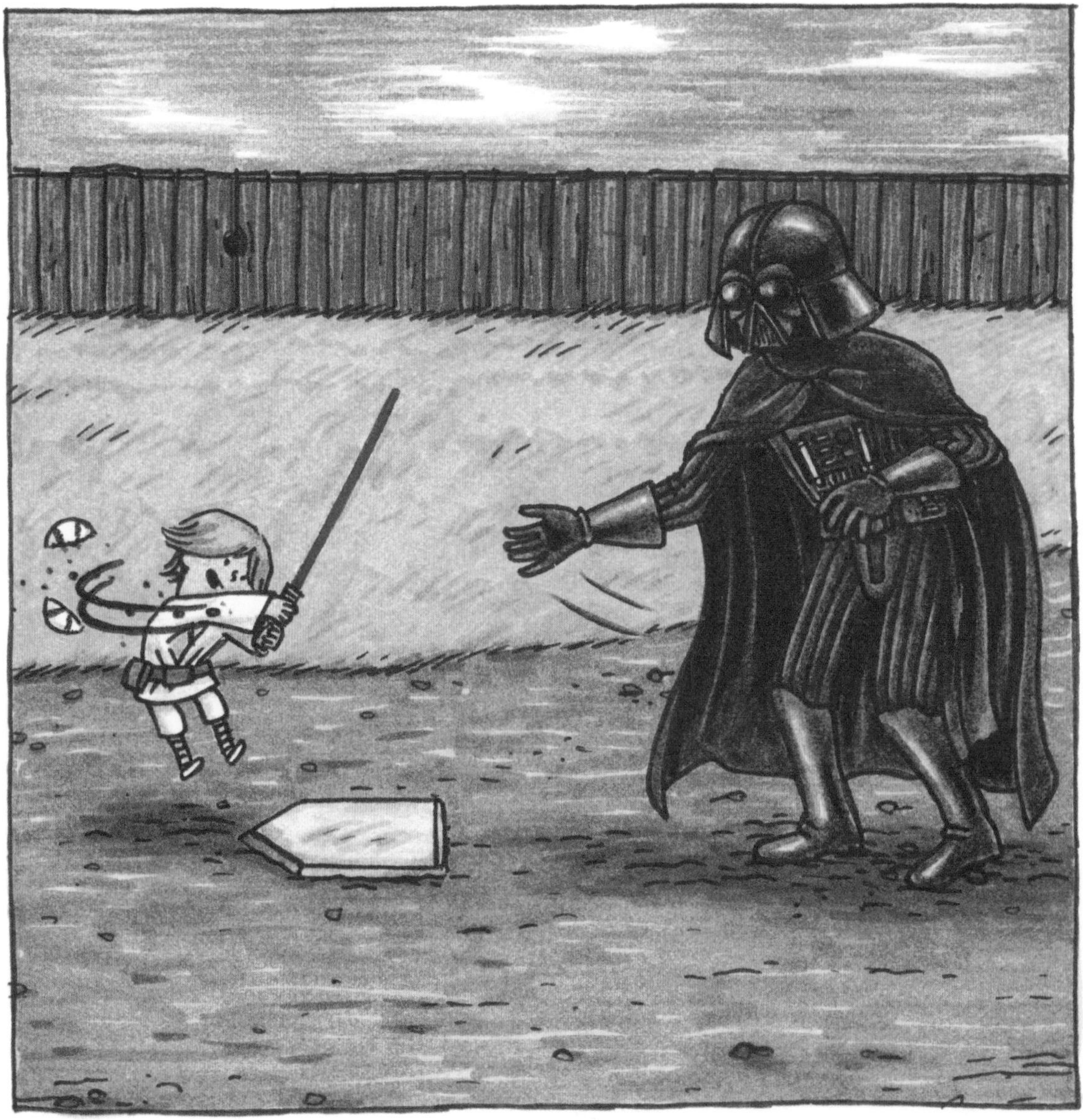

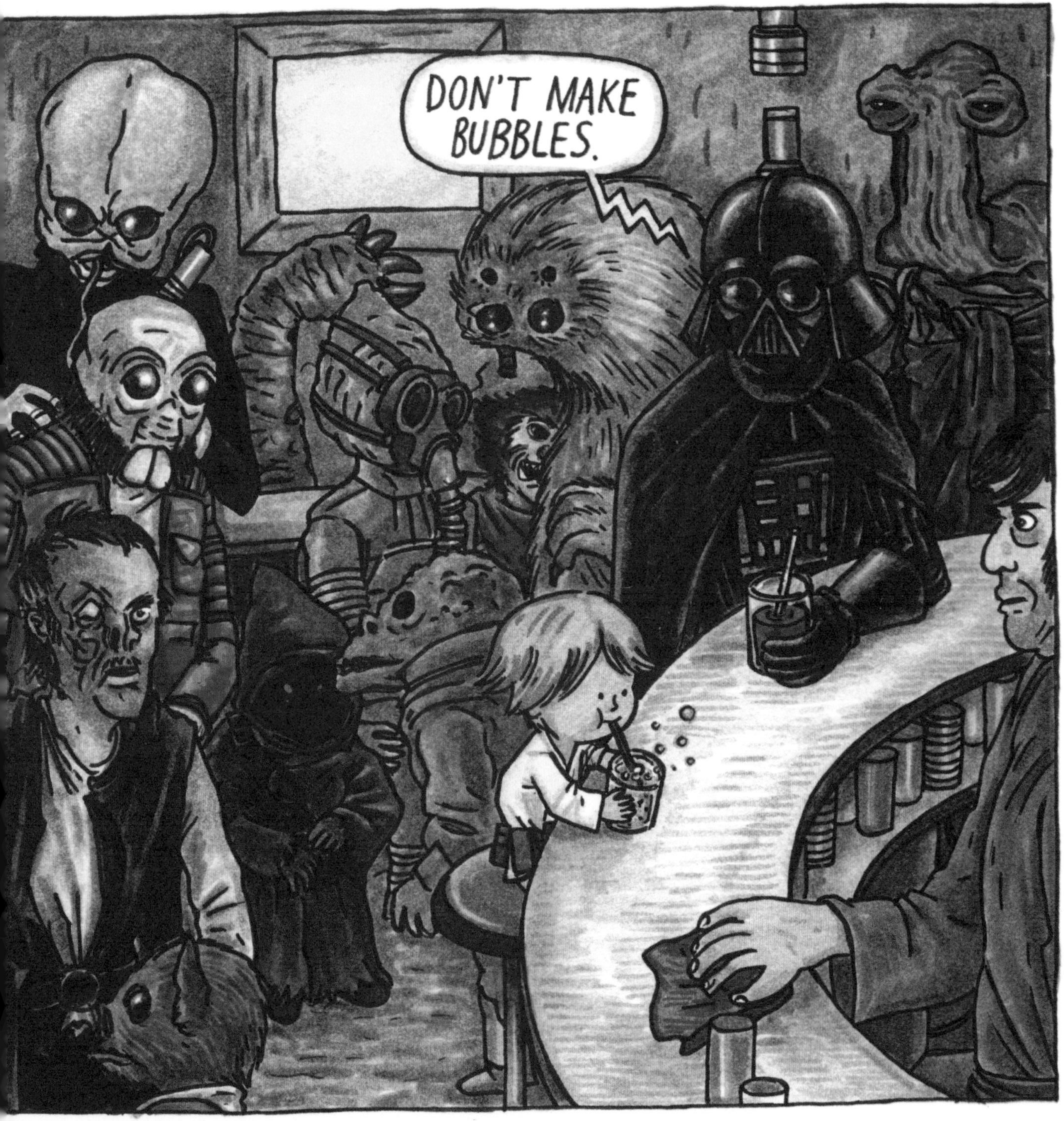
DON'T MAKE BUBBLES.

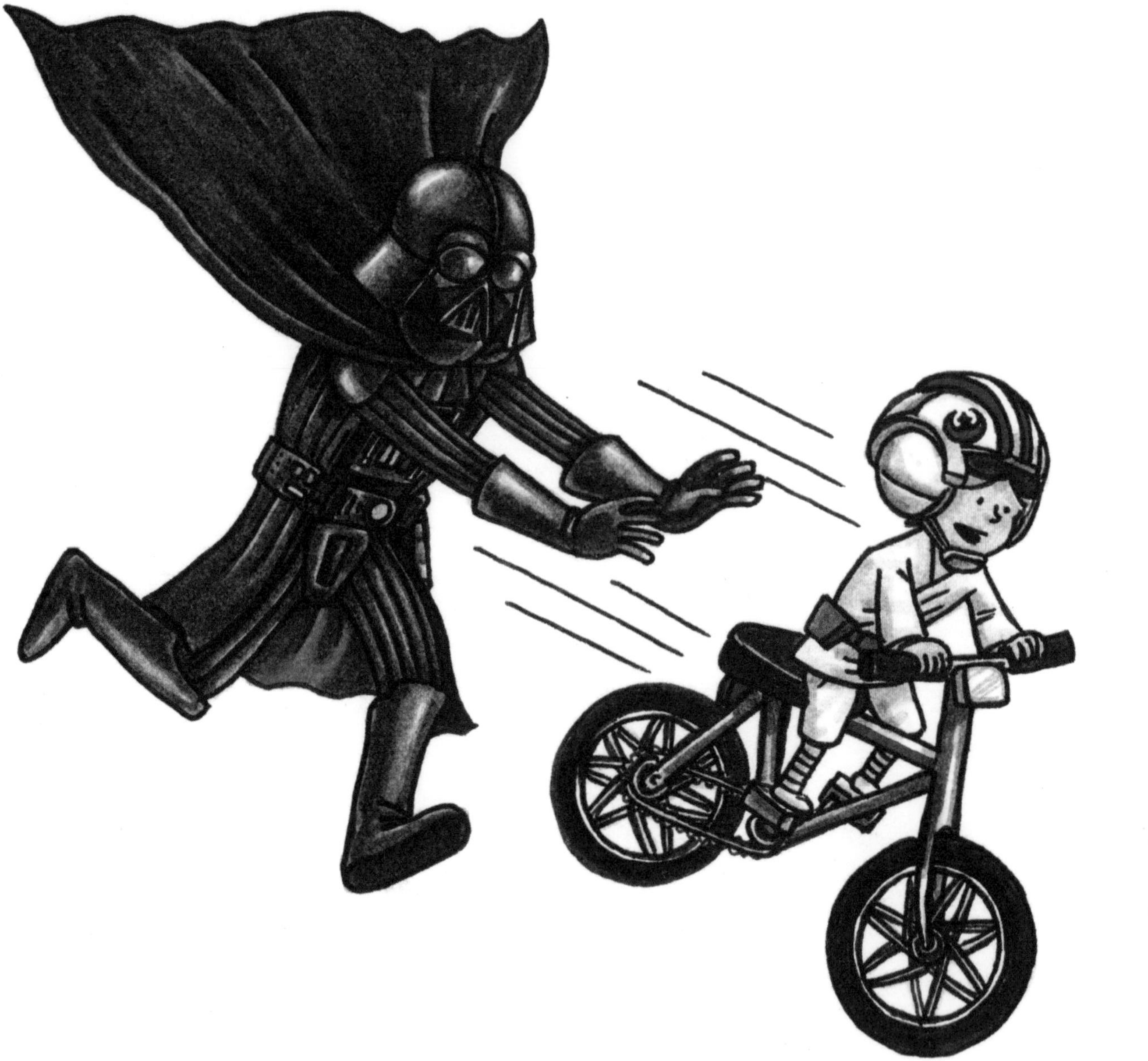

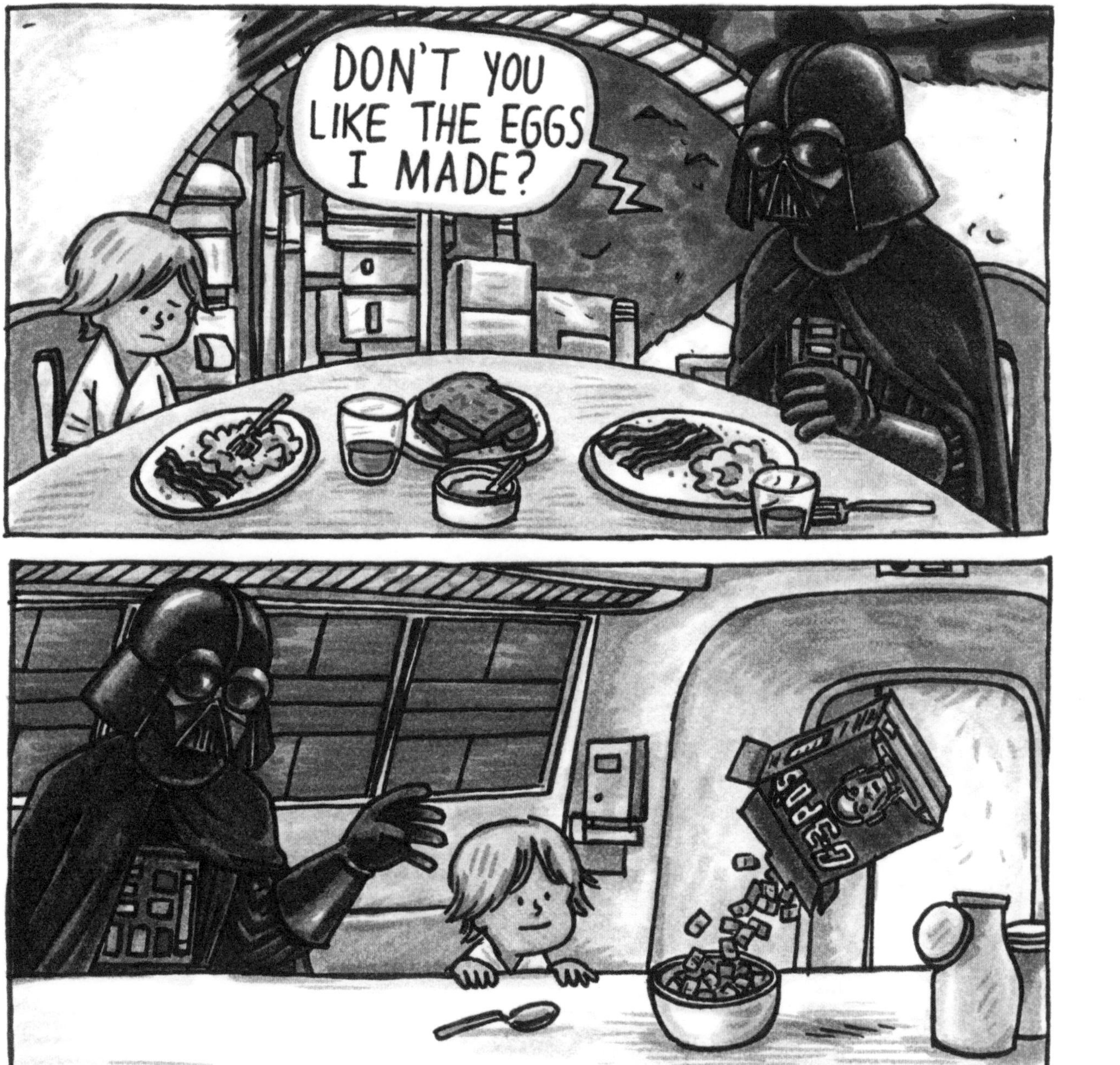
DON'T YOU LIKE THE EGGS I MADE?

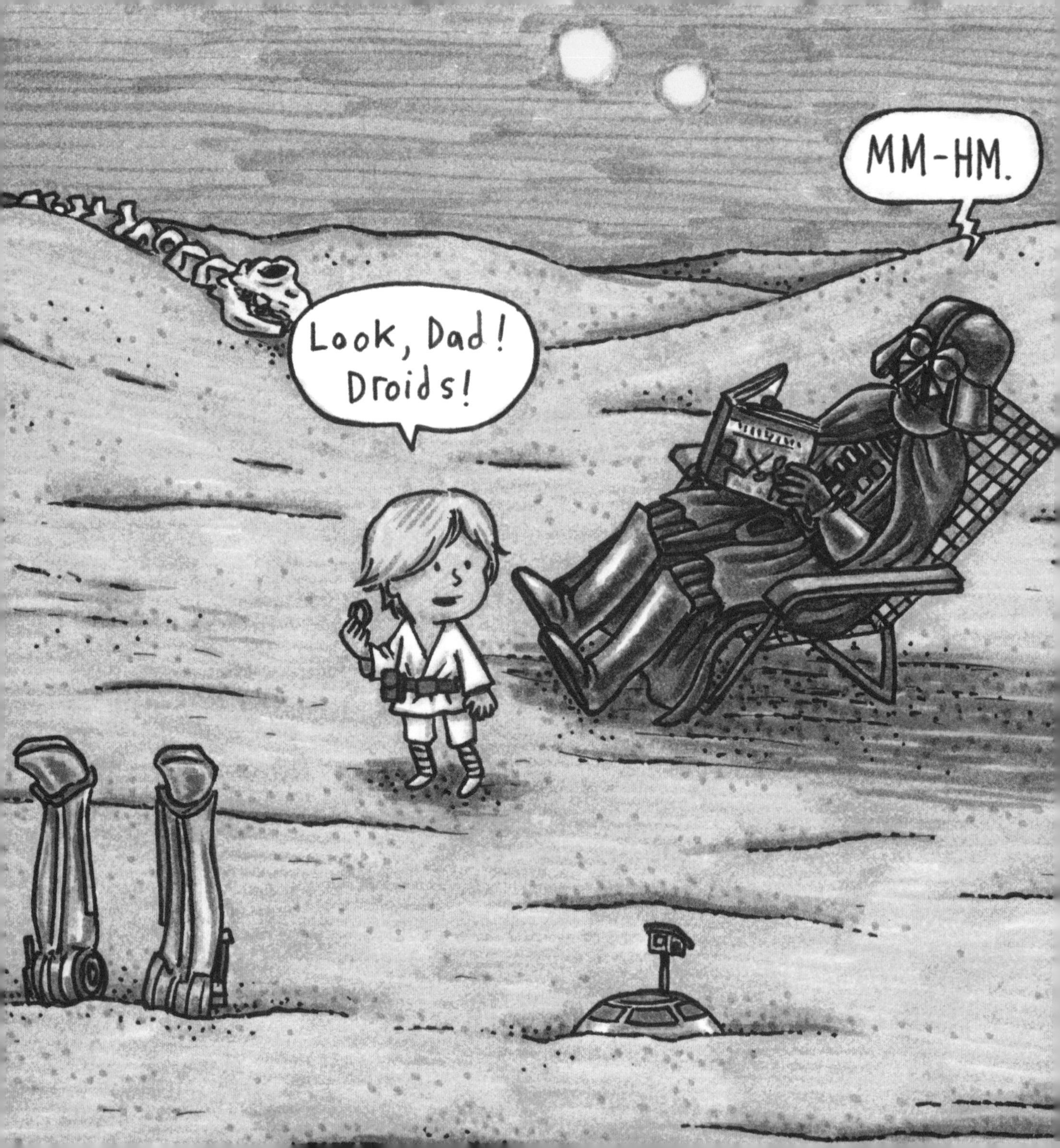
MM-HM.
Look, Dad!
Droids!

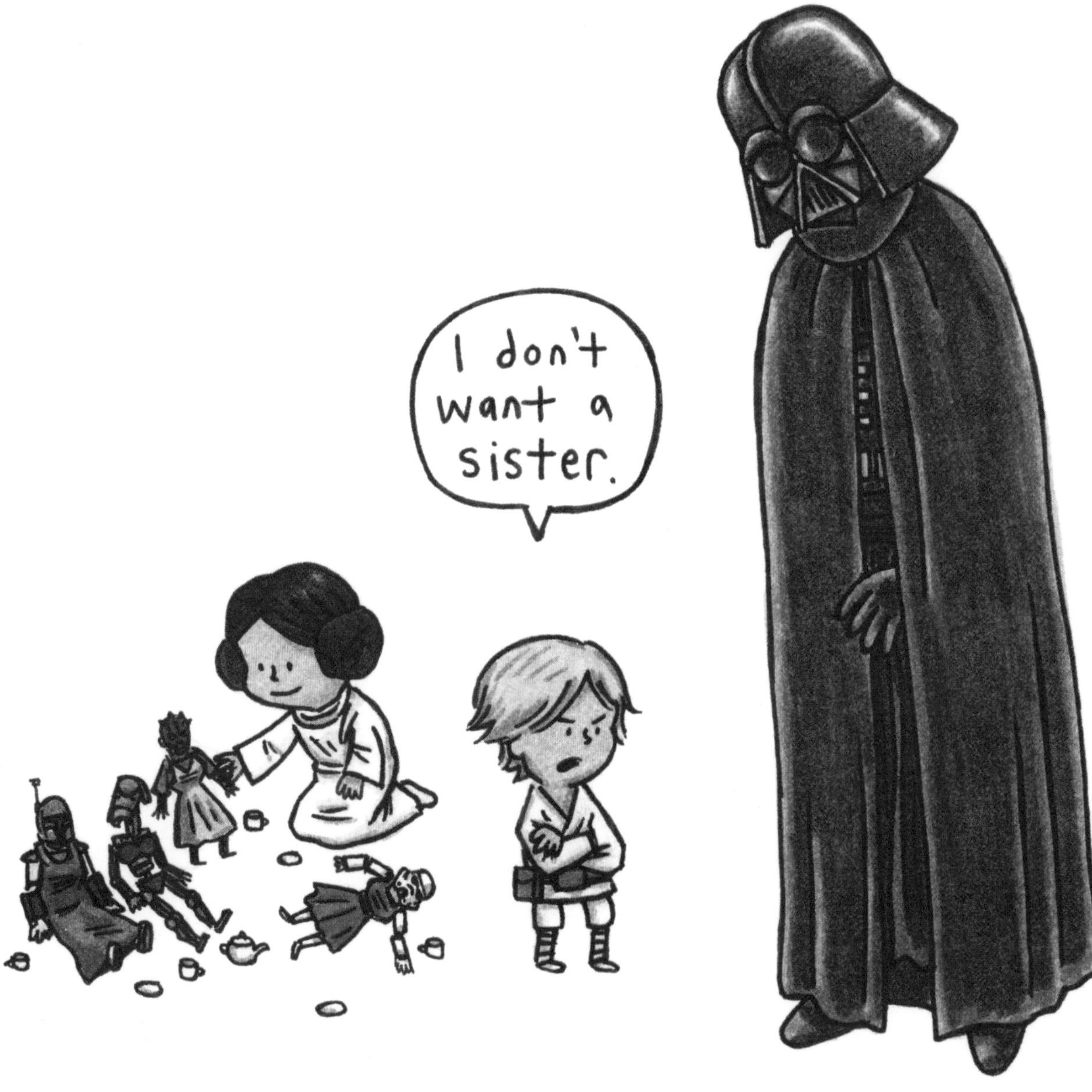
I don't want a sister.

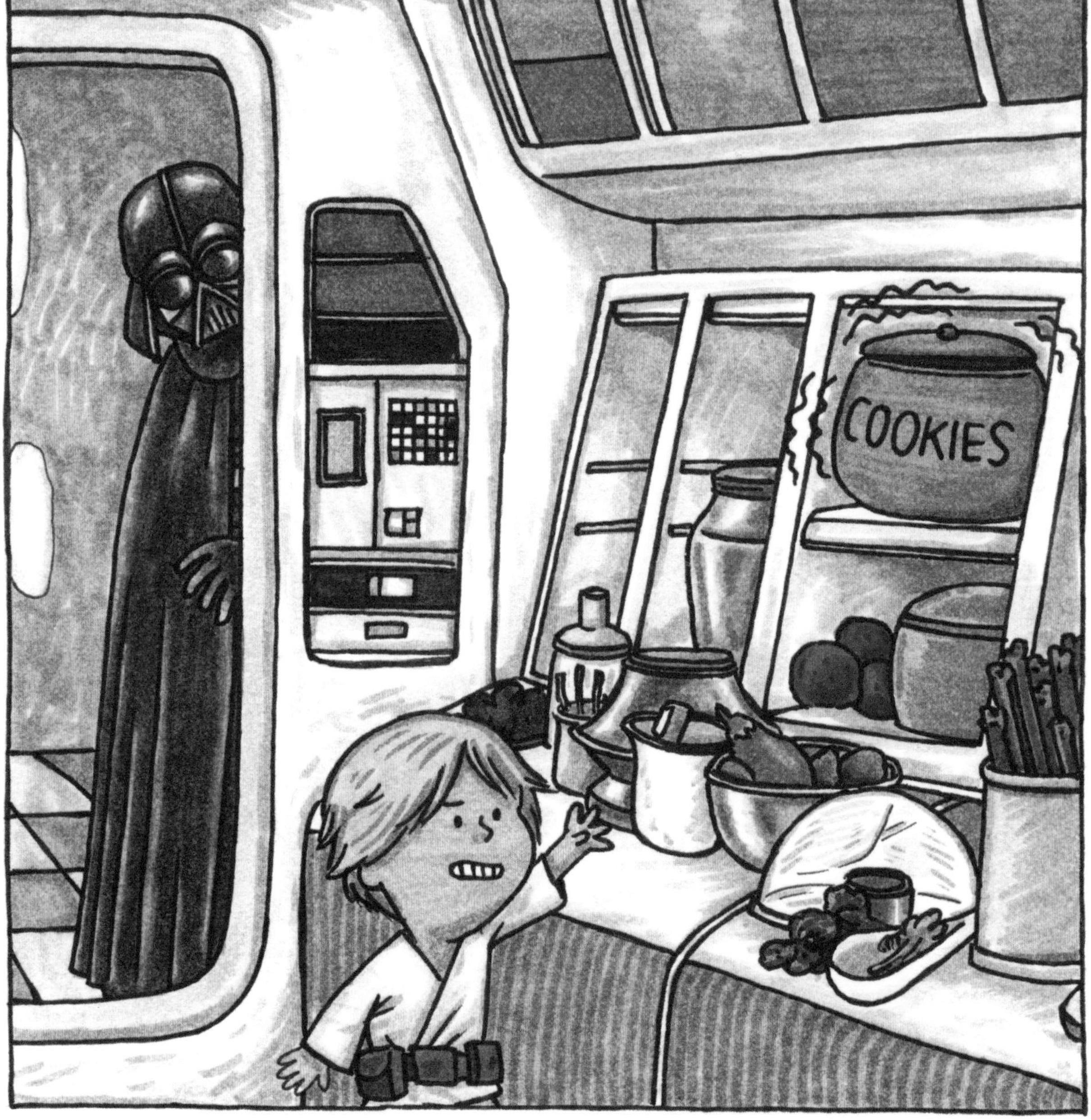
COOKIES

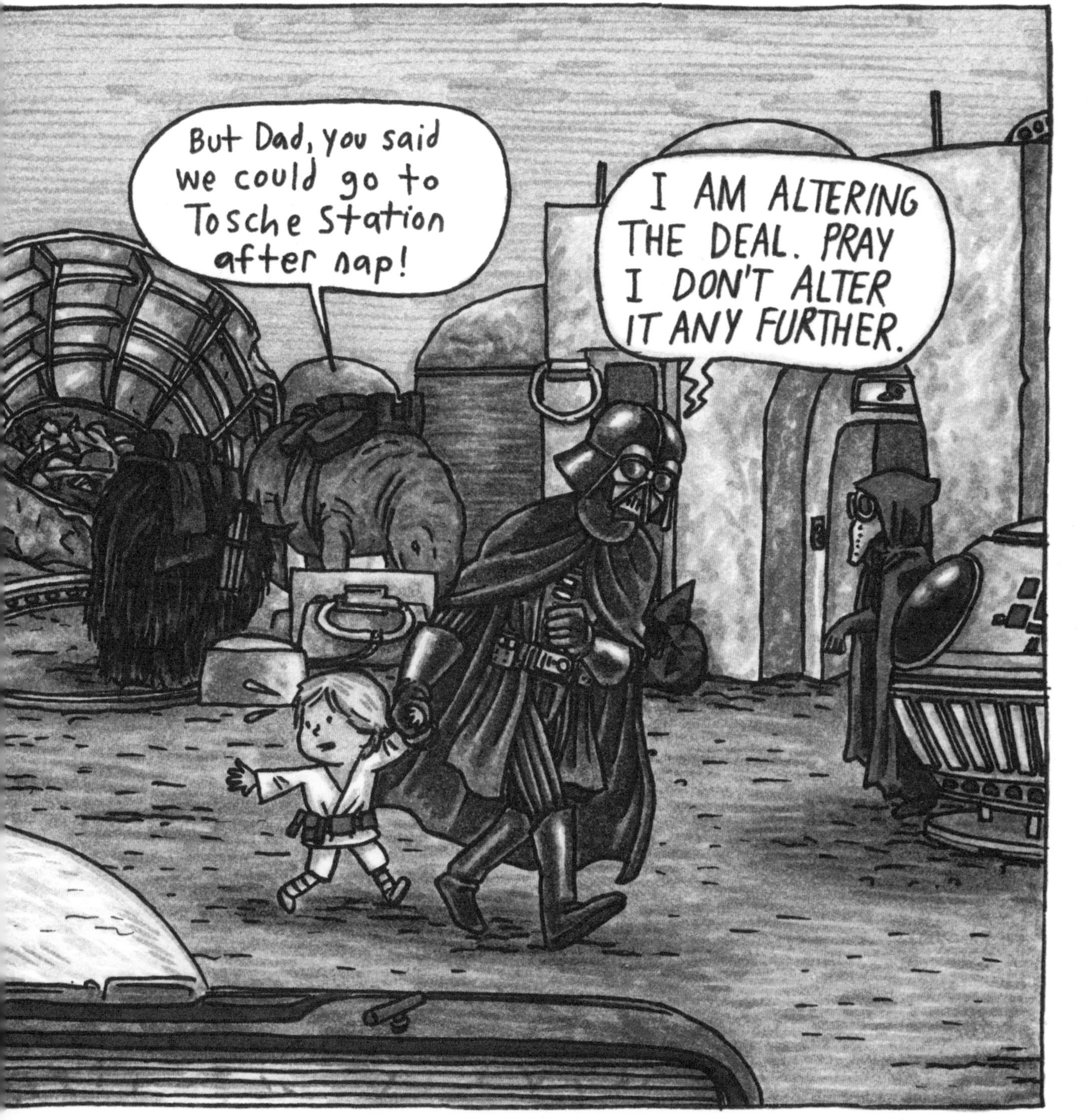
But Dad, you said we could go to Tosche Station after nap!
I AM ALTERING THE DEAL. PRAY I DON'T ALTER IT ANY FURTHER.

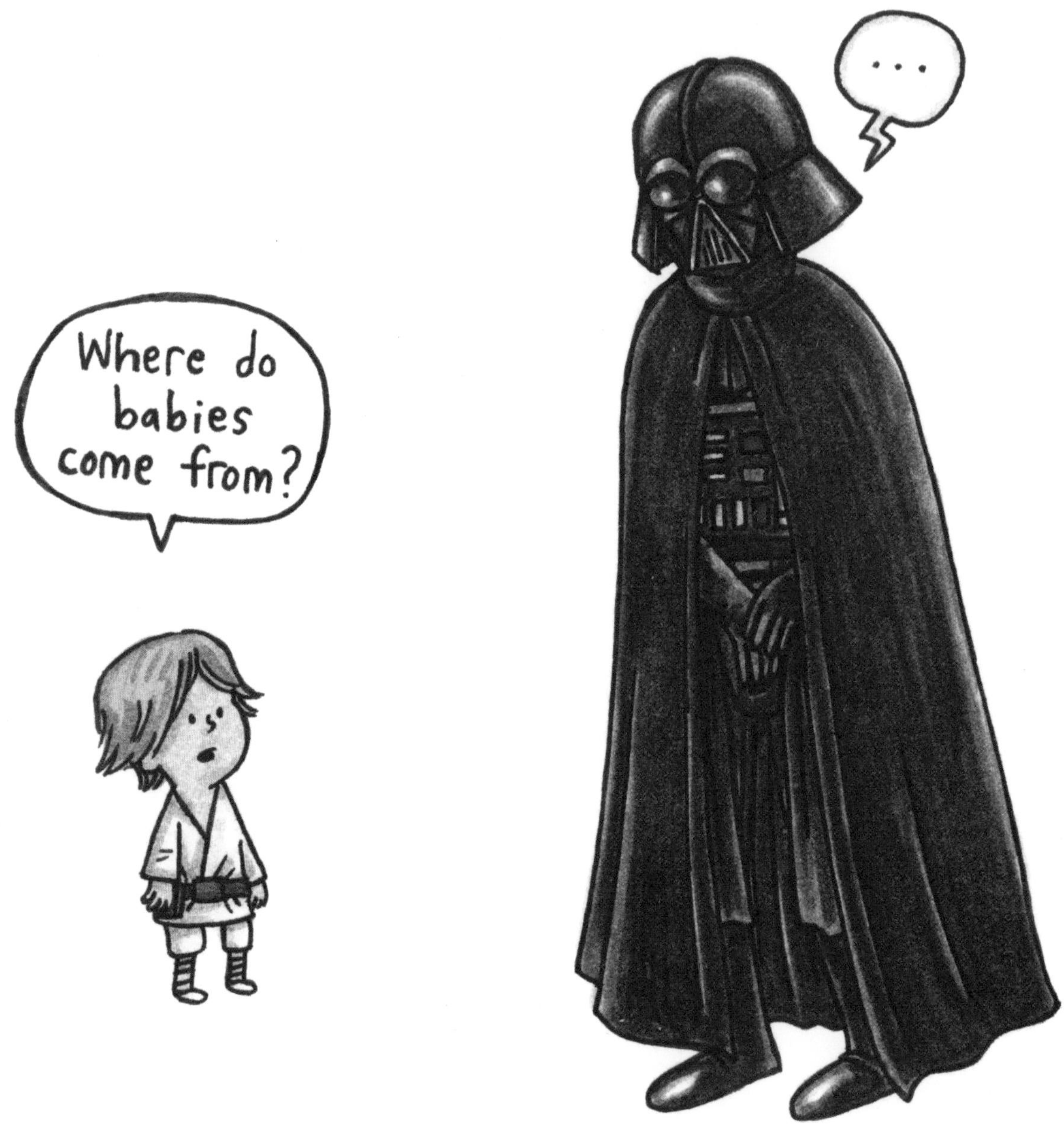
Where do babies come from?
...

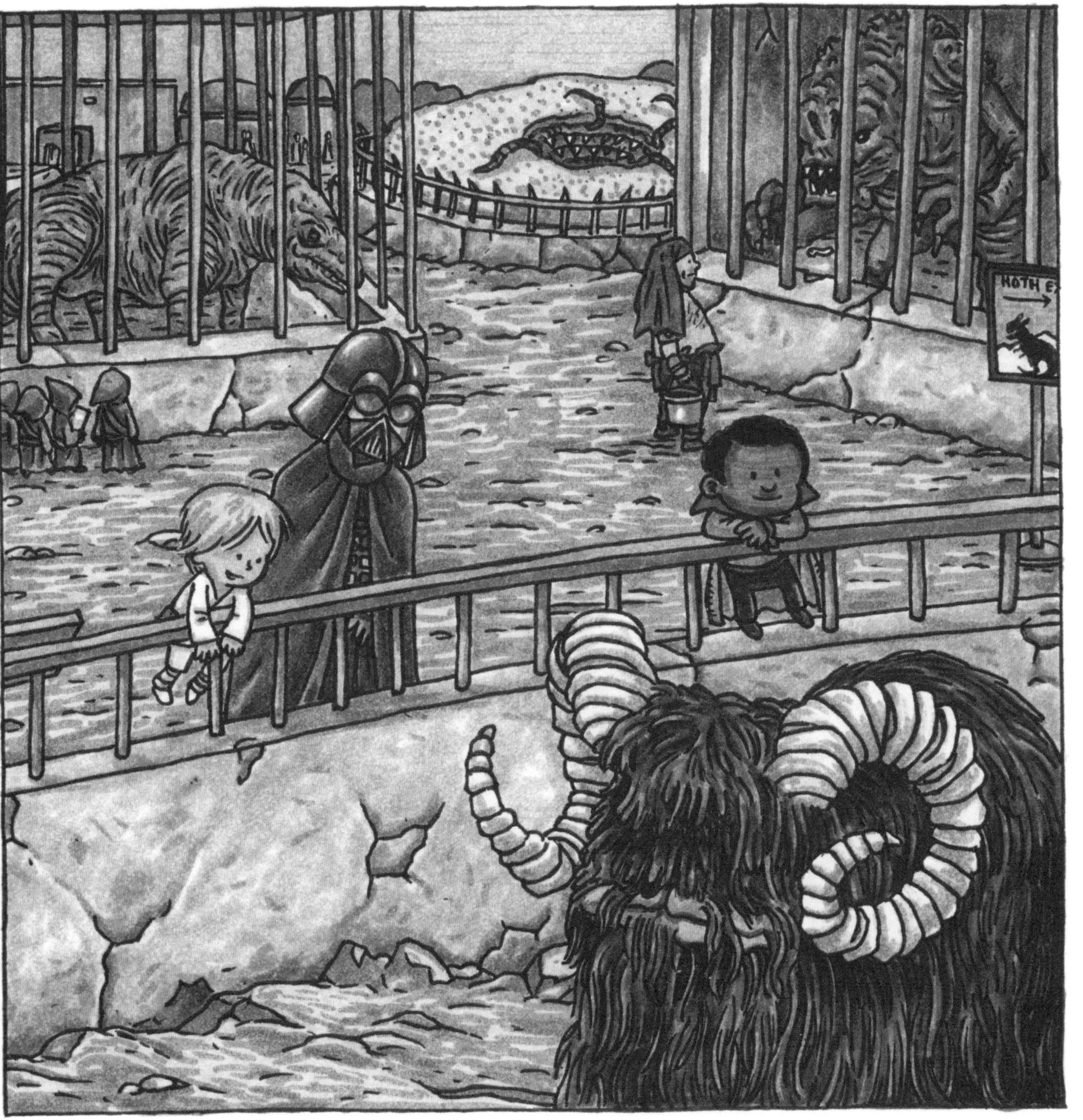
HOTH E

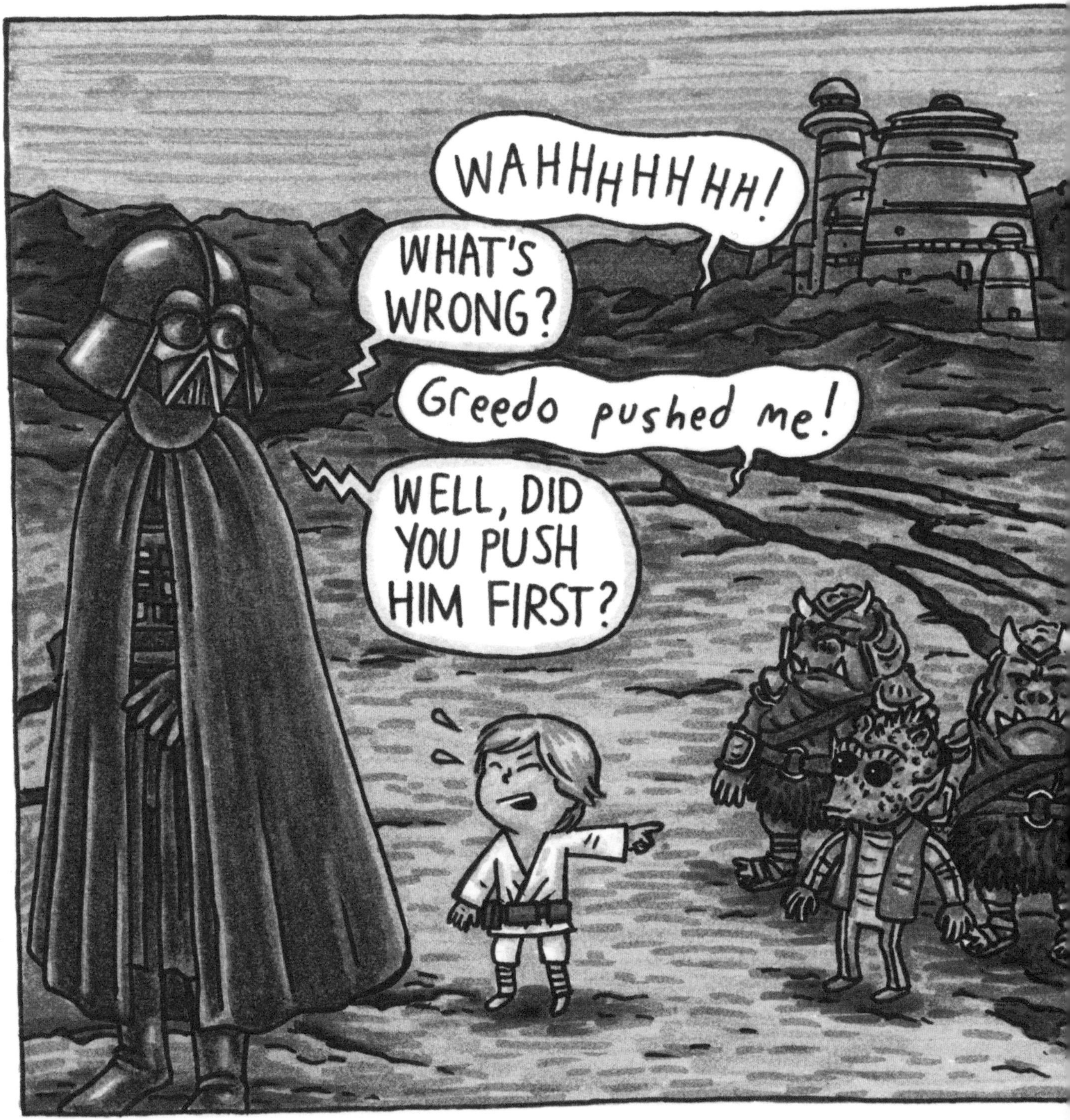
WAHHHHHHH!
WHAT'S WRONG?
Greedo pushed me!
WELL, DID YOU PUSH HIM FIRST?

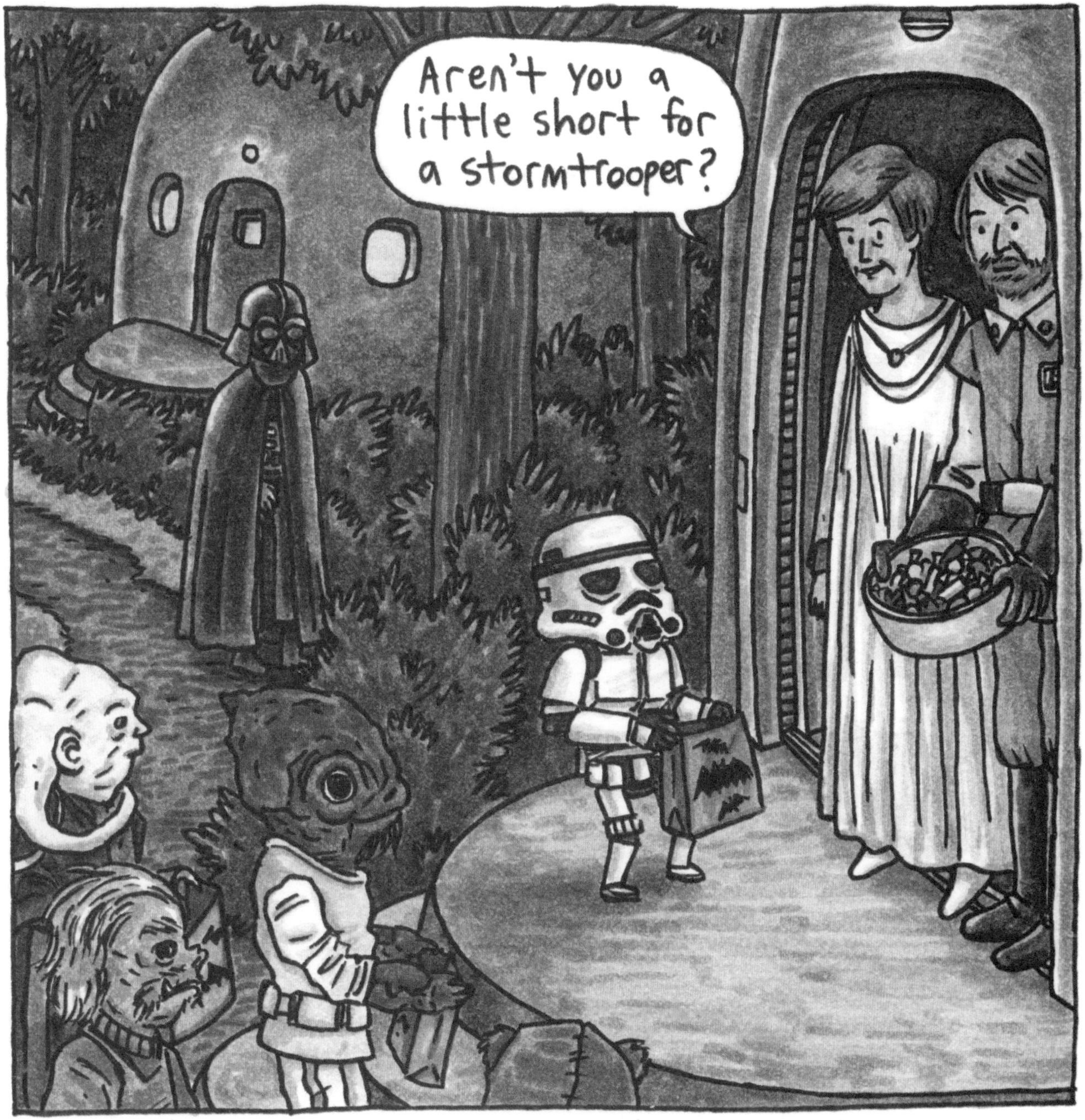
Aren't you a little short for a stormtrooper?

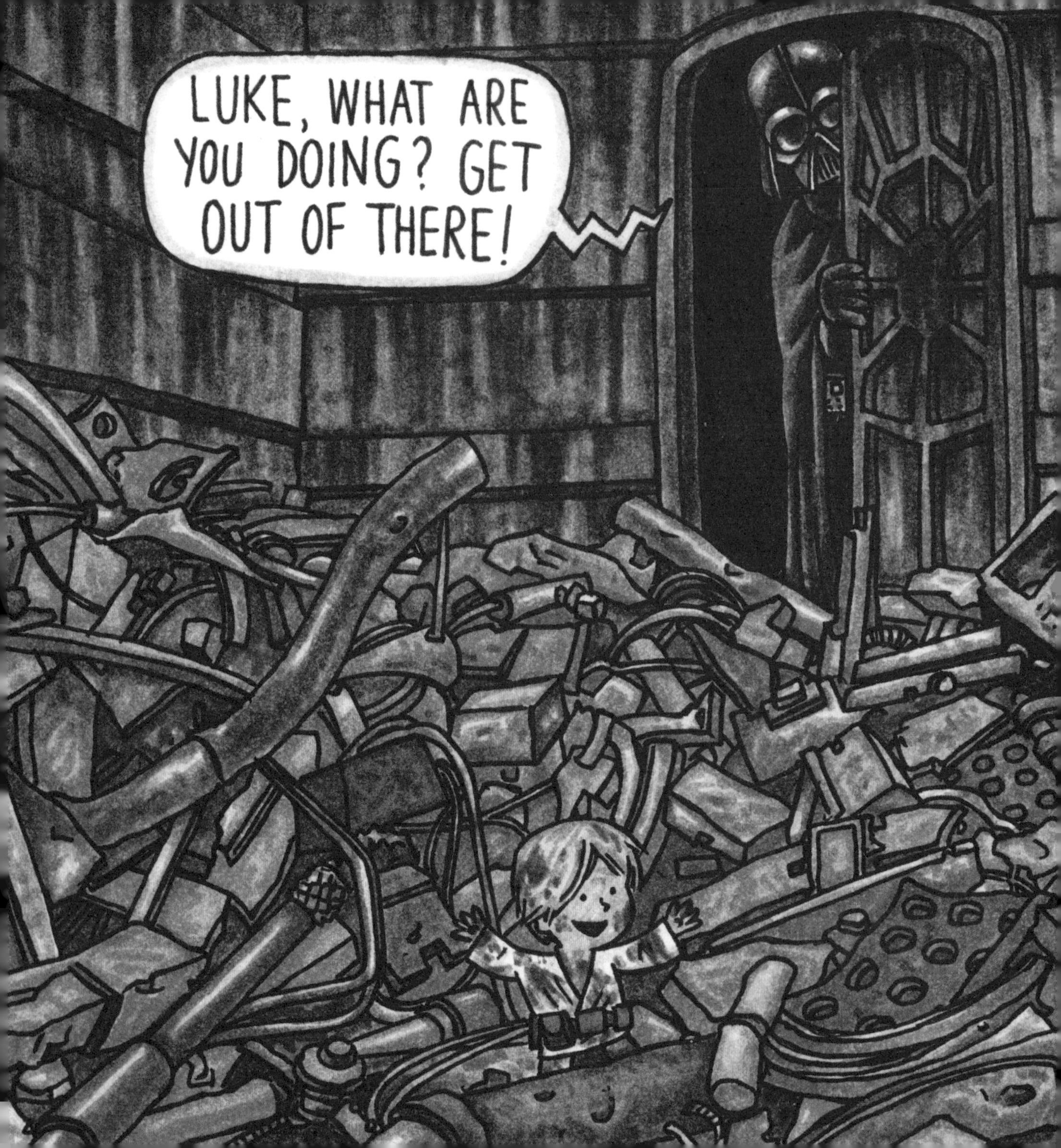
LUKE, WHAT ARE YOU DOING? GET OUT OF THERE!

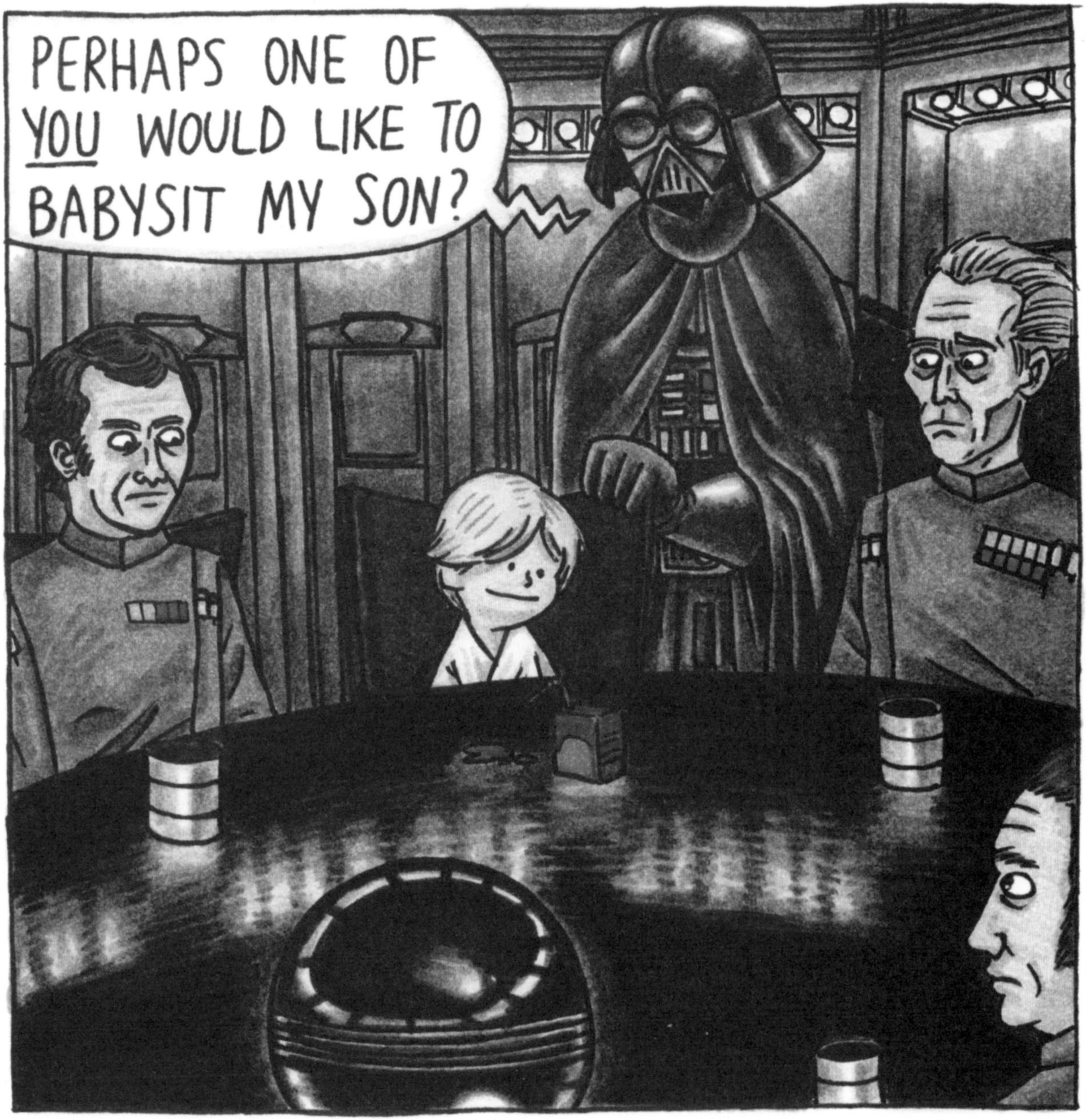
PERHAPS ONE OF YOU WOULD LIKE TO BABYSIT MY SON?

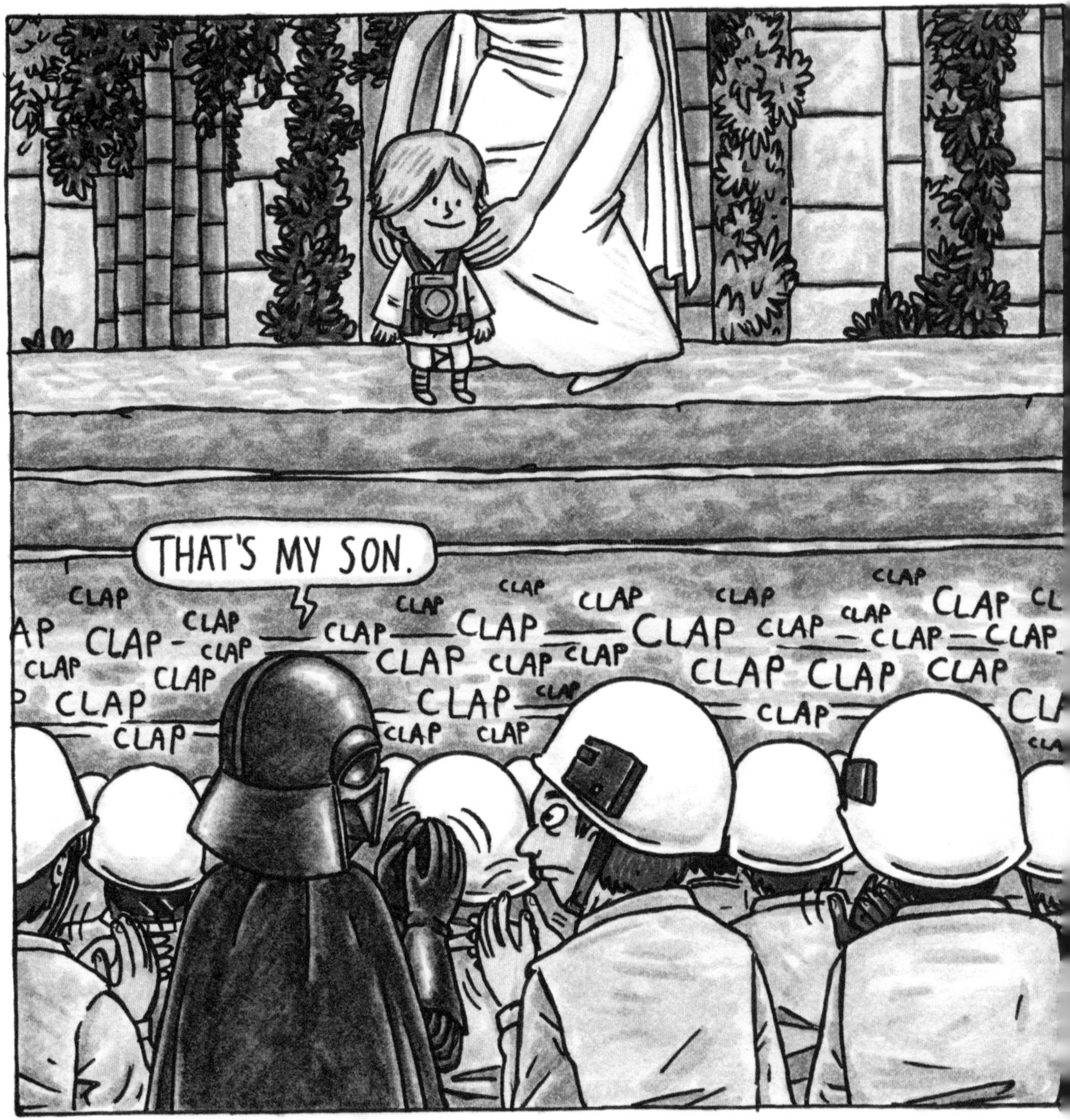
THAT'S MY SON.
CLAP CLAP CLAP CLAP CLAP CLAP

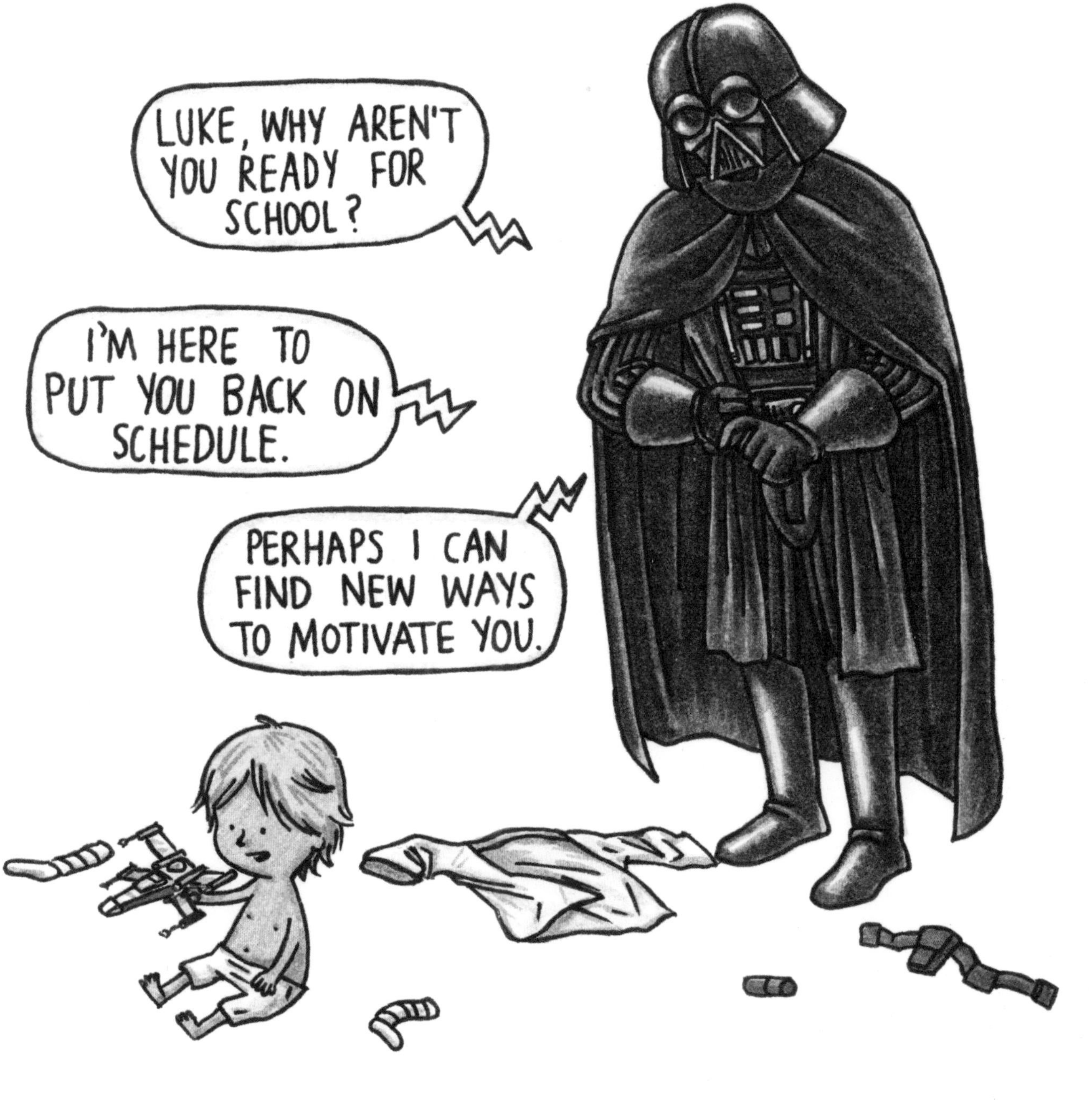
LUKE, WHY AREN'T YOU READY FOR SCHOOL?
I'M HERE TO PUT YOU BACK ON SCHEDULE.
PERHAPS I CAN FIND NEW WAYS TO MOTIVATE YOU.

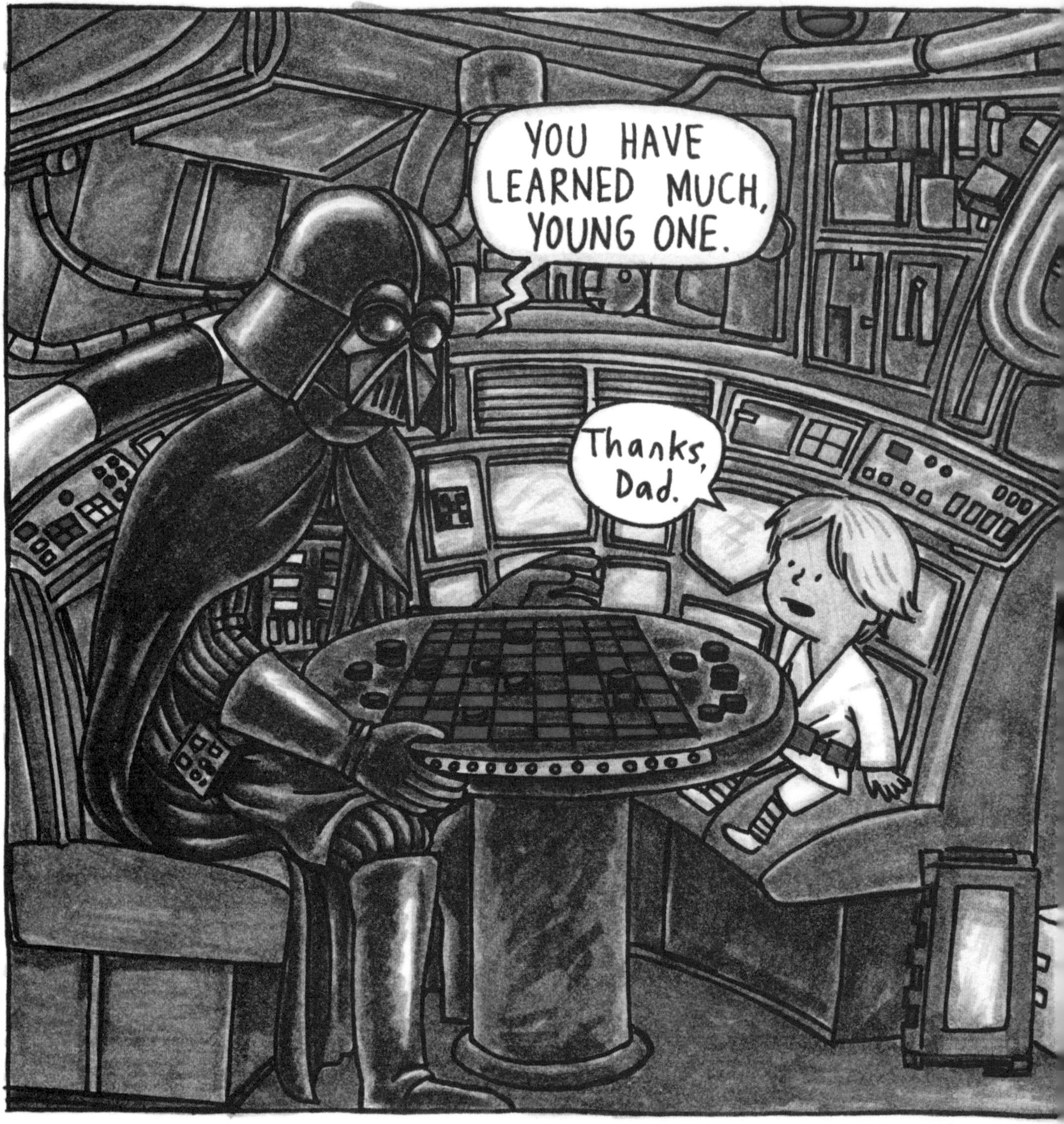
YOU HAVE LEARNED MUCH, YOUNG ONE.
Thanks, Dad.

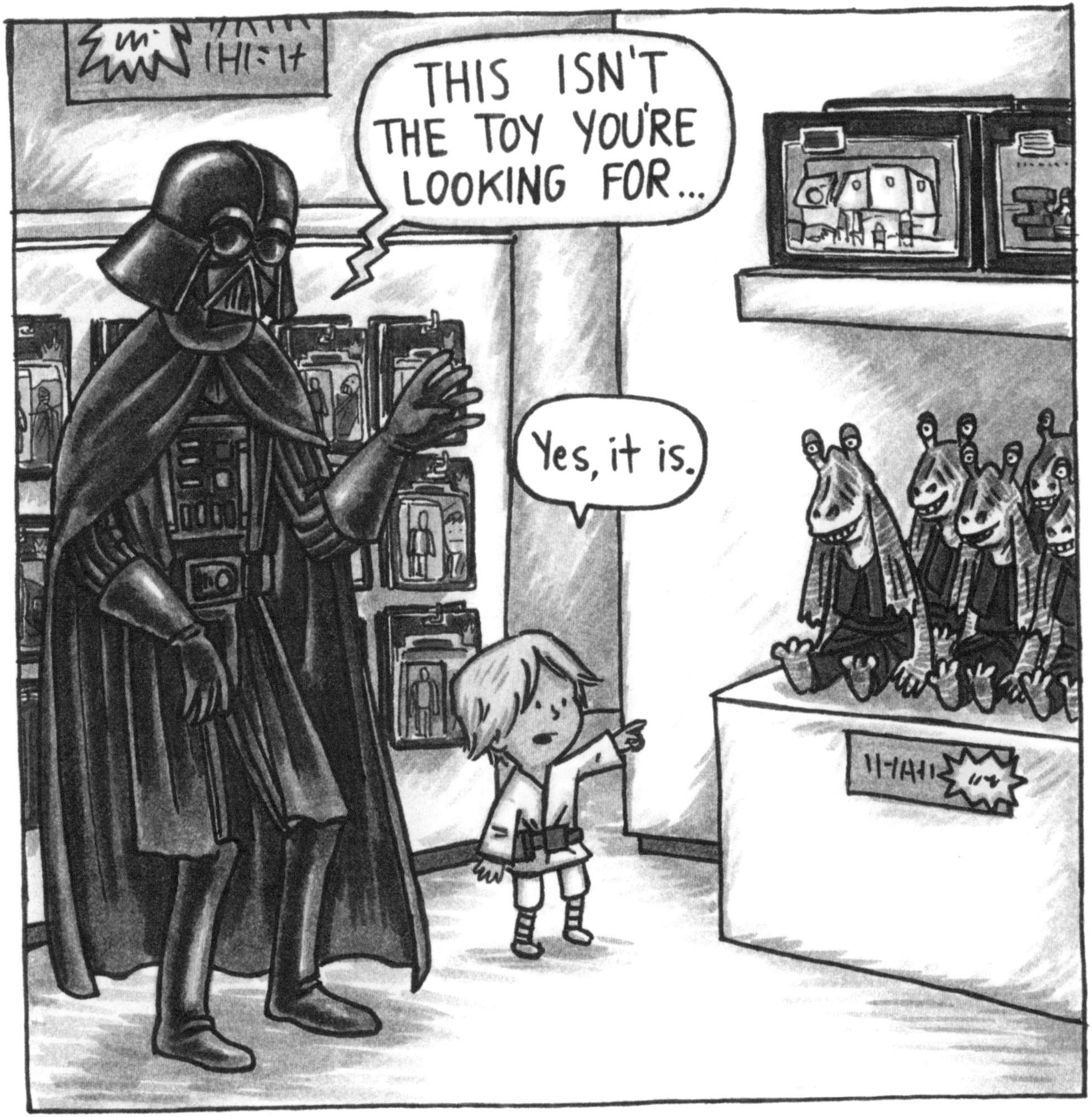
THIS ISN'T THE TOY YOU'RE LOOKING FOR...
Yes, it is.

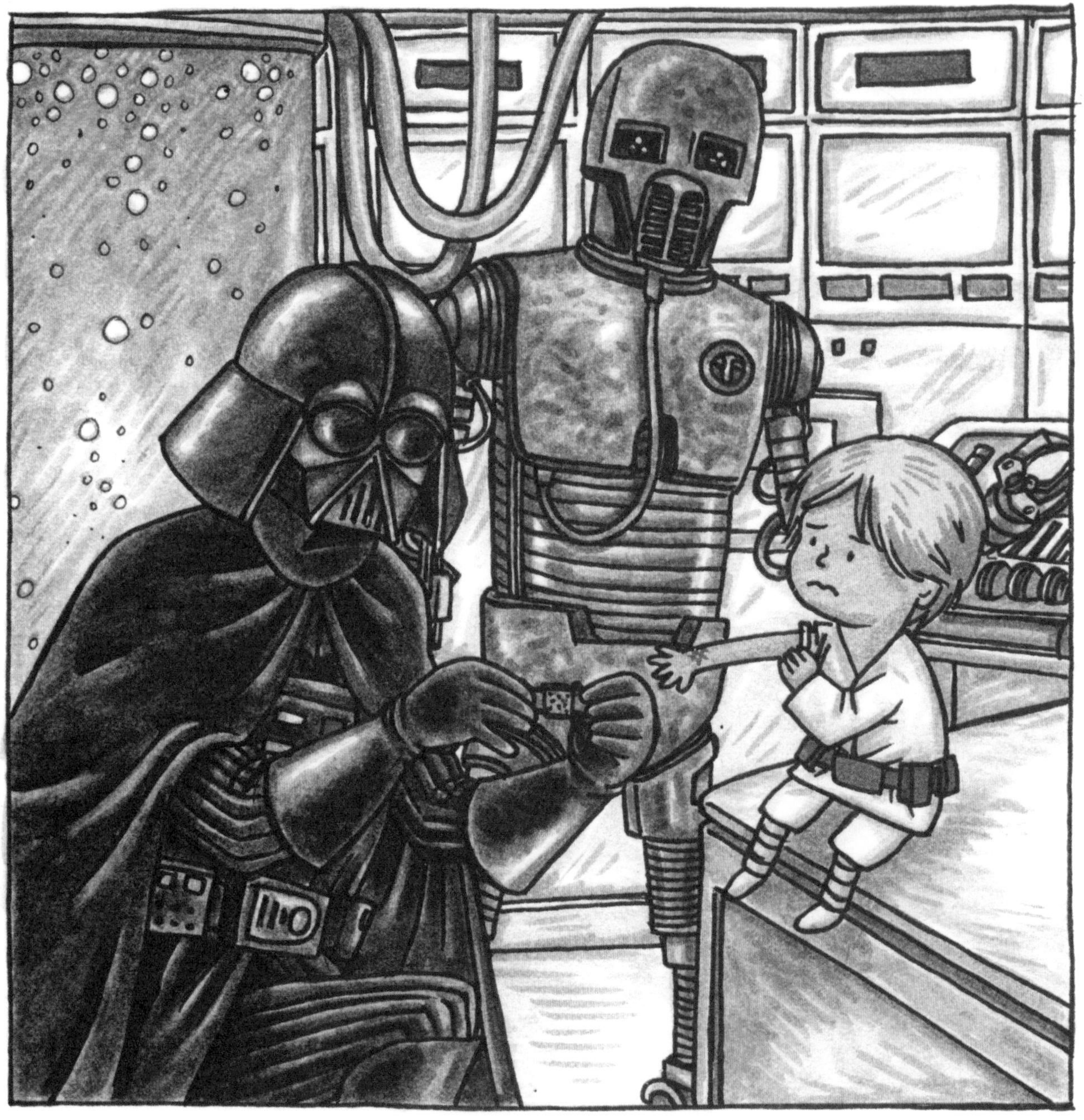

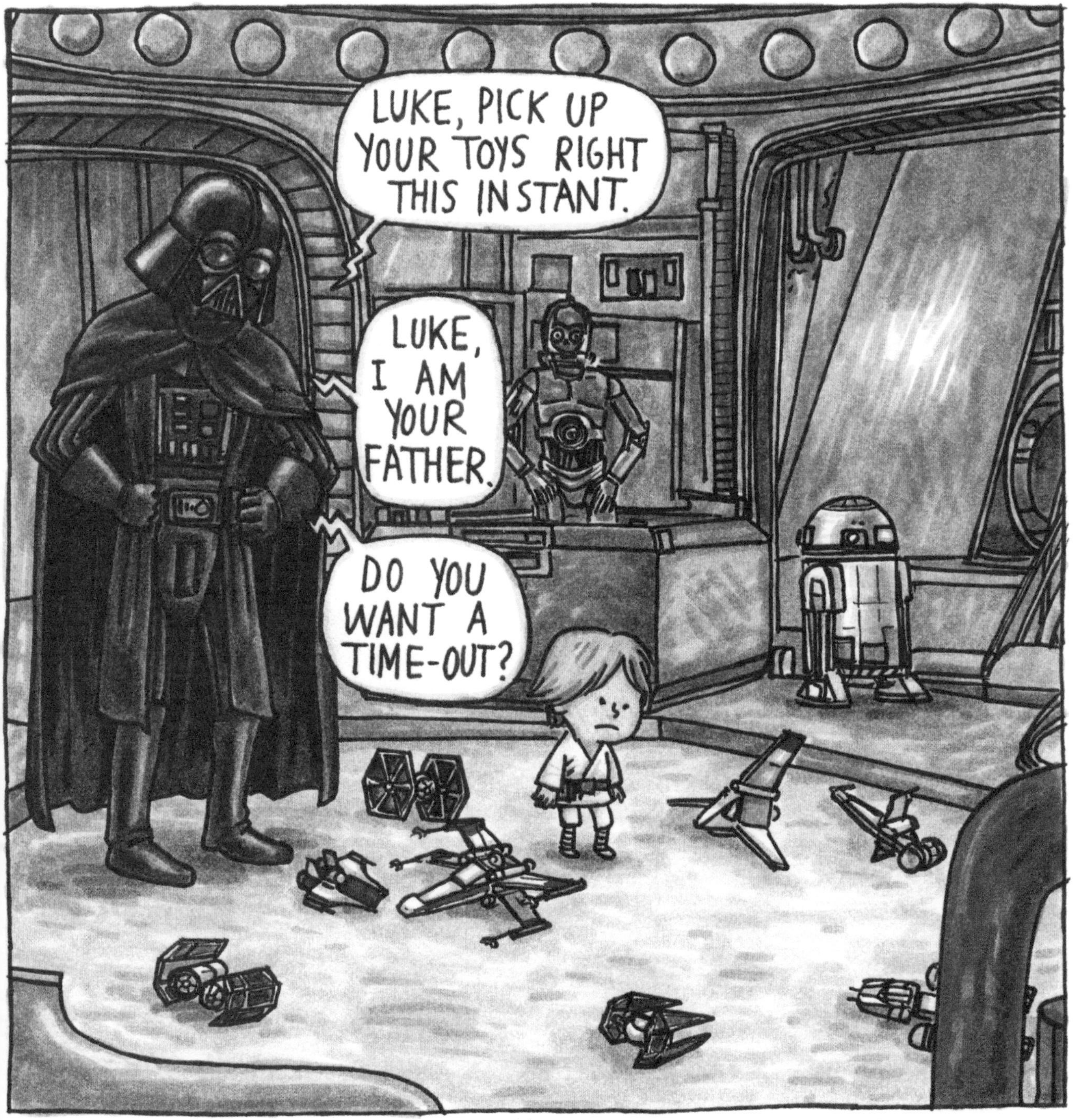
LUKE, PICK UP YOUR TOYS RIGHT THIS INSTANT.
LUKE, I AM YOUR FATHER.
DO YOU WANT A TIME-OUT?

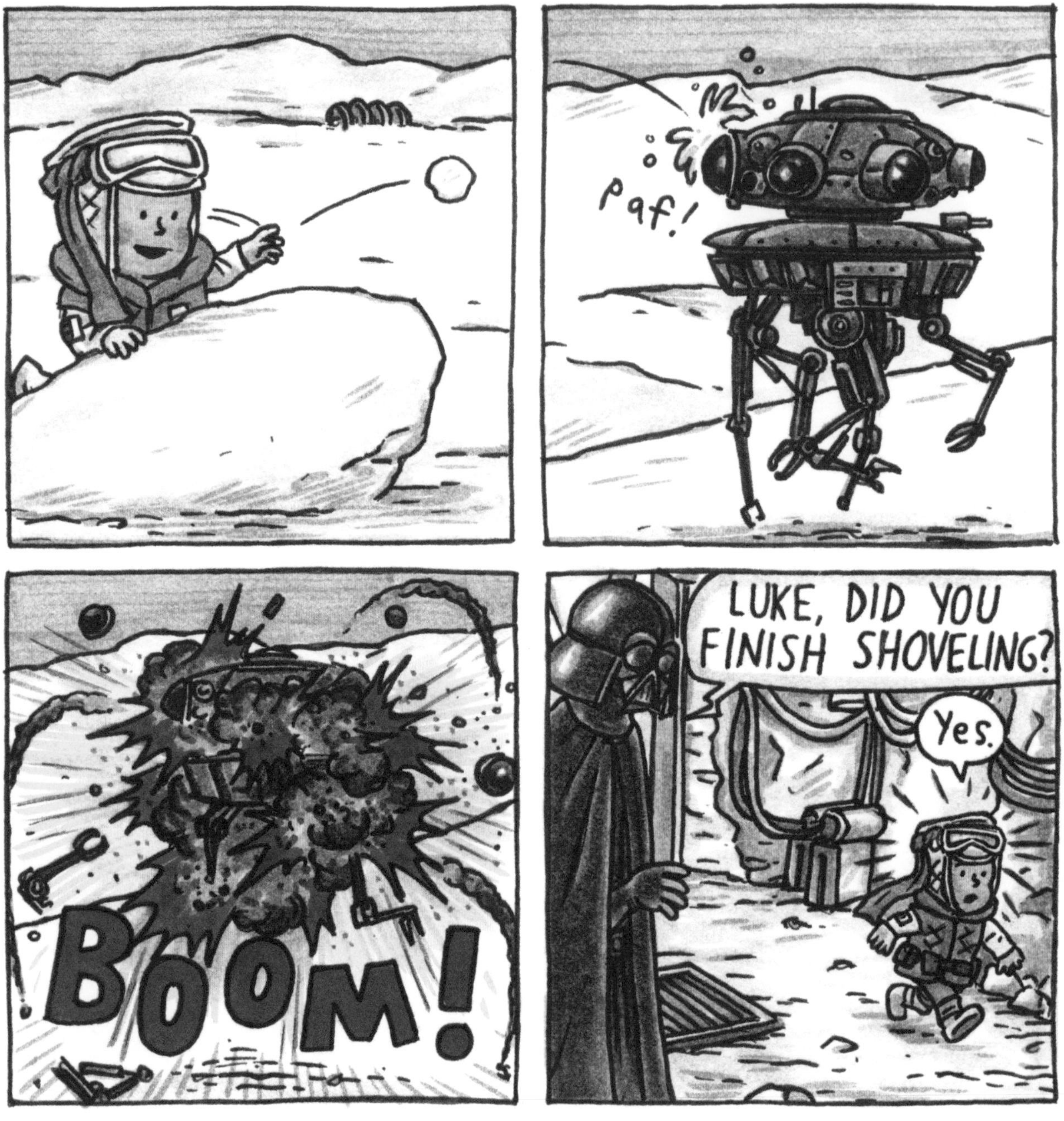
Paf!
BOOM!
LUKE, DID YOU FINISH SHOVELING?
Yes.

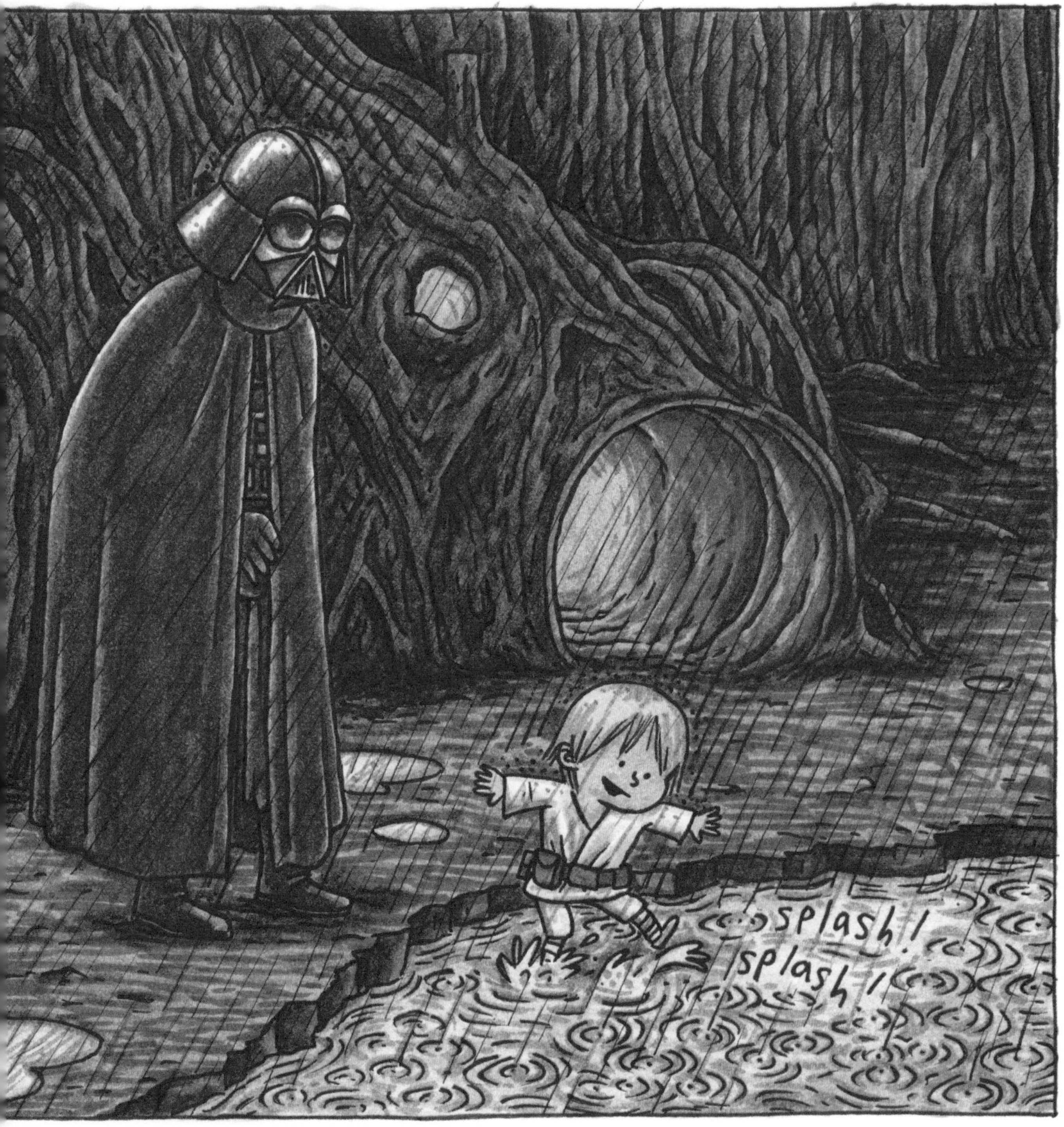
splash!
splash!

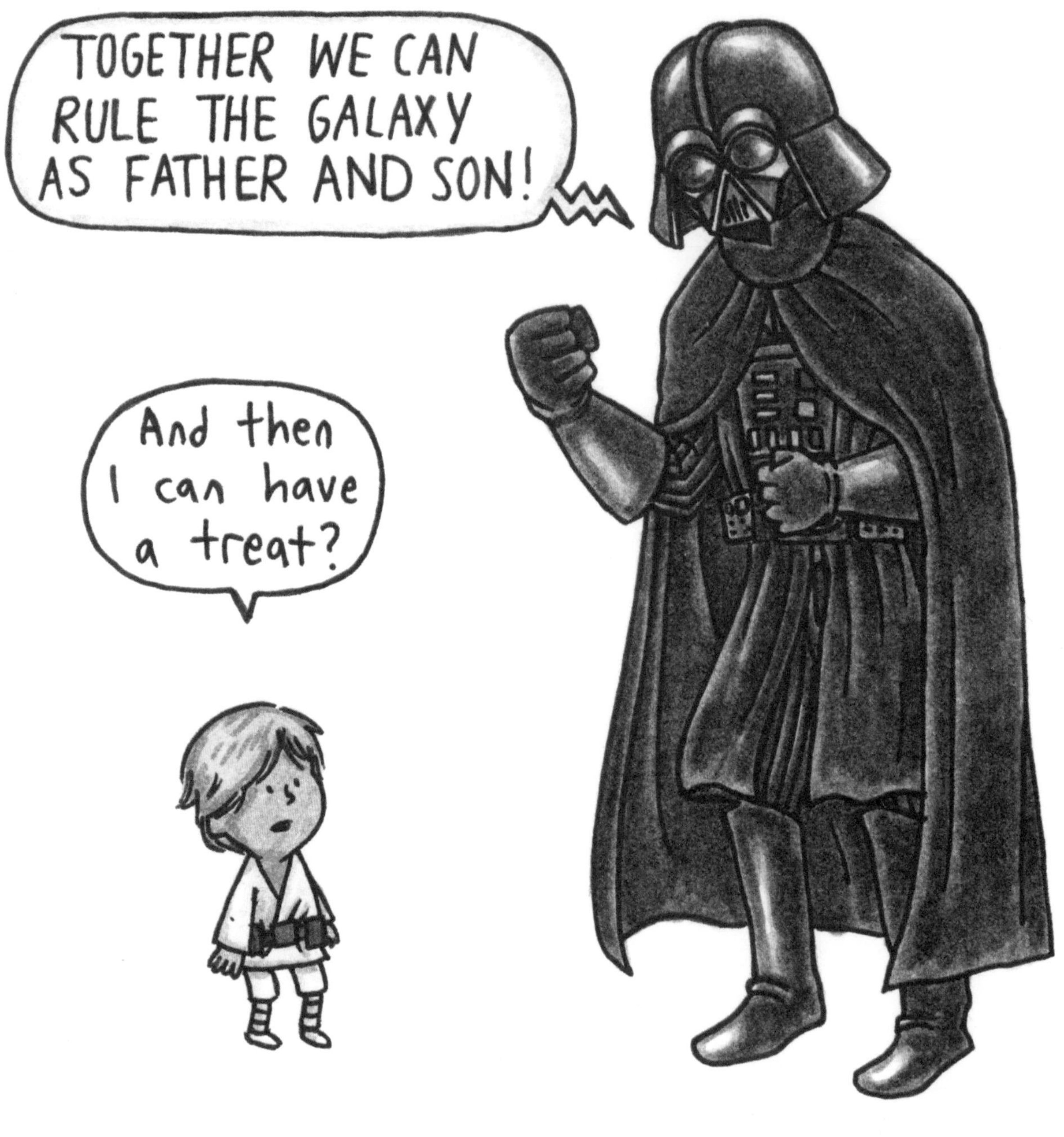
TOGETHER WE CAN RULE THE GALAXY AS FATHER AND SON!
And then I can have a treat?

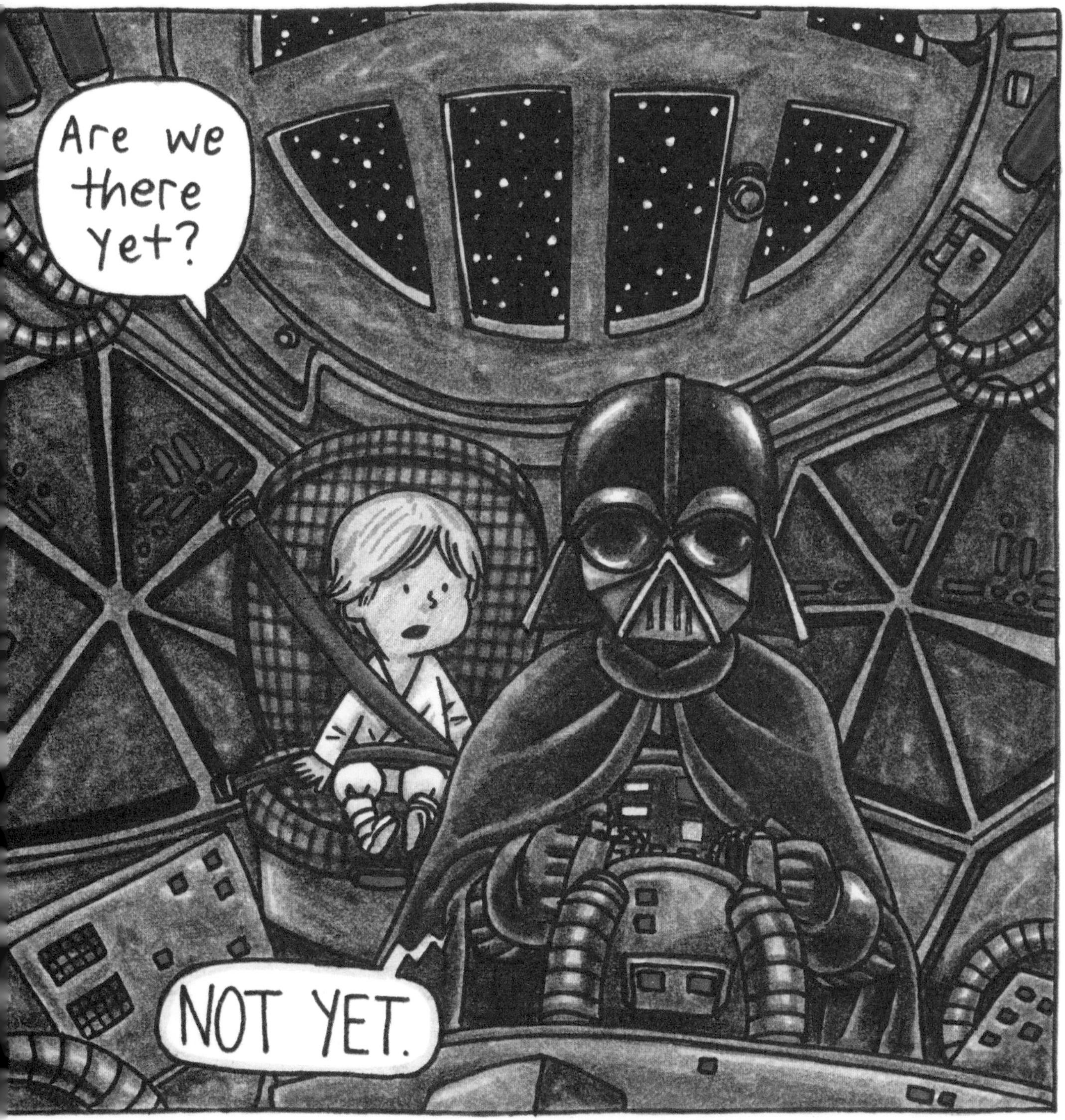
Are we there yet?
NOT YET.

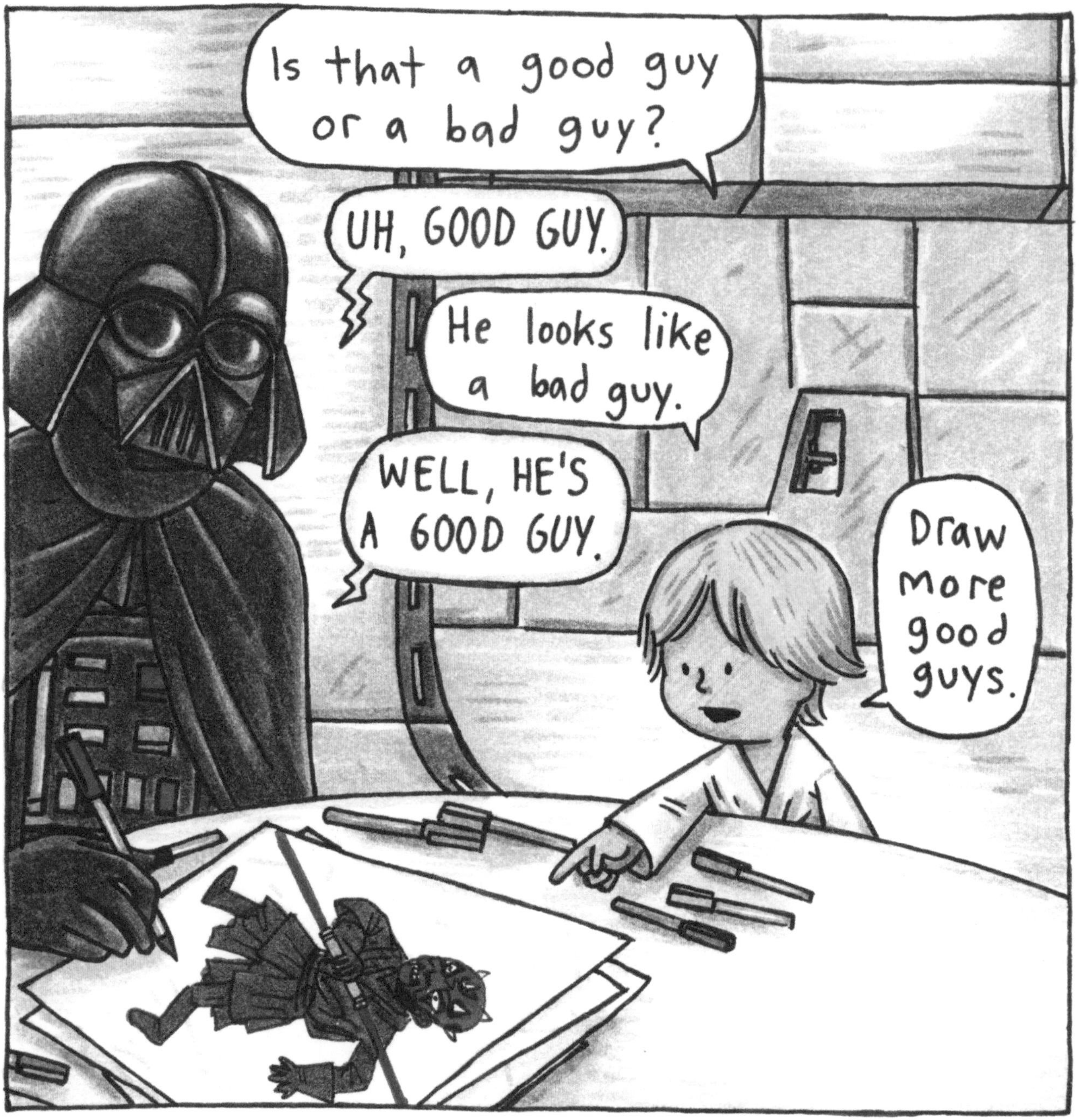
Is that a good guy or a bad guy?
UH, GOOD GUY.
He looks like a bad guy.
WELL, HE'S A GOOD GUY.
Draw more good guys.

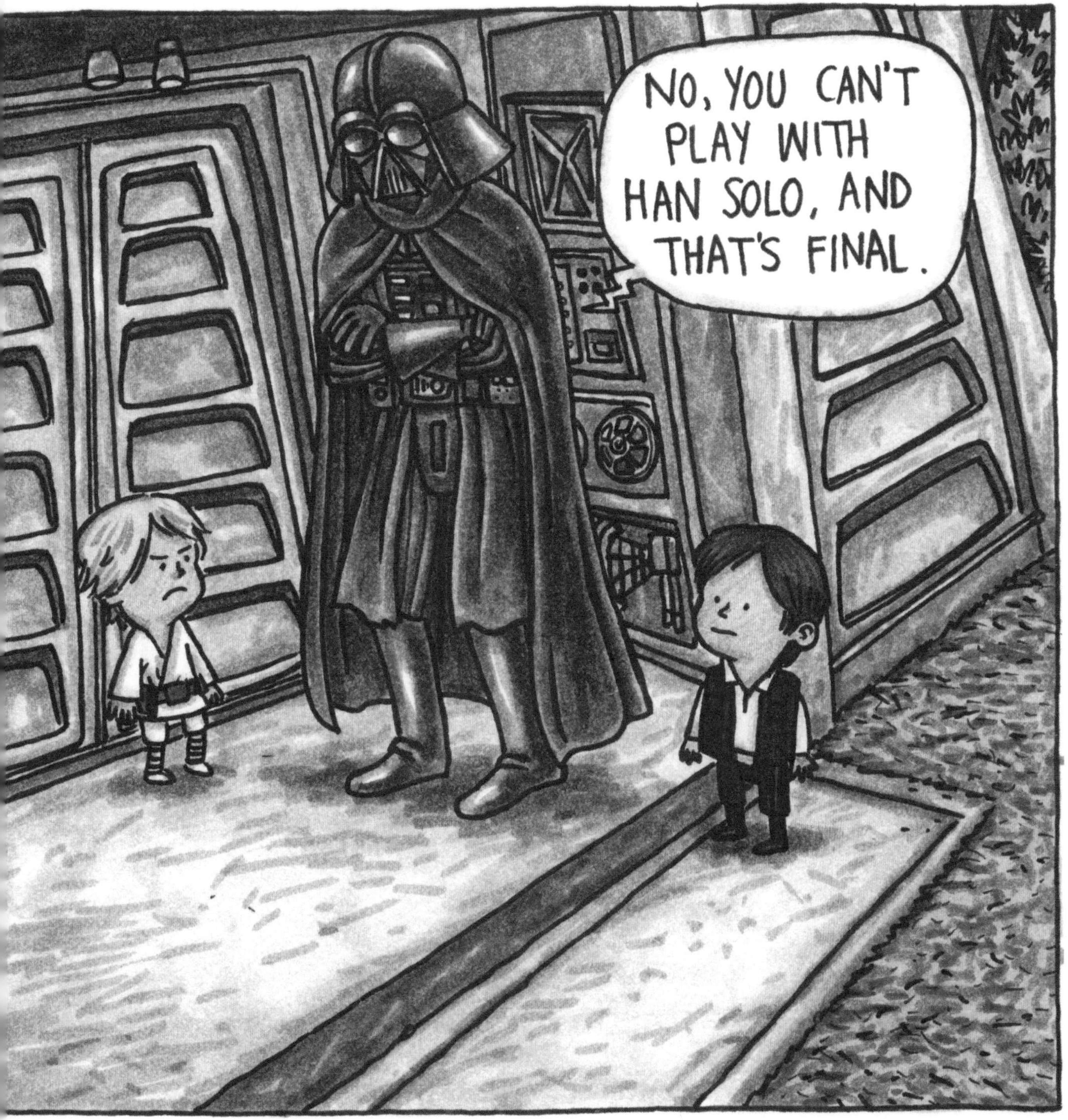
NO, YOU CAN'T PLAY WITH HAN SOLO, AND THAT'S FINAL.

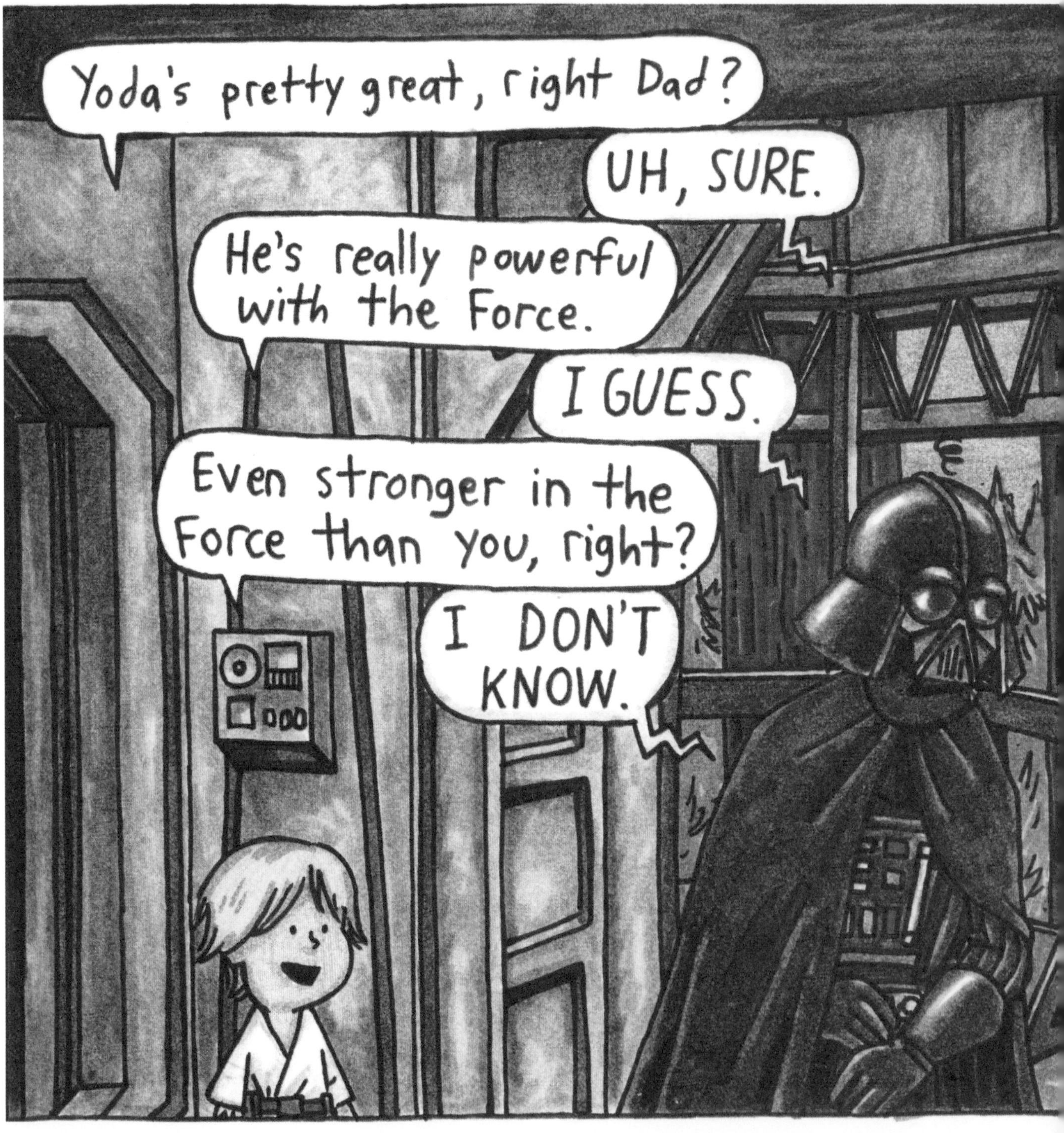
Yoda's pretty great, right Dad?
UH, SURE.
He's really powerful with the Force.
I GUESS.
Even stronger in the Force than you, right?
I DON'T KNOW.

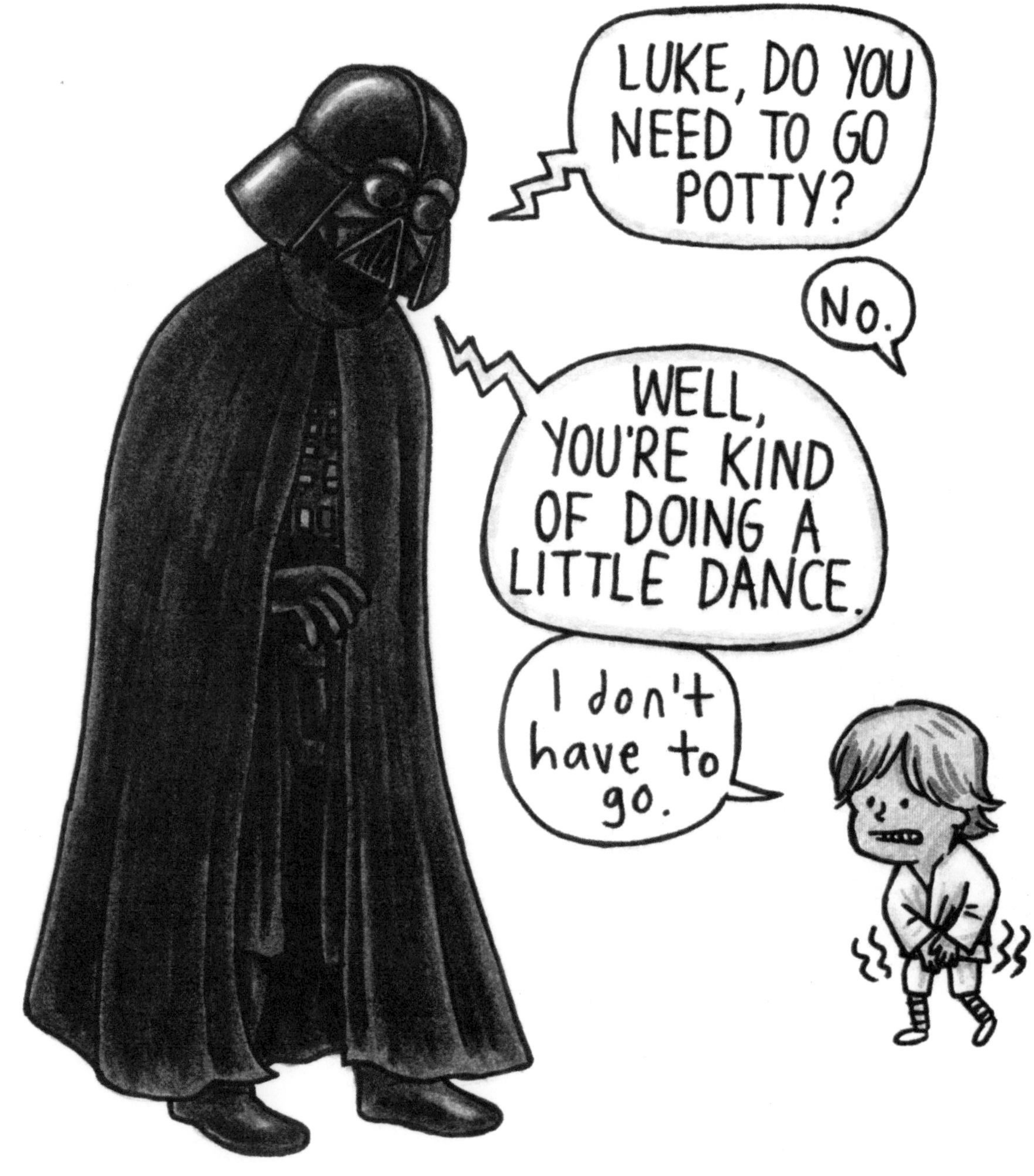
LUKE, DO YOU NEED TO GO POTTY?
No.
WELL, YOU'RE KIND OF DOING A LITTLE DANCE.
I don't have to go.

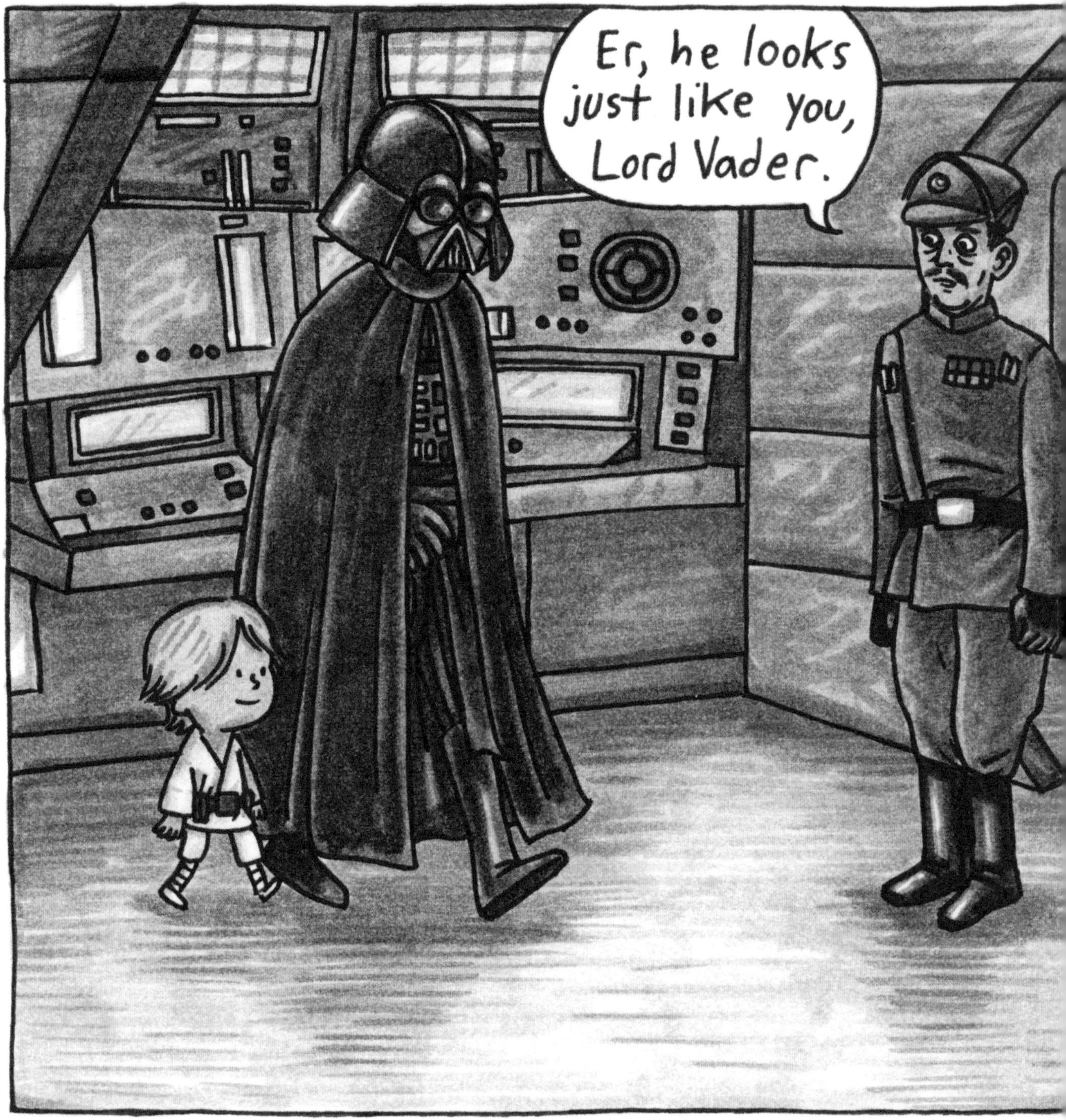
Er, he looks just like you, Lord Vader.

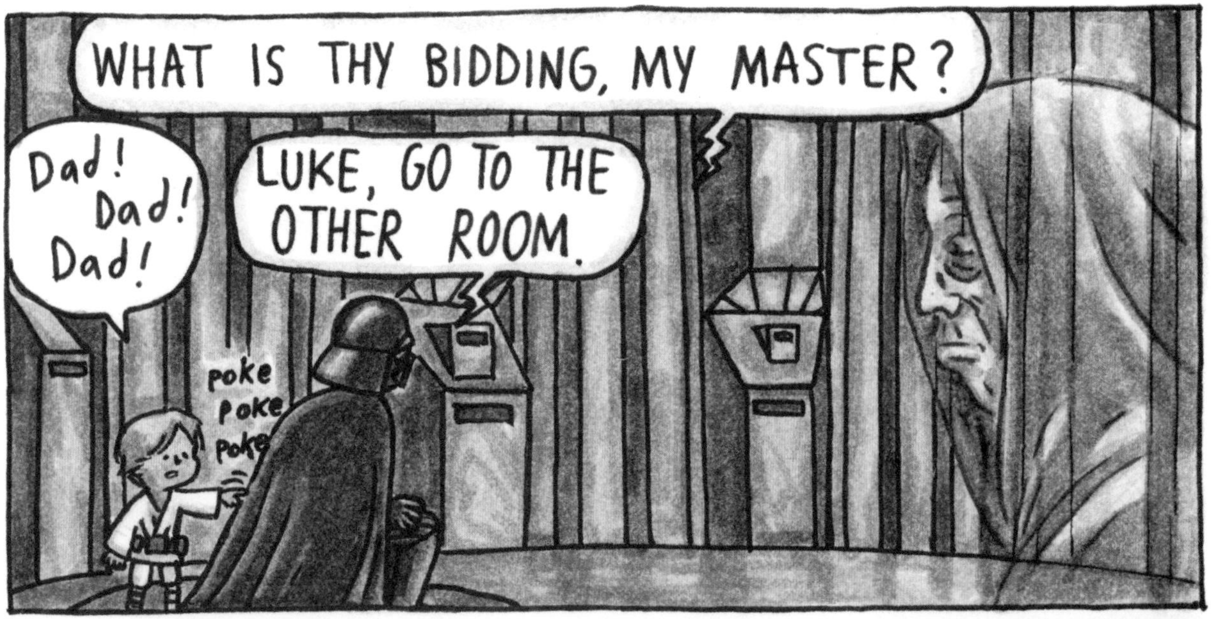
WHAT IS THY BIDDING, MY MASTER?
Dad! Dad! Dad!
LUKE, GO TO THE OTHER ROOM.
poke poke poke

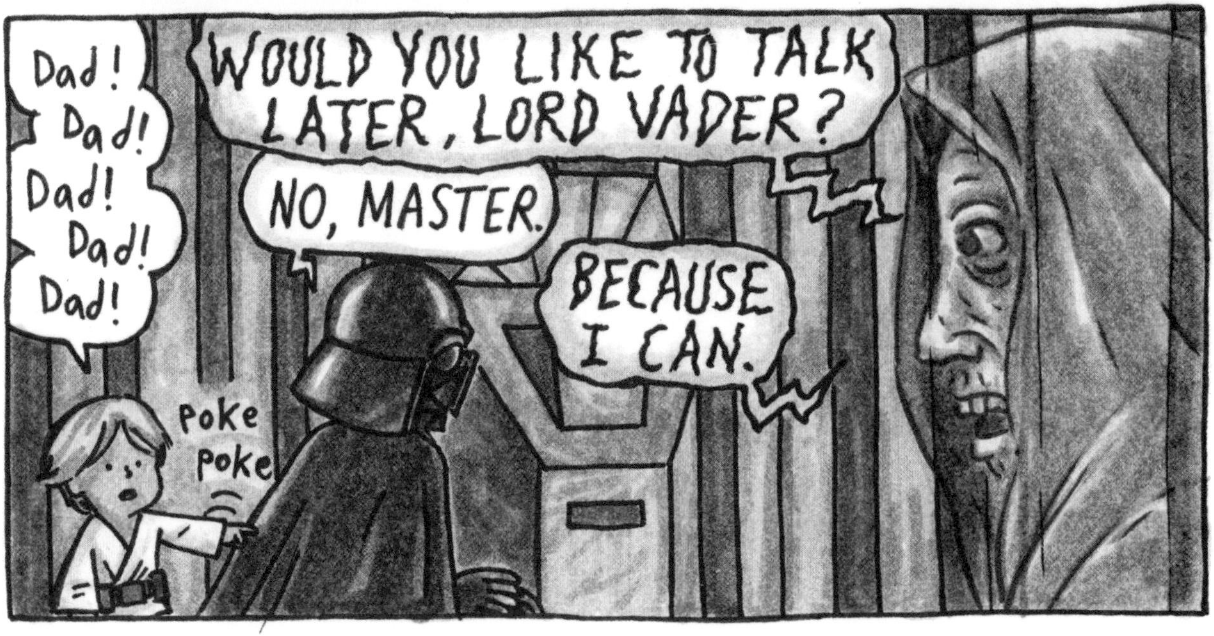
Dad! Dad! Dad! Dad! Dad!
WOULD YOU LIKE TO TALK LATER, LORD VADER?
NO, MASTER.
BECAUSE I CAN.
poke poke

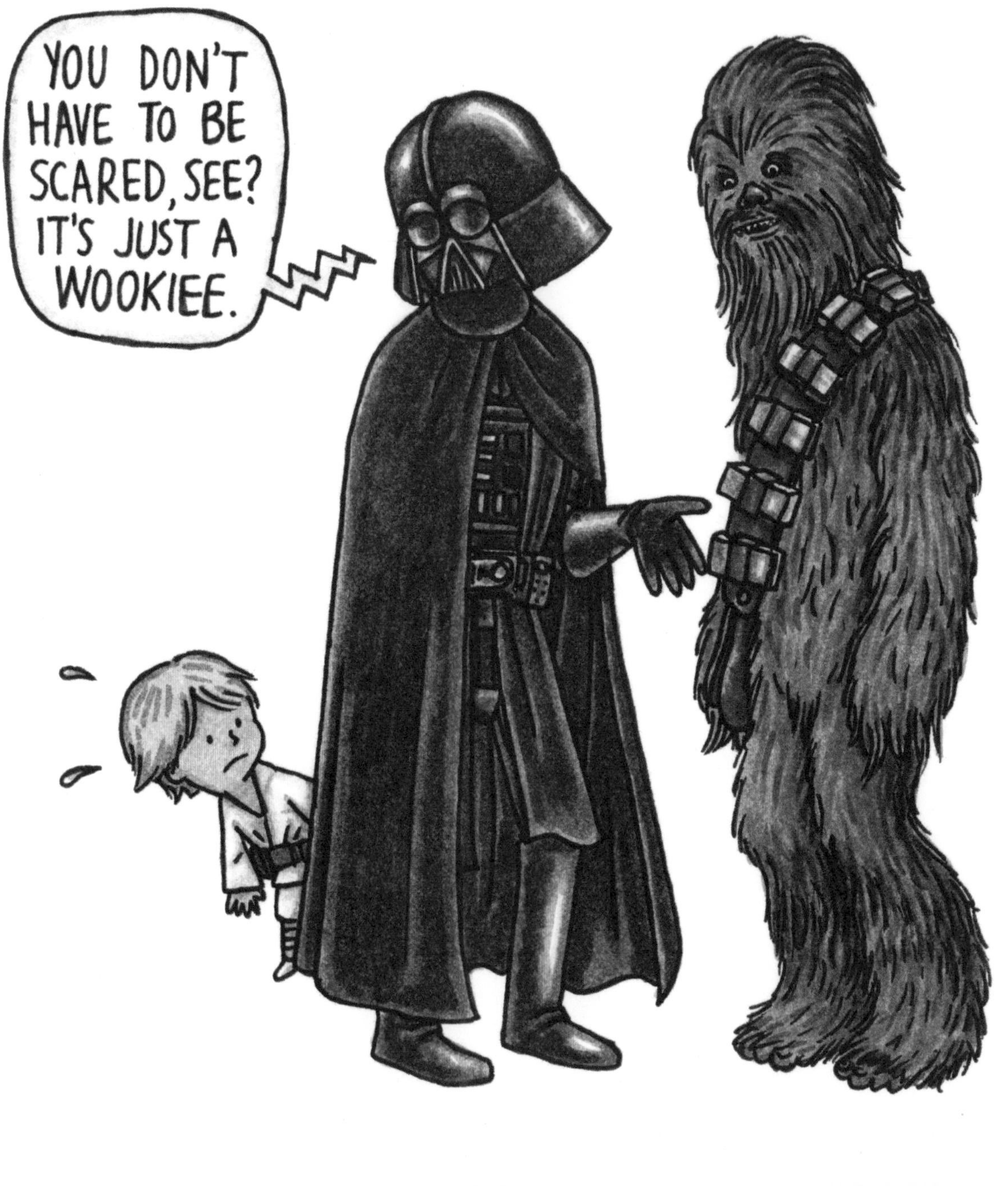
YOU DON'T HAVE TO BE SCARED, SEE? IT'S JUST A WOOKIEE.

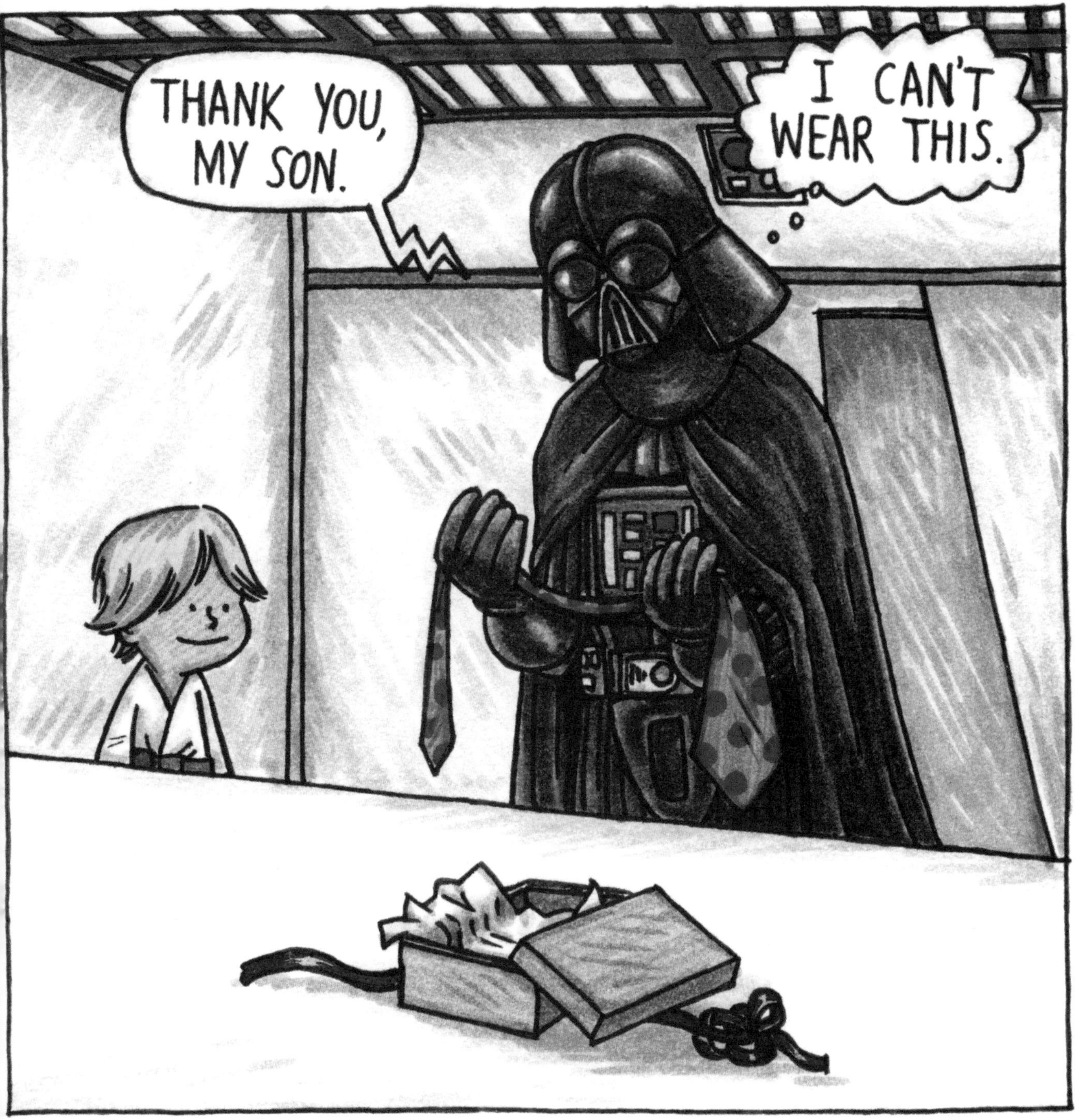
THANK YOU, MY SON.
I CAN'T WEAR THIS.

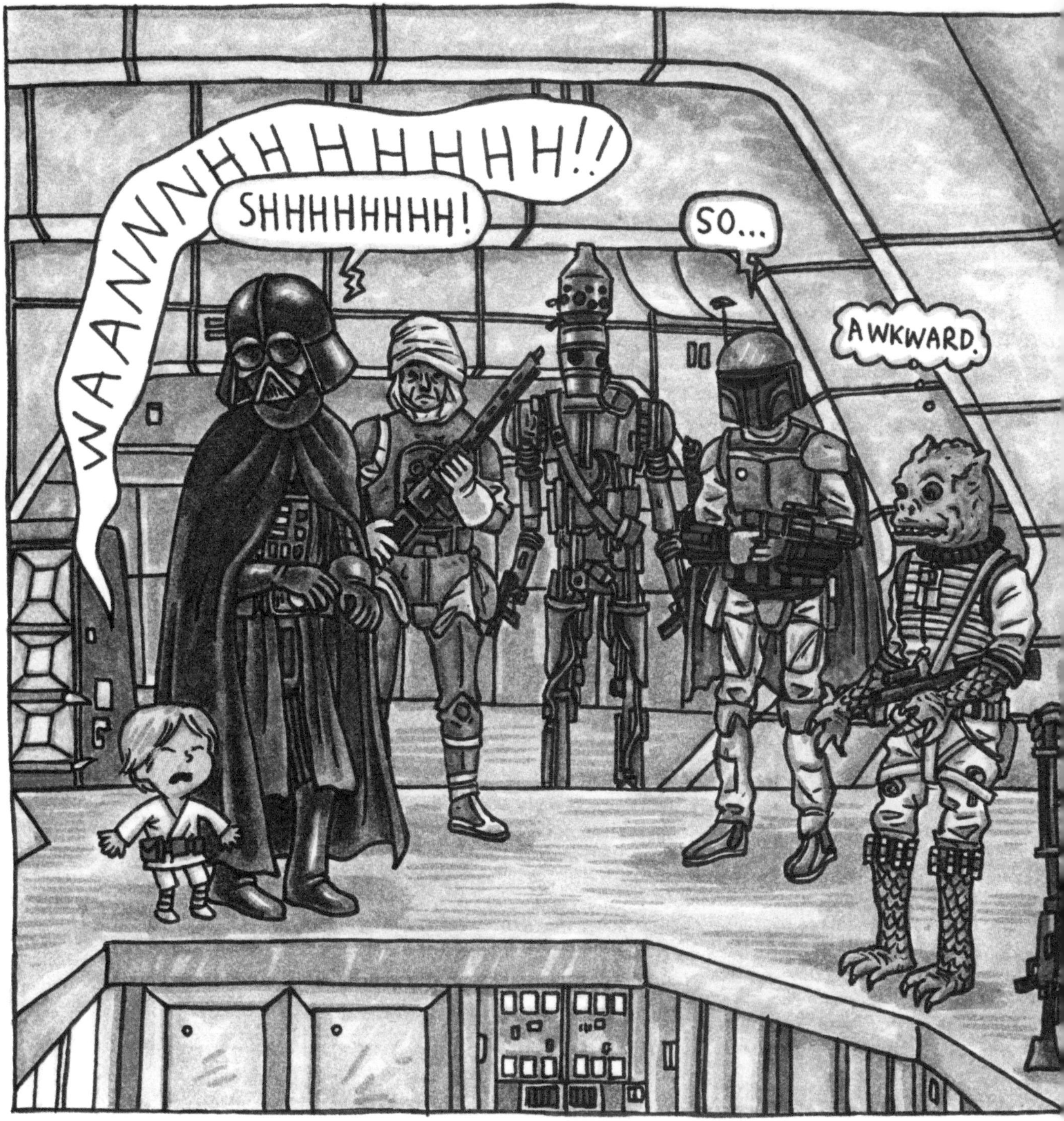
WAANNHHHHHHH!!
SHHHHHHHH!
SO...
AWKWARD.

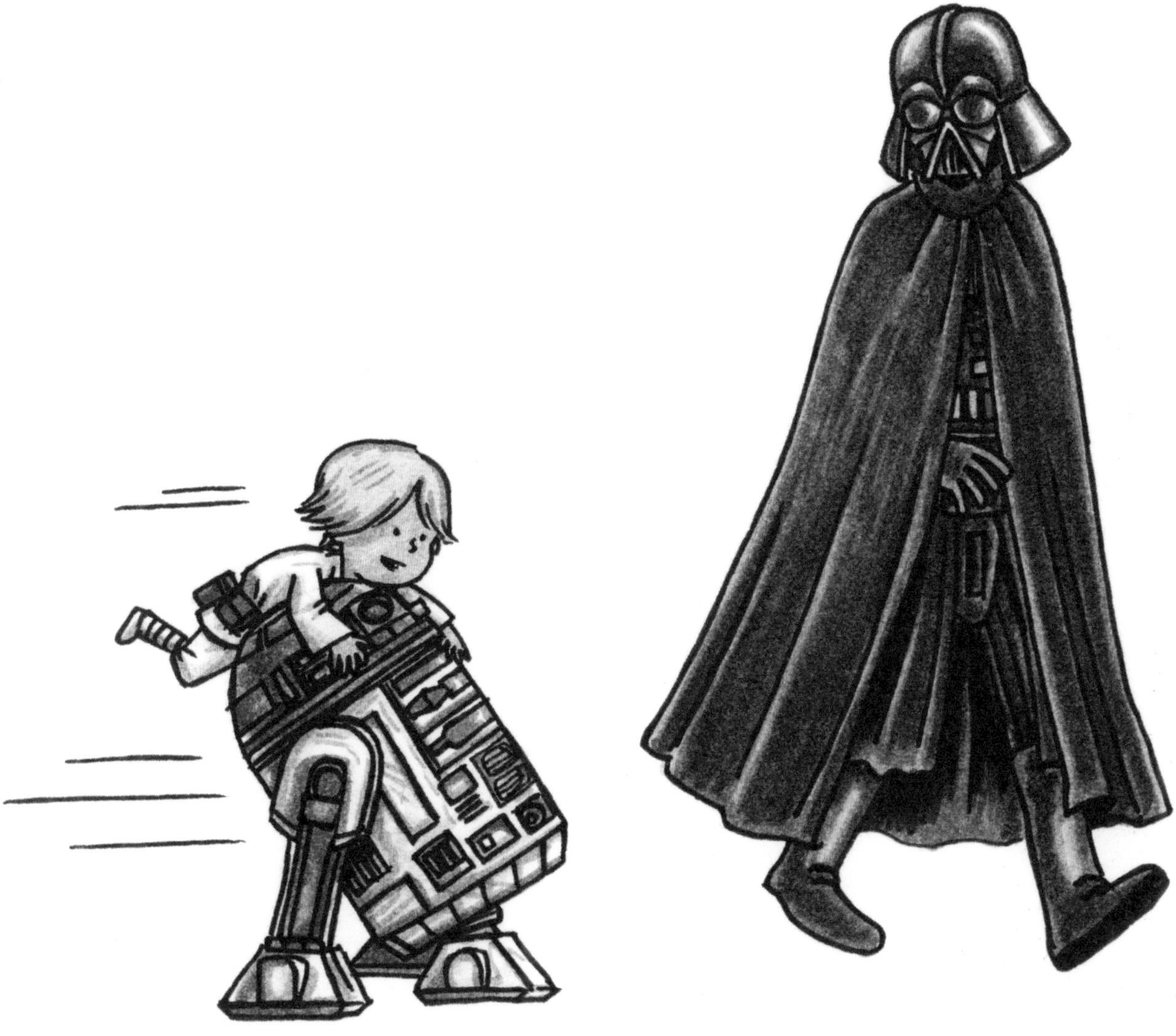

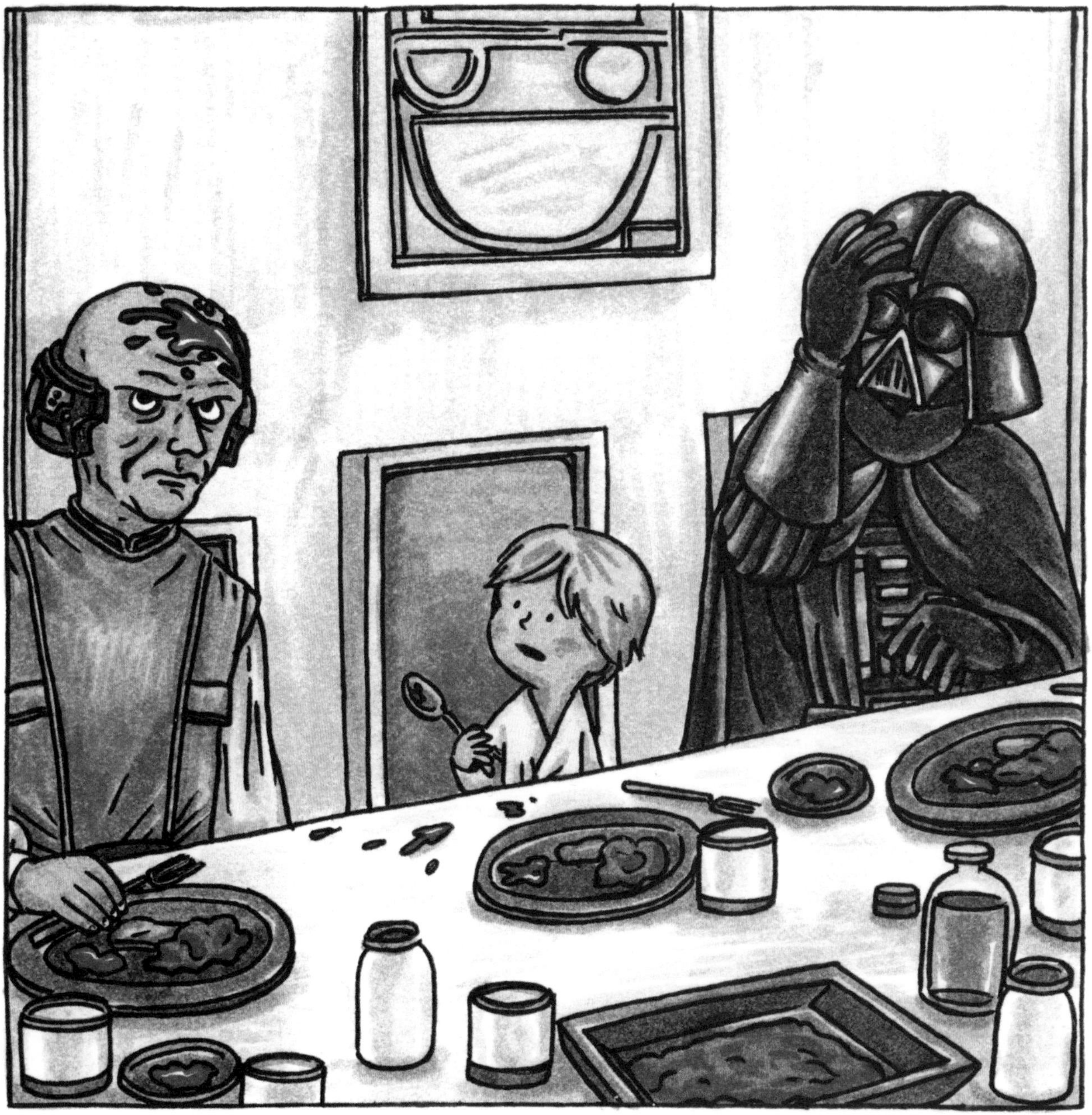

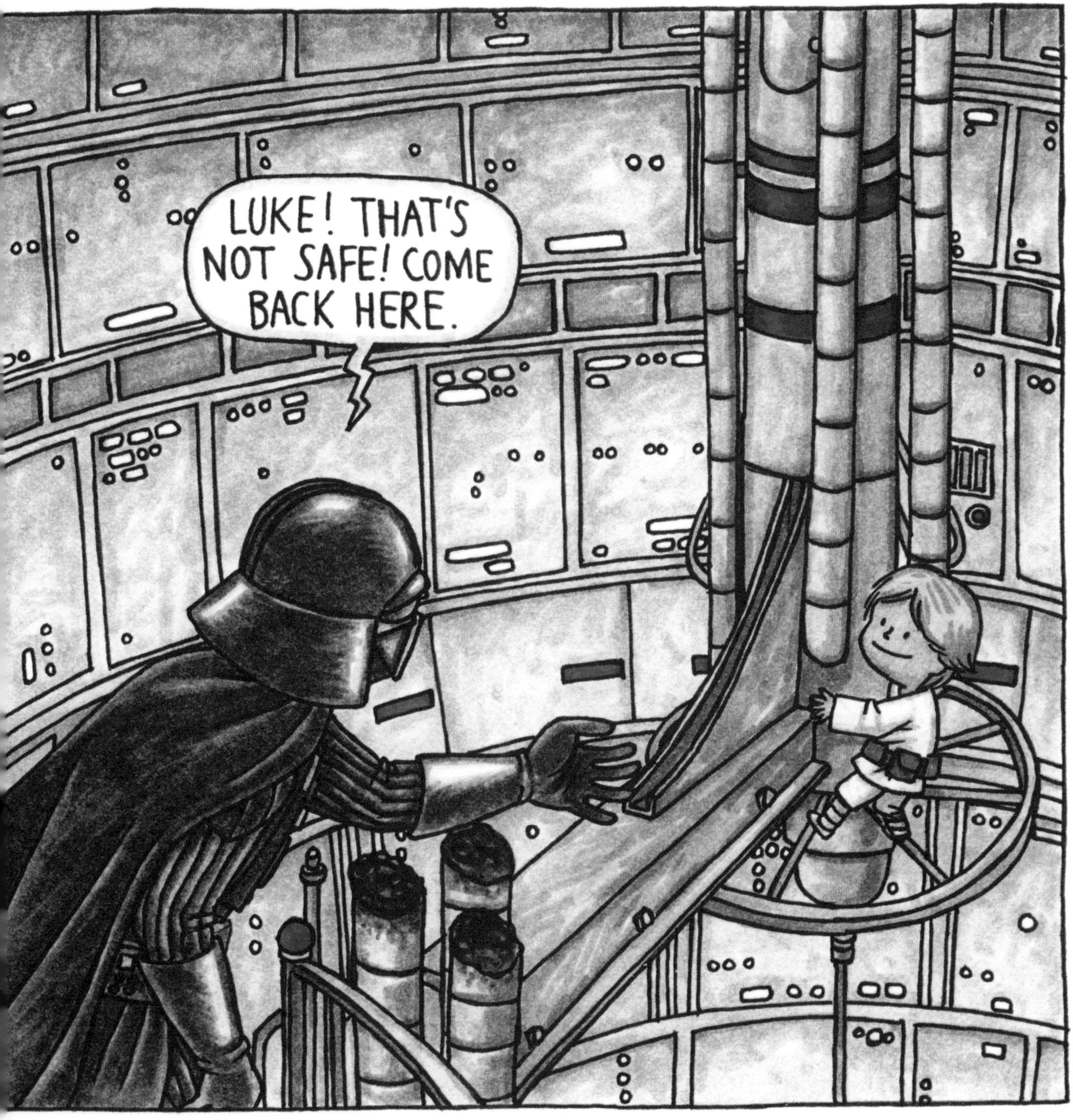
LUKE! THAT'S NOT SAFE! COME BACK HERE.

PLEEEASSSSE, Dad? Can we go now? Can we? I'm ready to go home. Pleassse?
I FIND YOUR LACK OF PATIENCE DISTURBING.

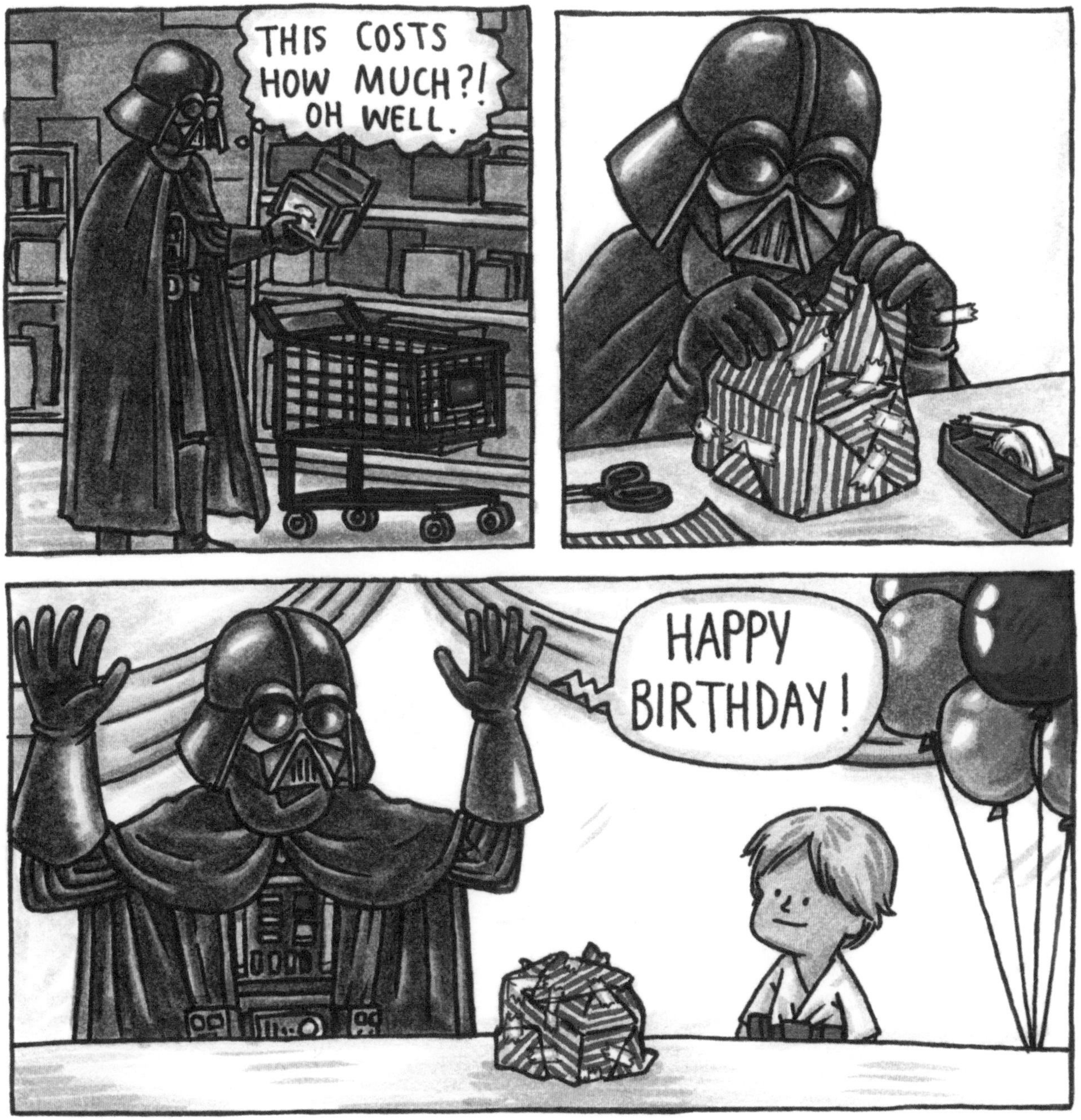
THIS COSTS HOW MUCH?! OH WELL.
HAPPY BIRTHDAY!

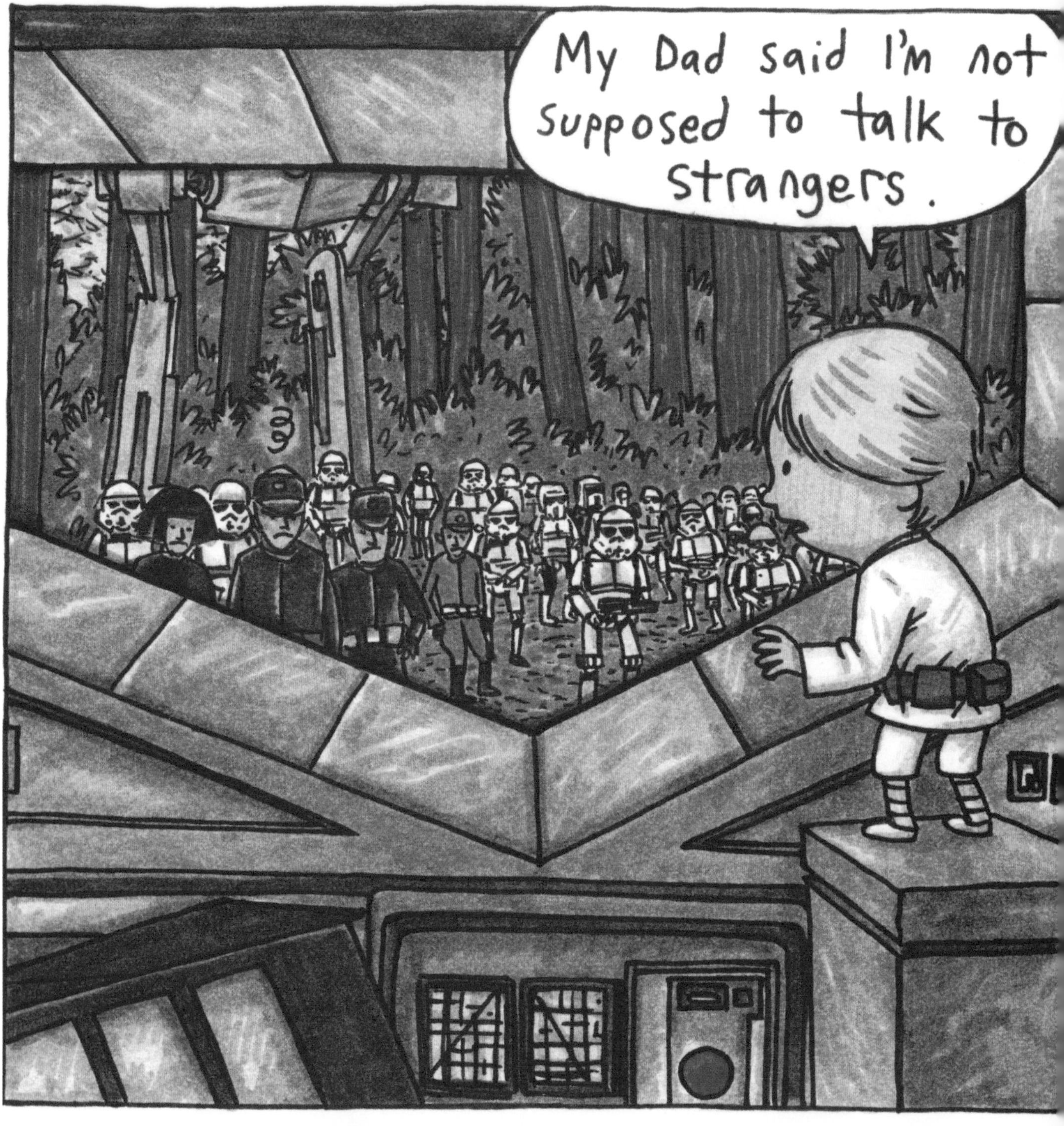
My Dad said I'm not supposed to talk to strangers.

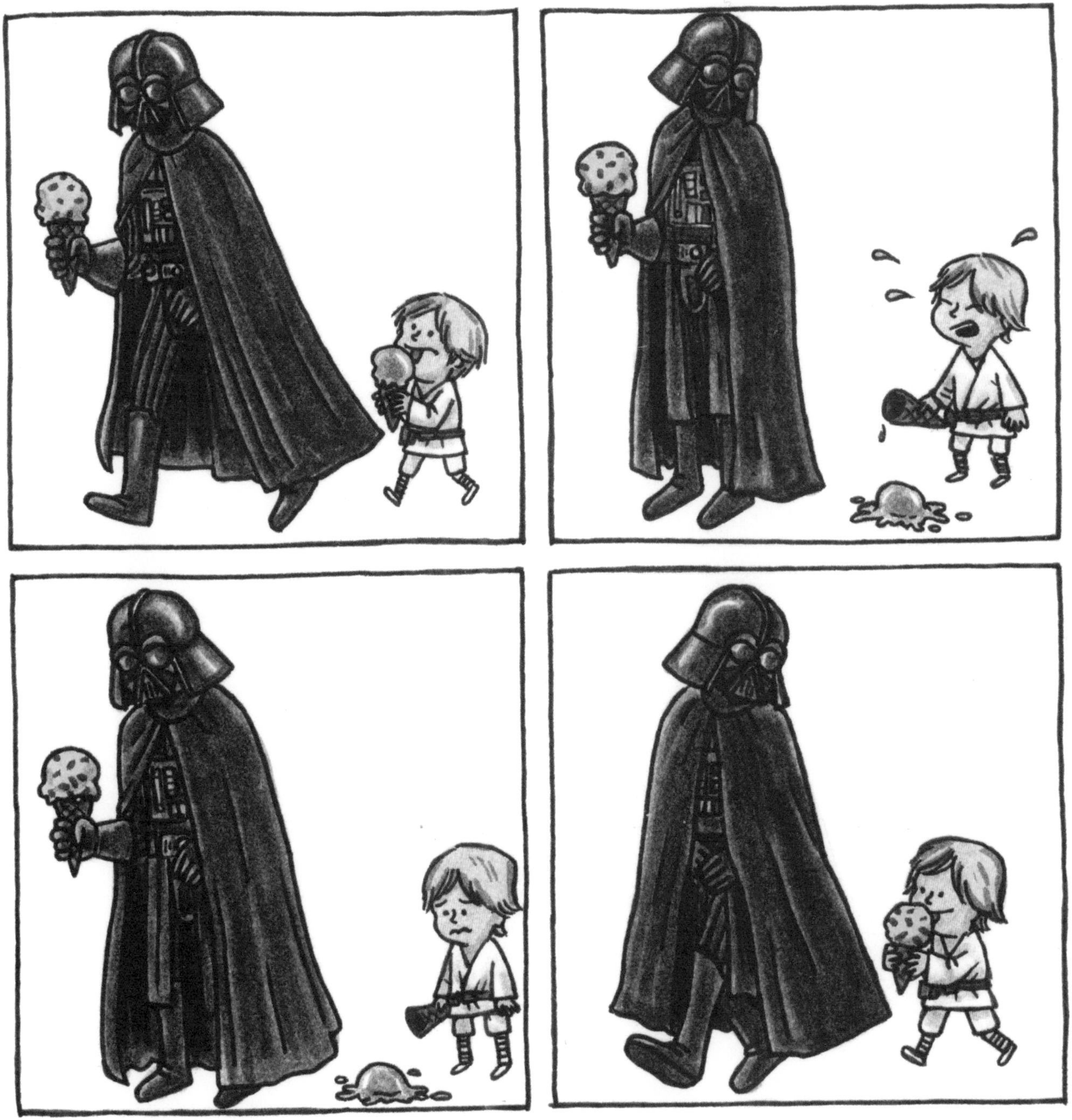

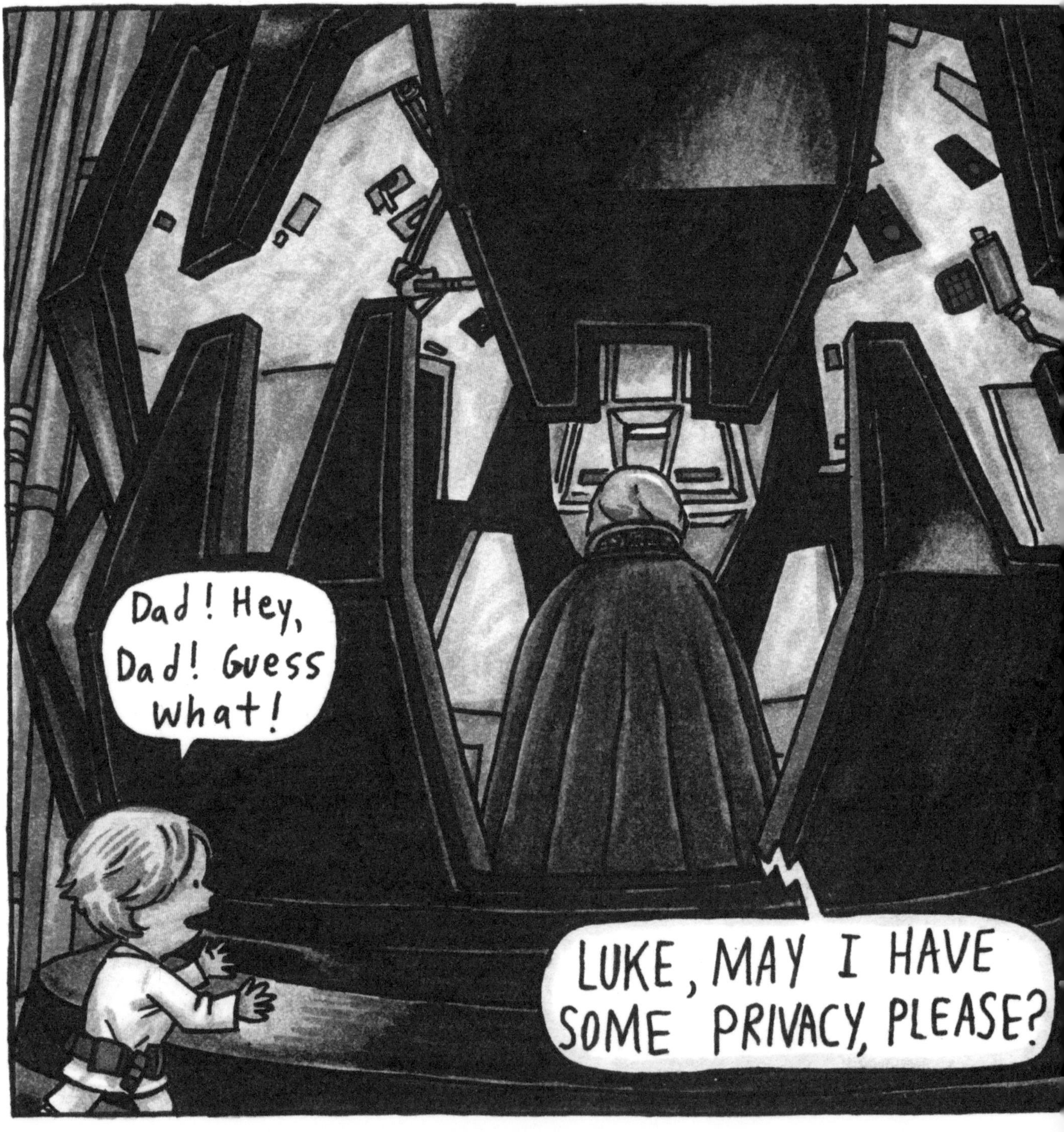
Dad! Hey, Dad! Guess what!
LUKE, MAY I HAVE SOME PRIVACY, PLEASE?

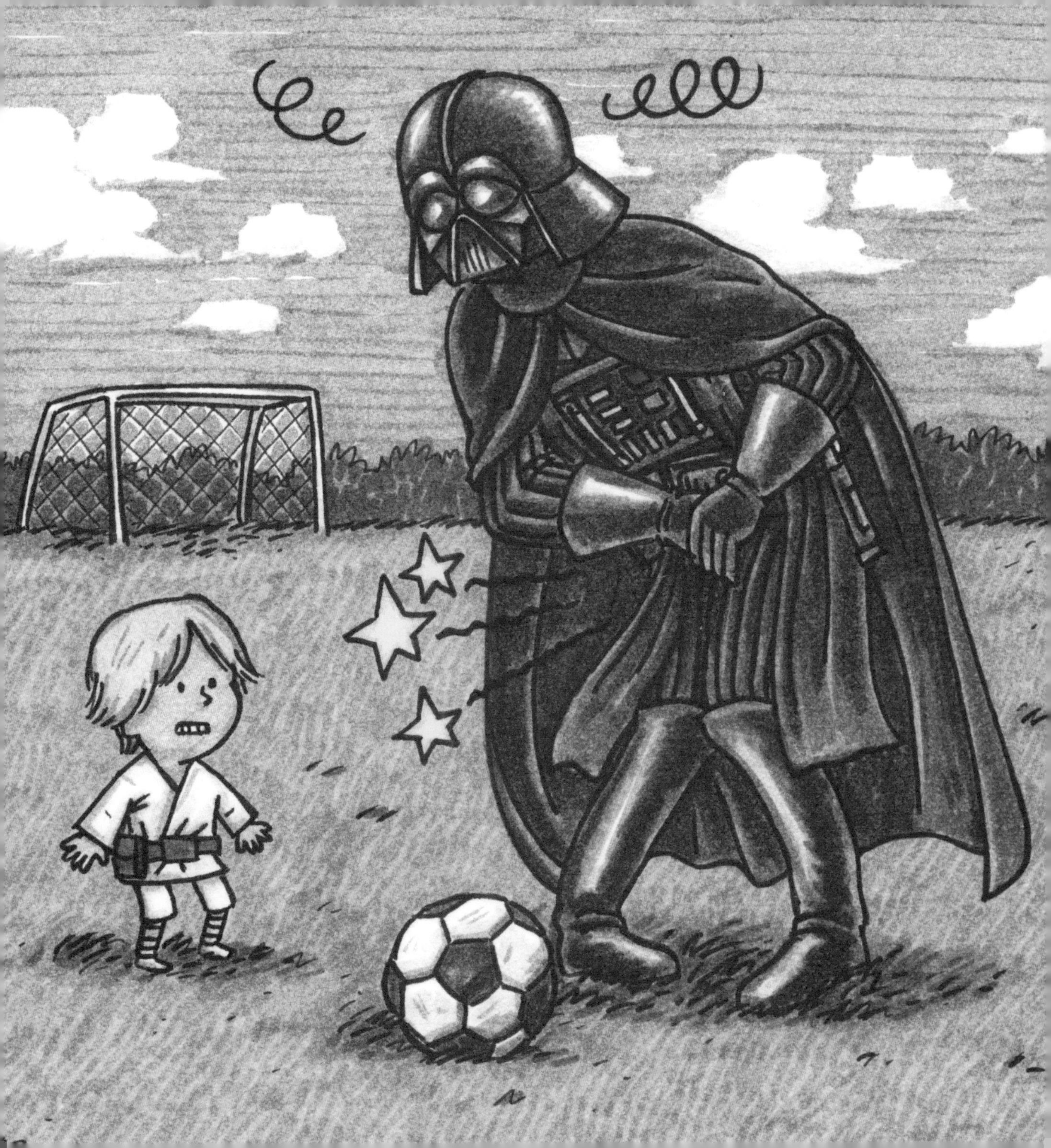

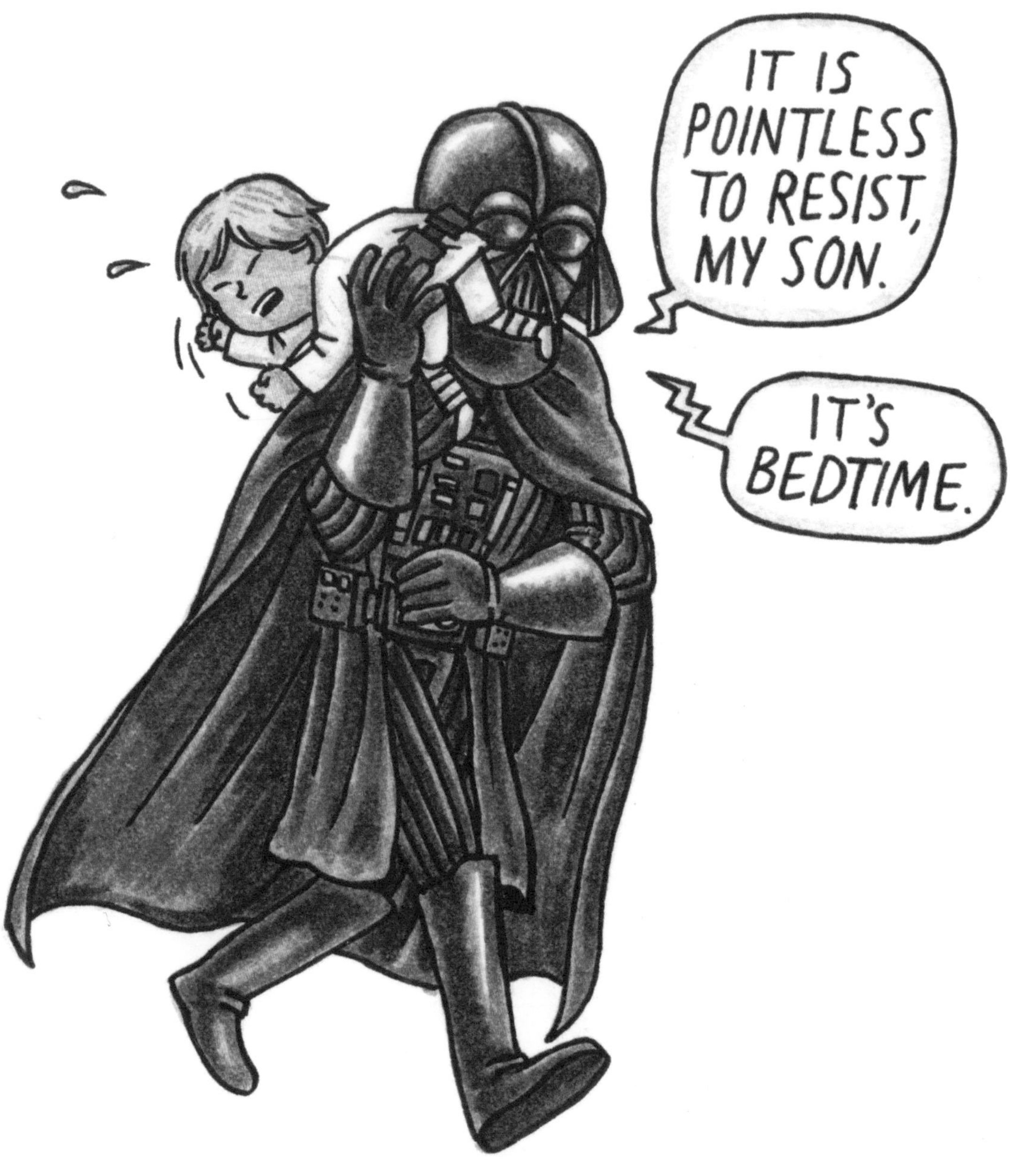
IT IS POINTLESS TO RESIST, MY SON.
IT'S BEDTIME.

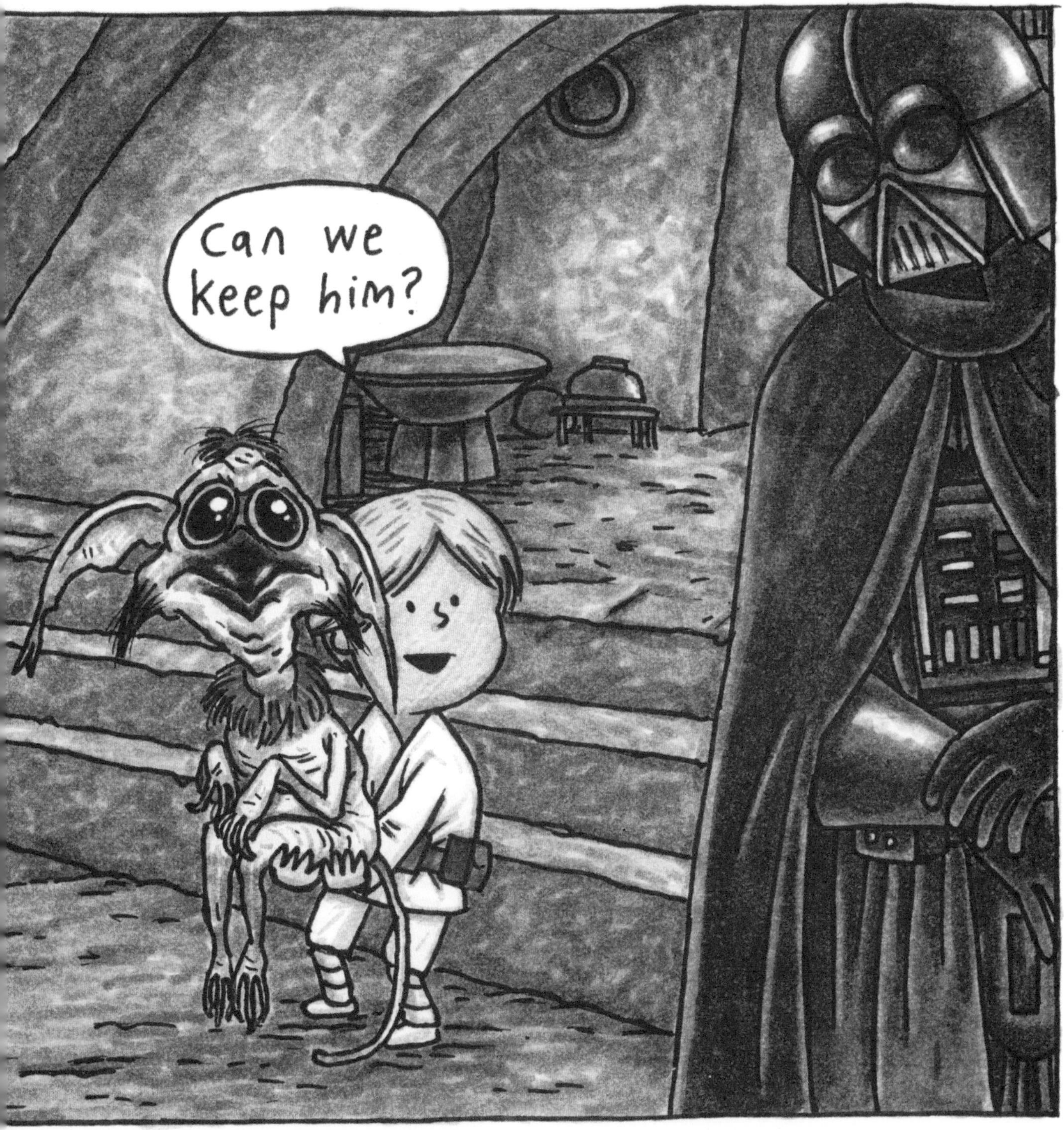
Can we keep him?

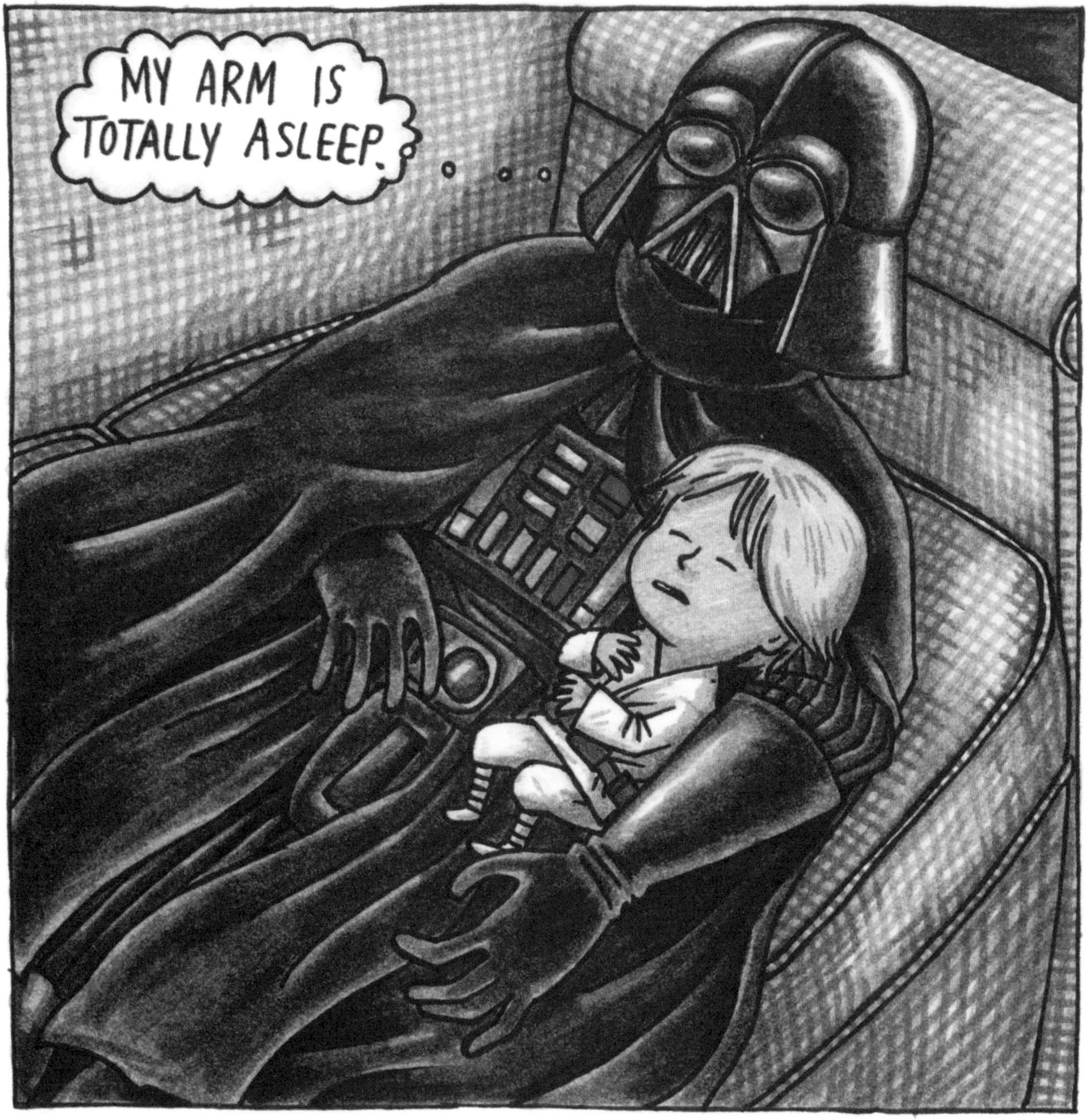
MY ARM IS TOTALLY ASLEEP.

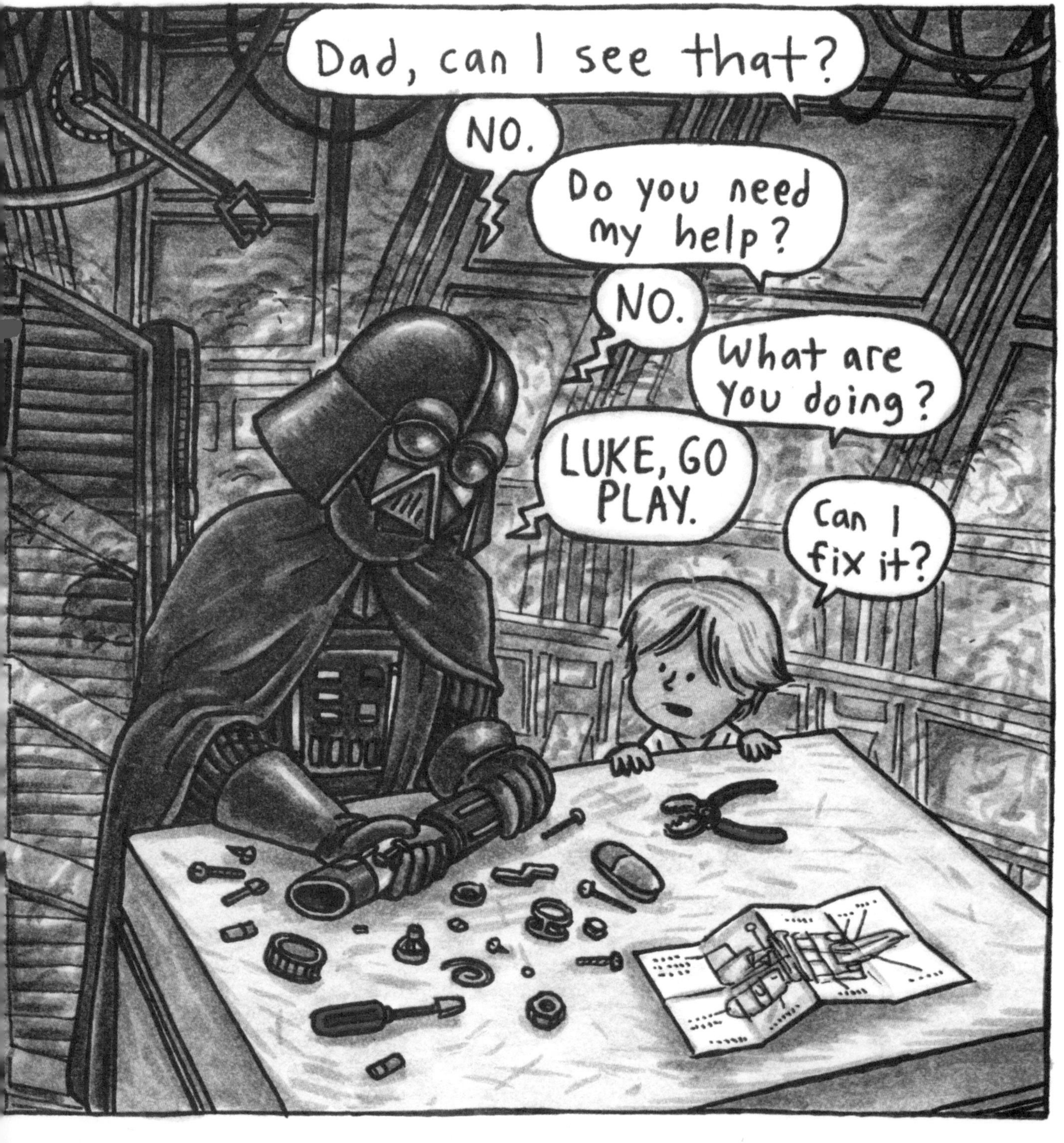
Dad, can I see that?
NO.
Do you need my help?
NO.
What are you doing?
LUKE, GO PLAY.
Can I fix it?

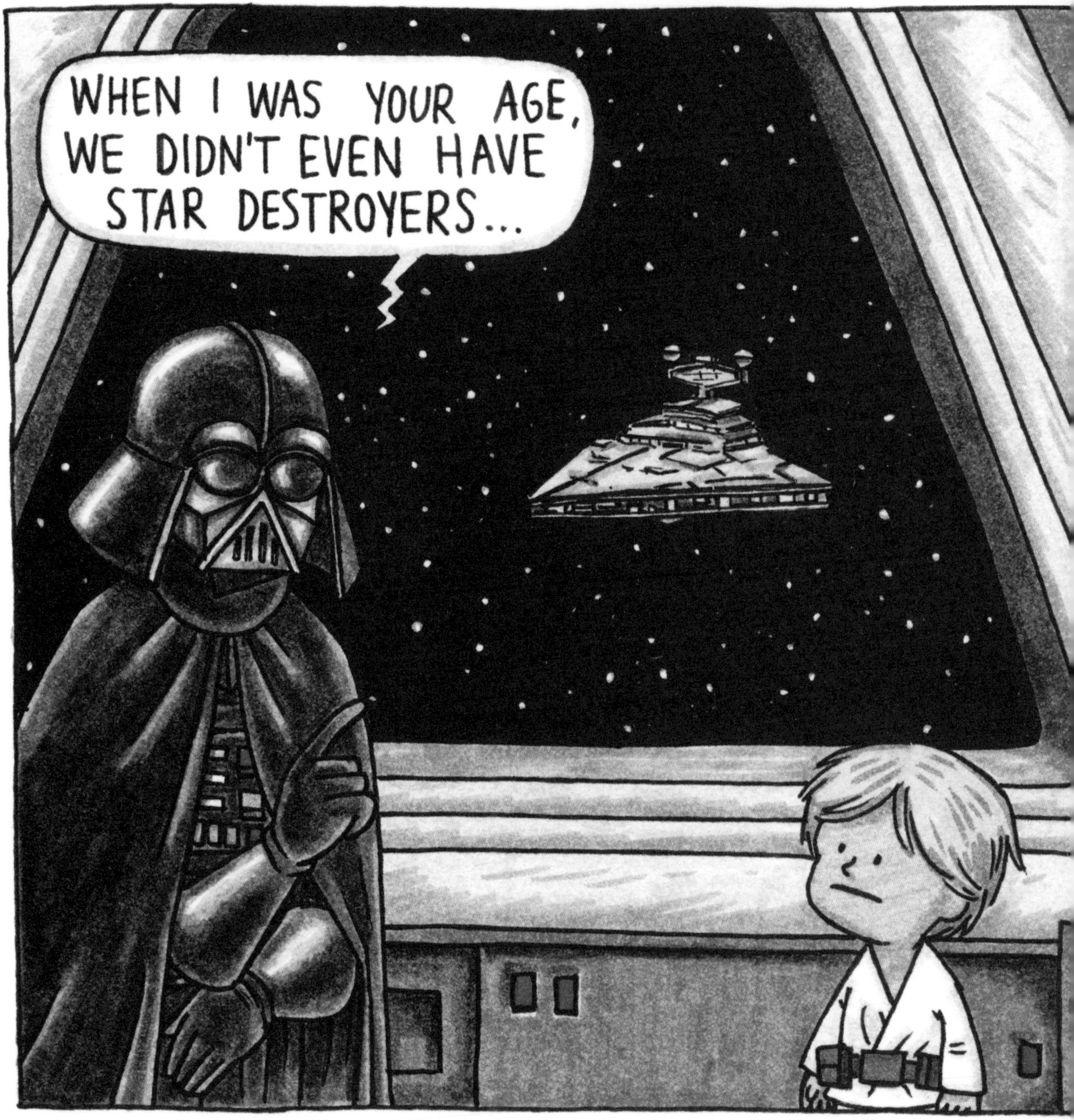
WHEN I WAS YOUR AGE, WE DIDN'T EVEN HAVE STAR DESTROYERS...

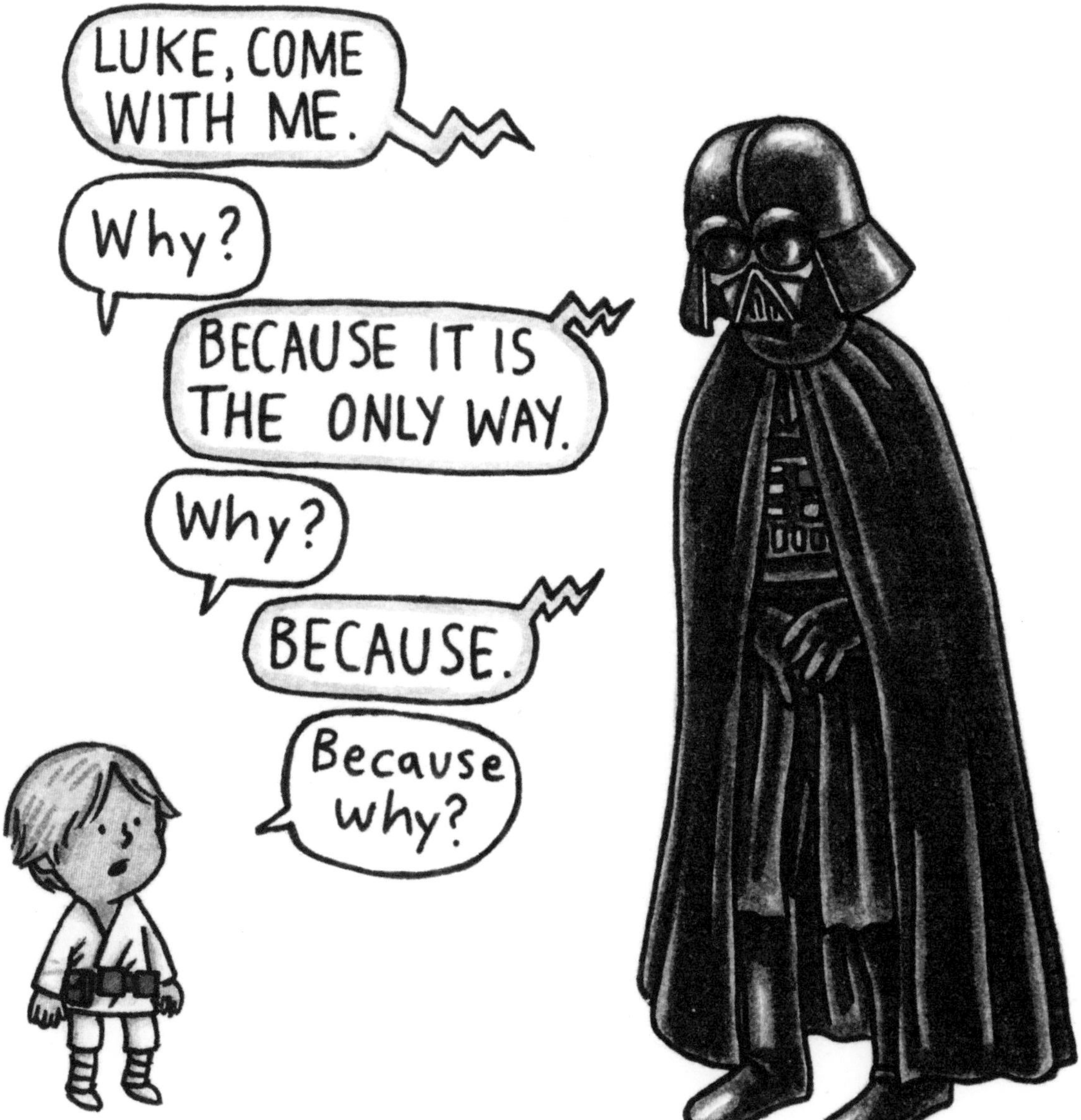
LUKE, COME WITH ME.
Why?
BECAUSE IT IS THE ONLY WAY.
Why?
BECAUSE.
Because why?

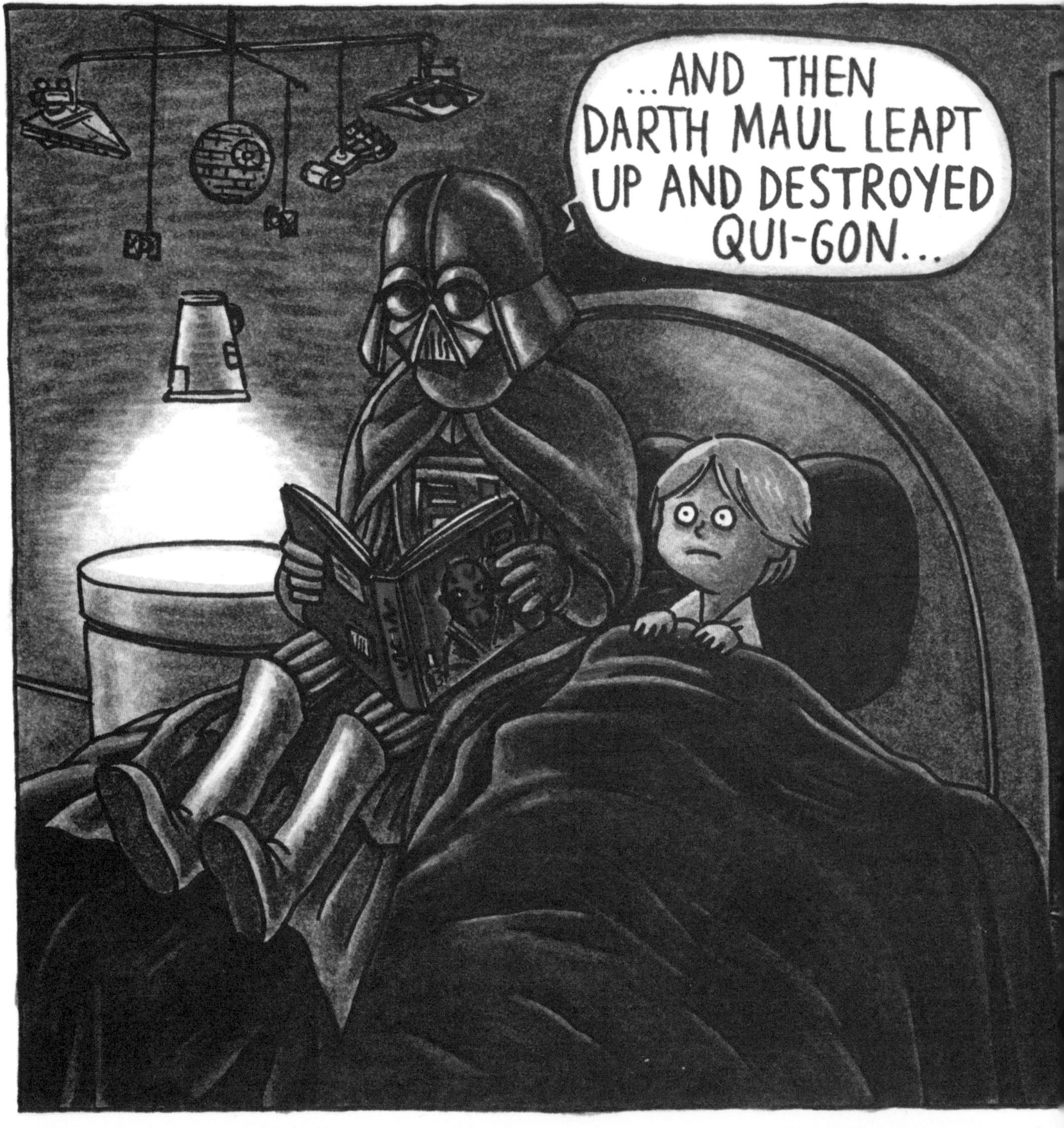
...AND THEN DARTH MAUL LEAPT UP AND DESTROYED QUI-GON...

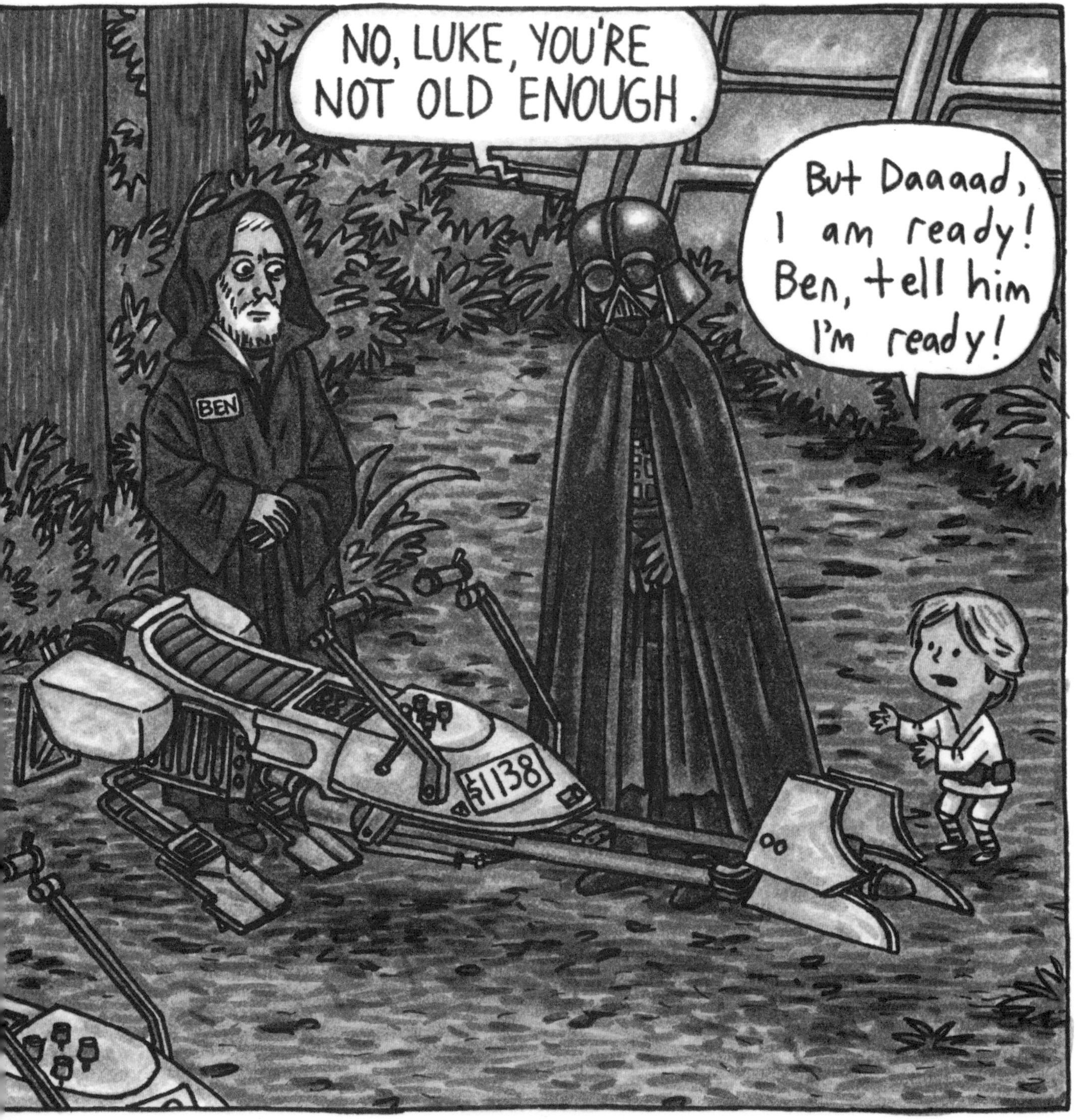
NO, LUKE, YOU'RE NOT OLD ENOUGH.
But Daaaad, I am ready! Ben, tell him I'm ready!
BEN
S1138

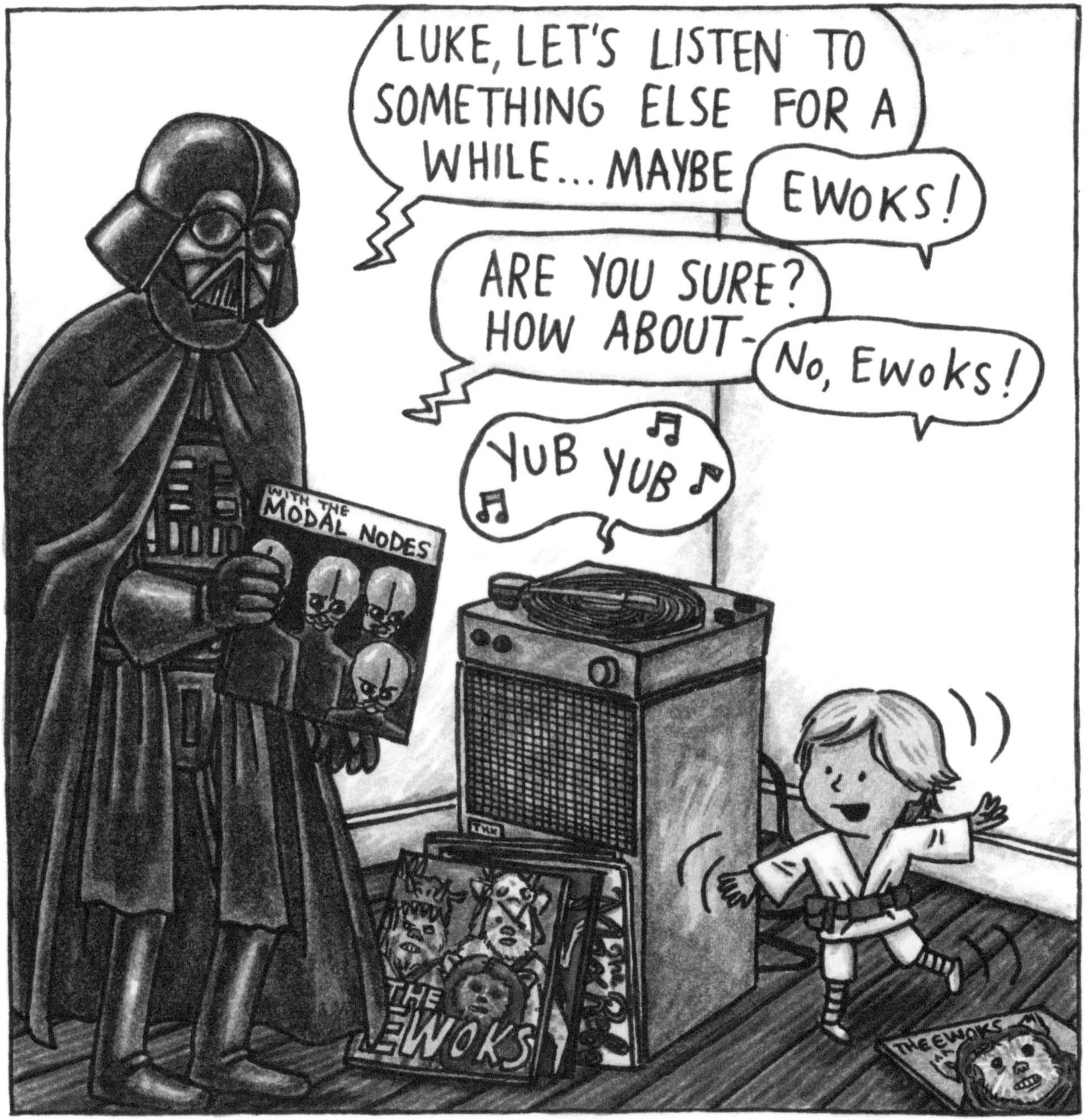
LUKE, LET'S LISTEN TO SOMETHING ELSE FOR A WHILE... MAYBE
EWOKS!
ARE YOU SURE? HOW ABOUT-
No, Ewoks!
YUB YUB
WITH THE MODAL NODES
THE EWOKS
THE EWOKS

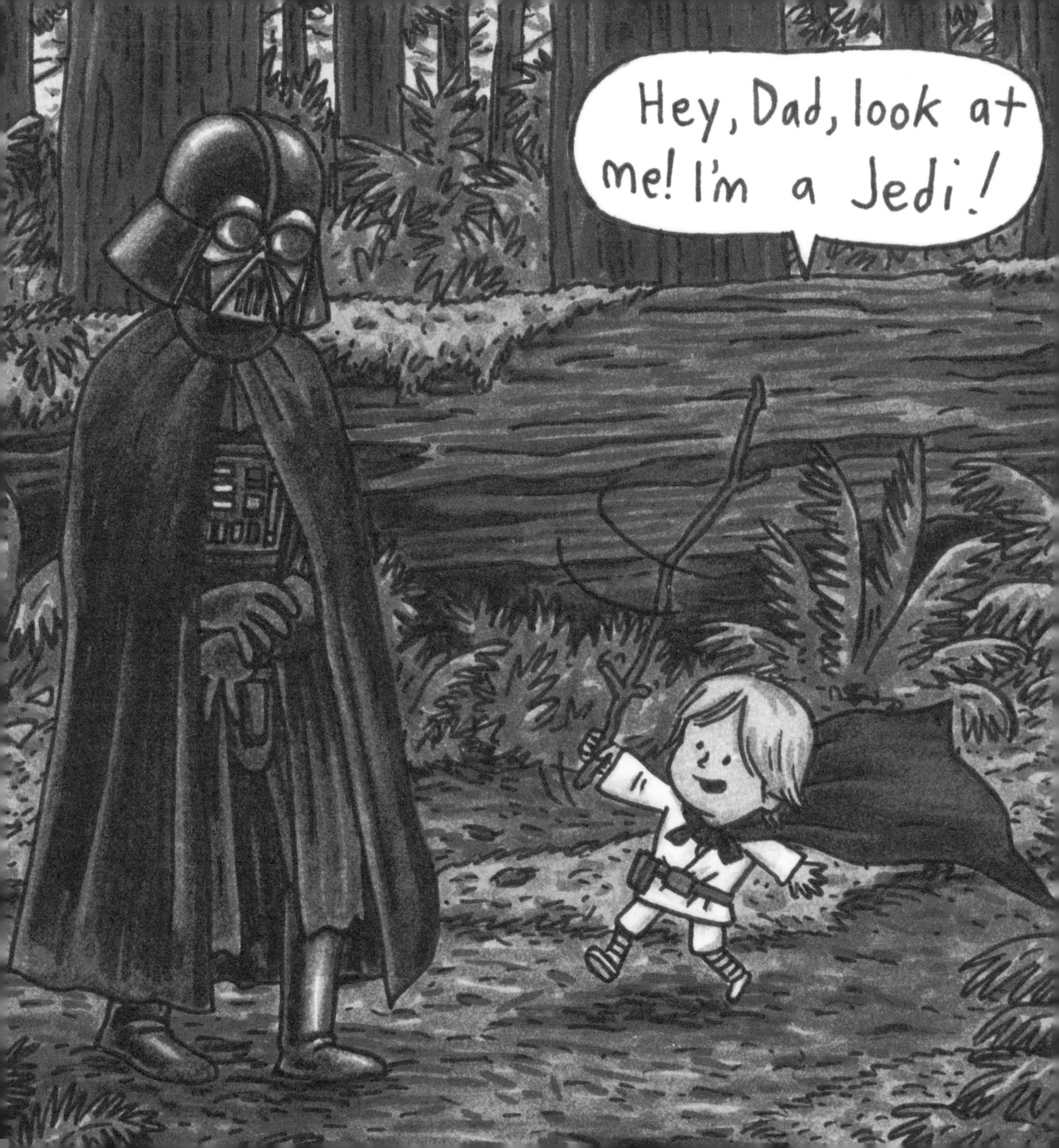
Hey, Dad, look at me! I'm a Jedi!

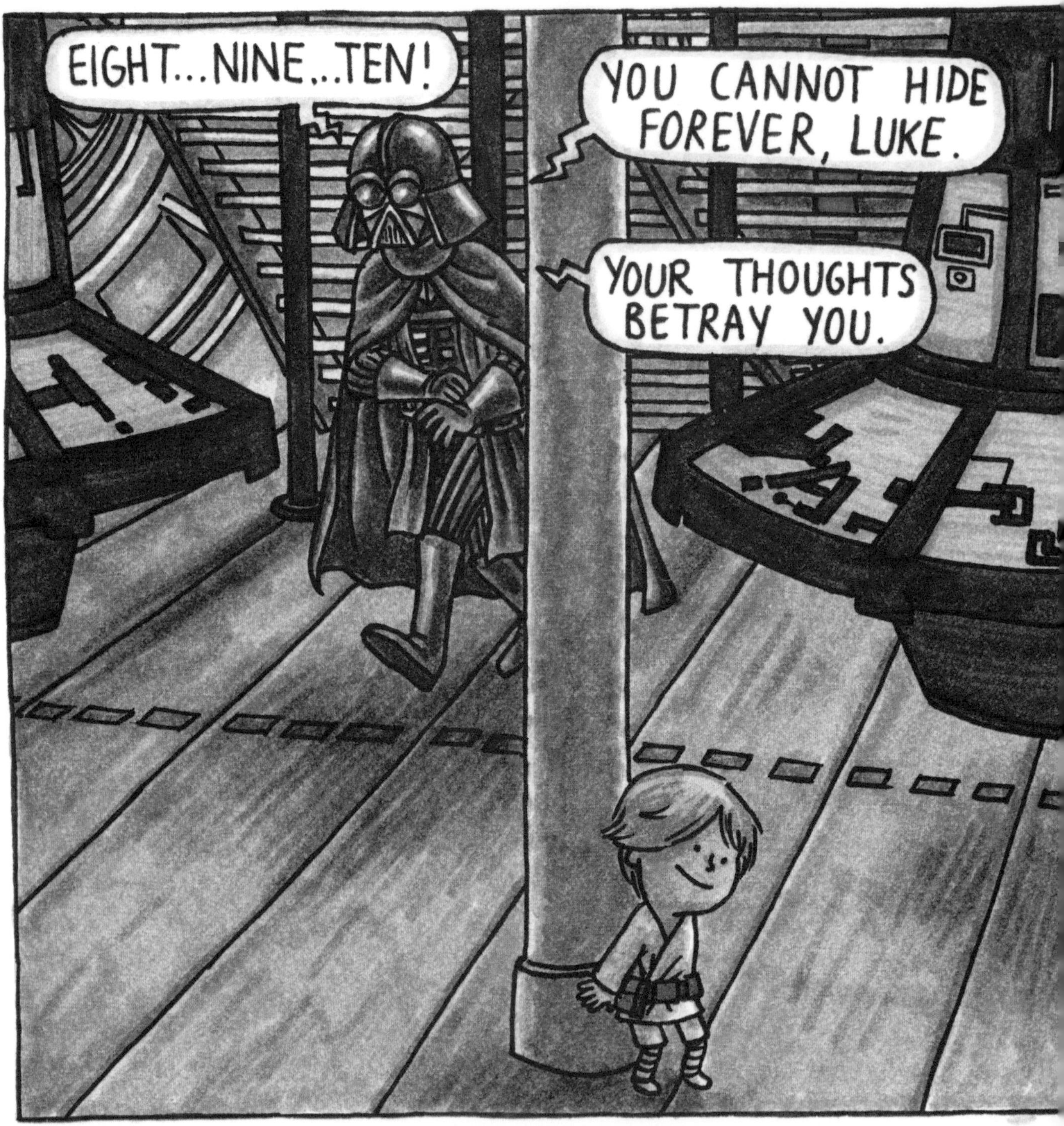
EIGHT...NINE...TEN!
YOU CANNOT HIDE FOREVER, LUKE.
YOUR THOUGHTS BETRAY YOU.

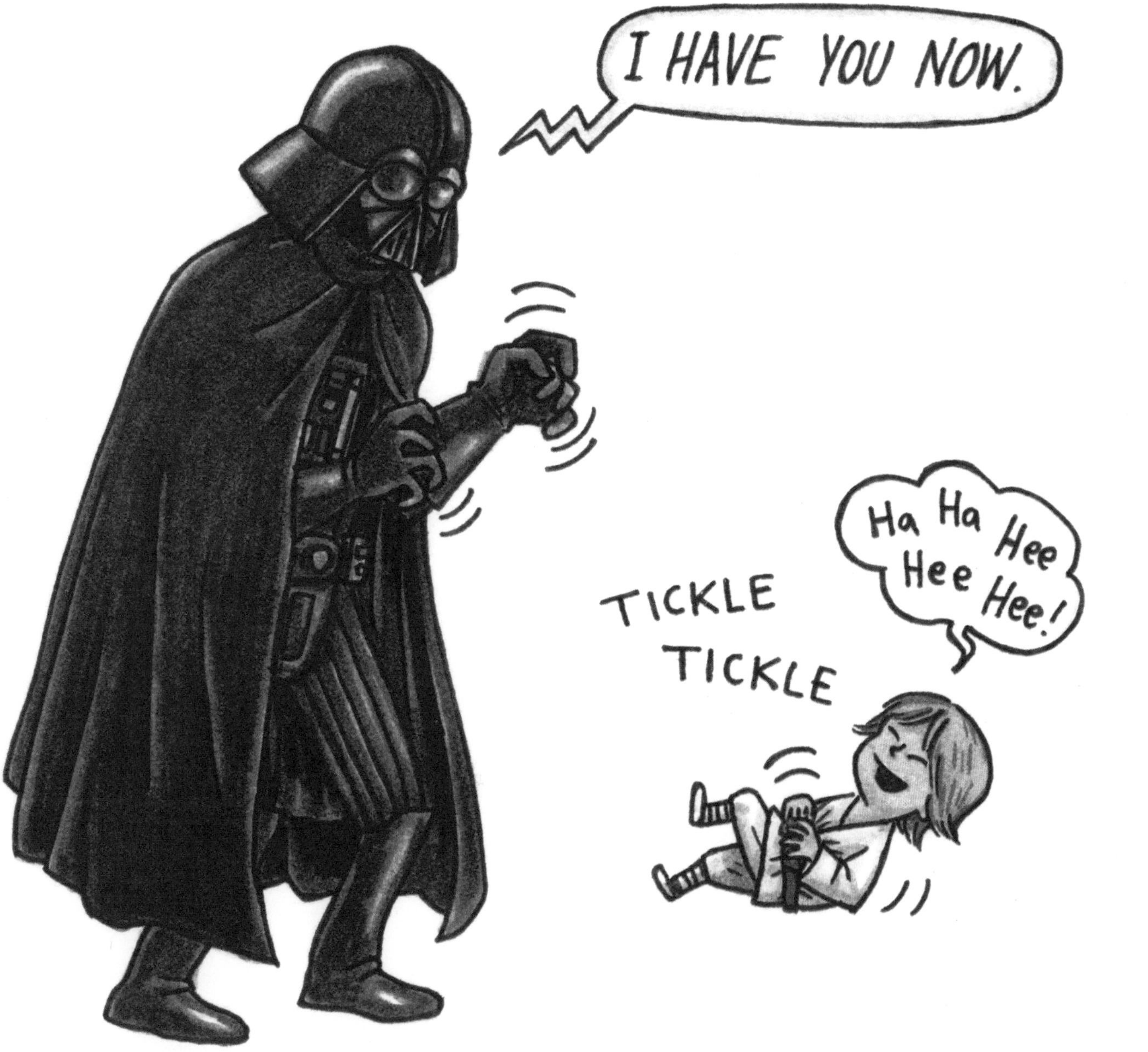

I HAVE YOU NOW.
TICKLE TICKLE
Ha Ha Hee Hee Hee!

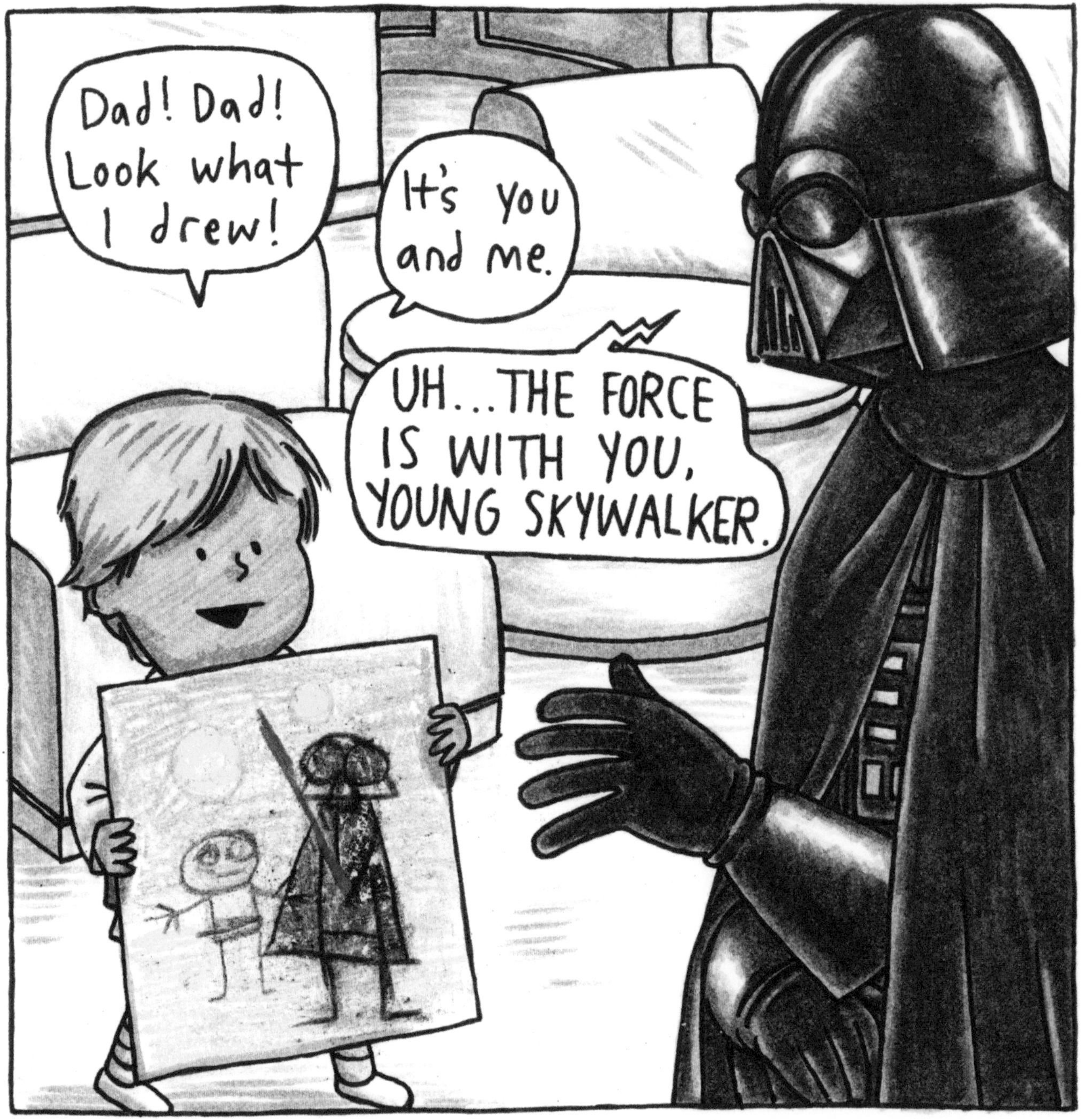
Dad! Dad! Look what I drew!
It's you and me.
UH...THE FORCE IS WITH YOU, YOUNG SKYWALKER.

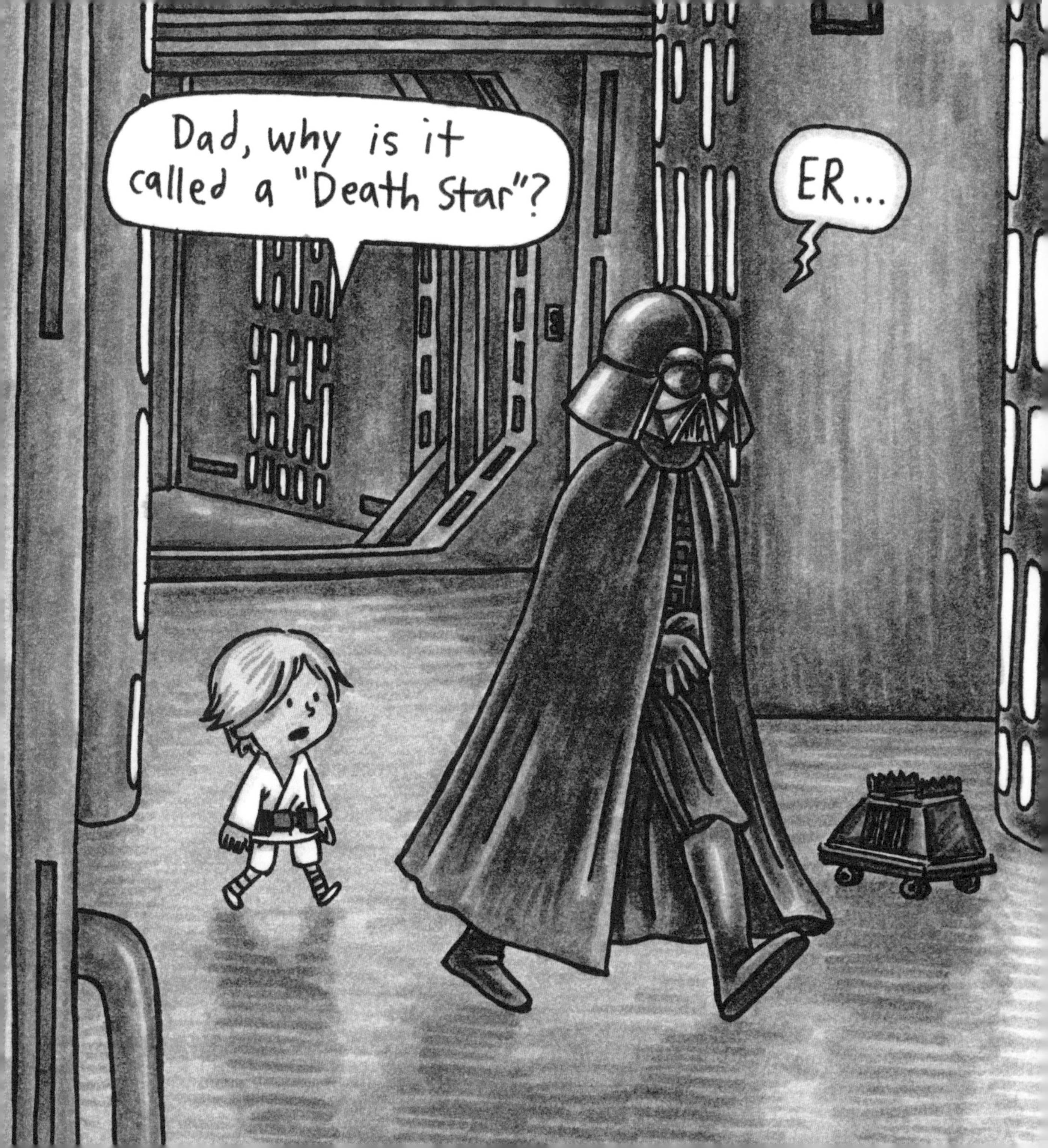
Dad, why is it called a "Death Star"?
ER...

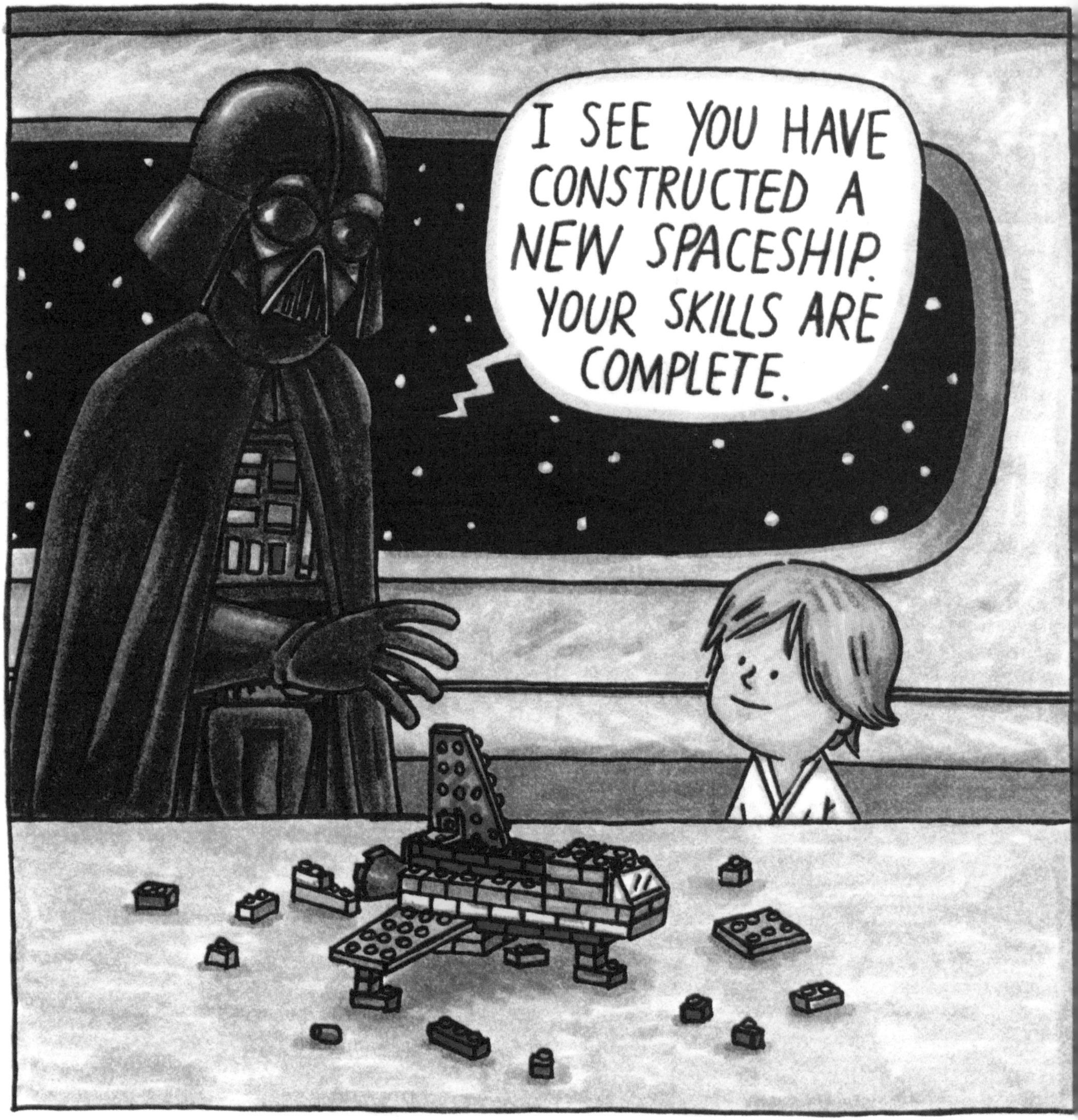
I SEE YOU HAVE CONSTRUCTED A NEW SPACESHIP. YOUR SKILLS ARE COMPLETE.

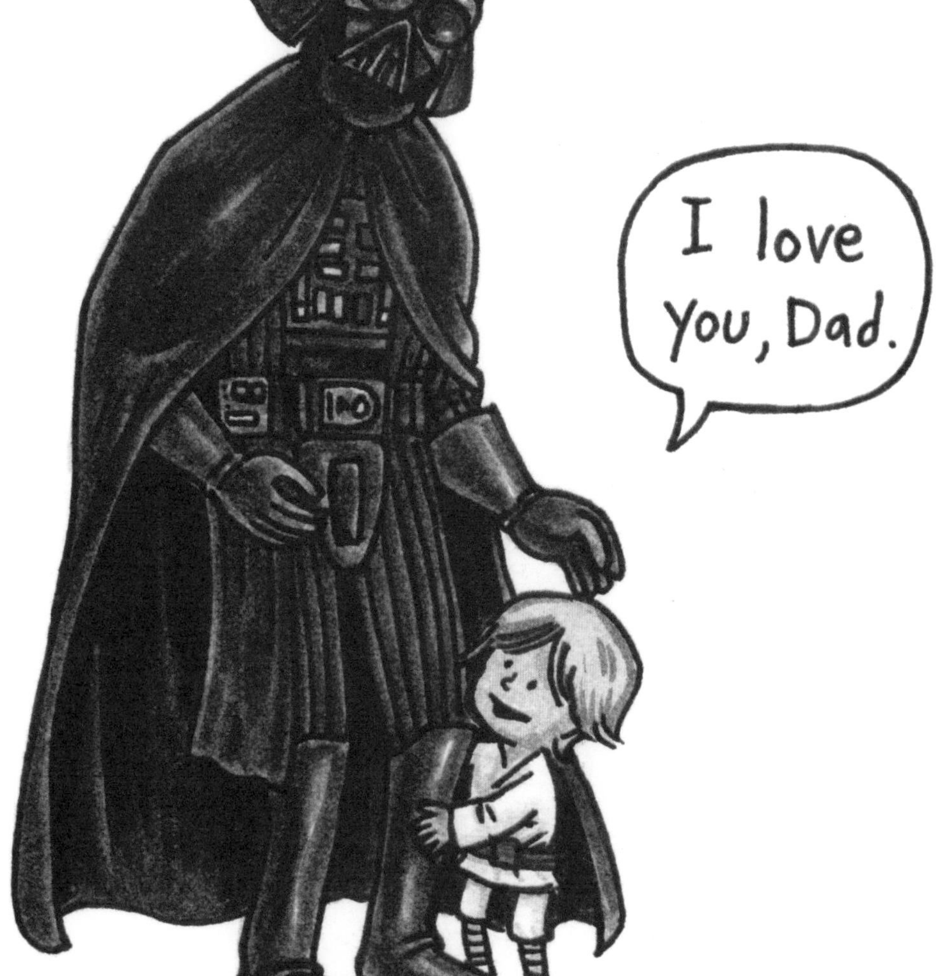
I love you, Dad.

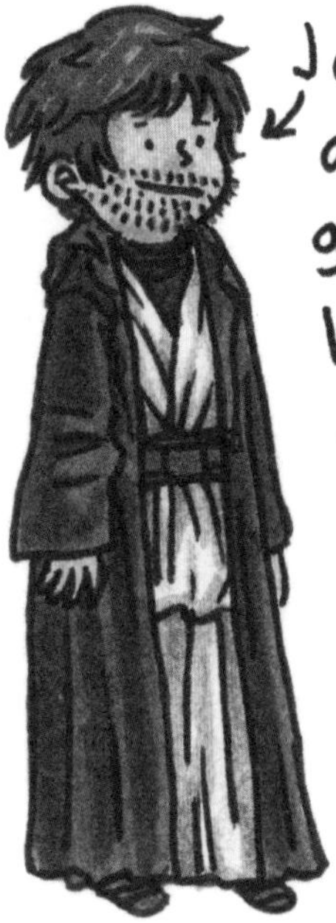

Jeffrey Brown is best known for his autobiographical comics and humorous graphic novels. He grew up watching Star Wars, playing with Star Wars action figures, and collecting Star Wars trading cards. He lives in Chicago with his wife, Jennifer, and sons, Oscar and Simon. →

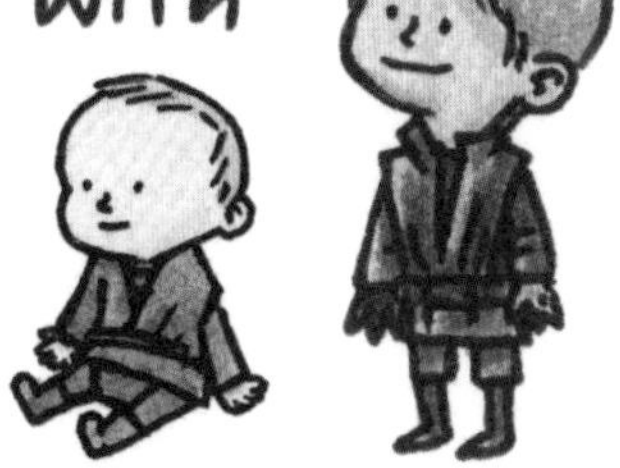

WWW.JEFFREYBROWNCOMICS.COM
P.O.BOX 120 DEERFIELD IL 60015-0120 USA

MORE BOOKS BY JEFFREY BROWN

From Chronicle (WWW.CHRONICLEBOOKS.COM):

Cat Getting Out Of A Bag
Cats Are Weird
Vader's Little Princess

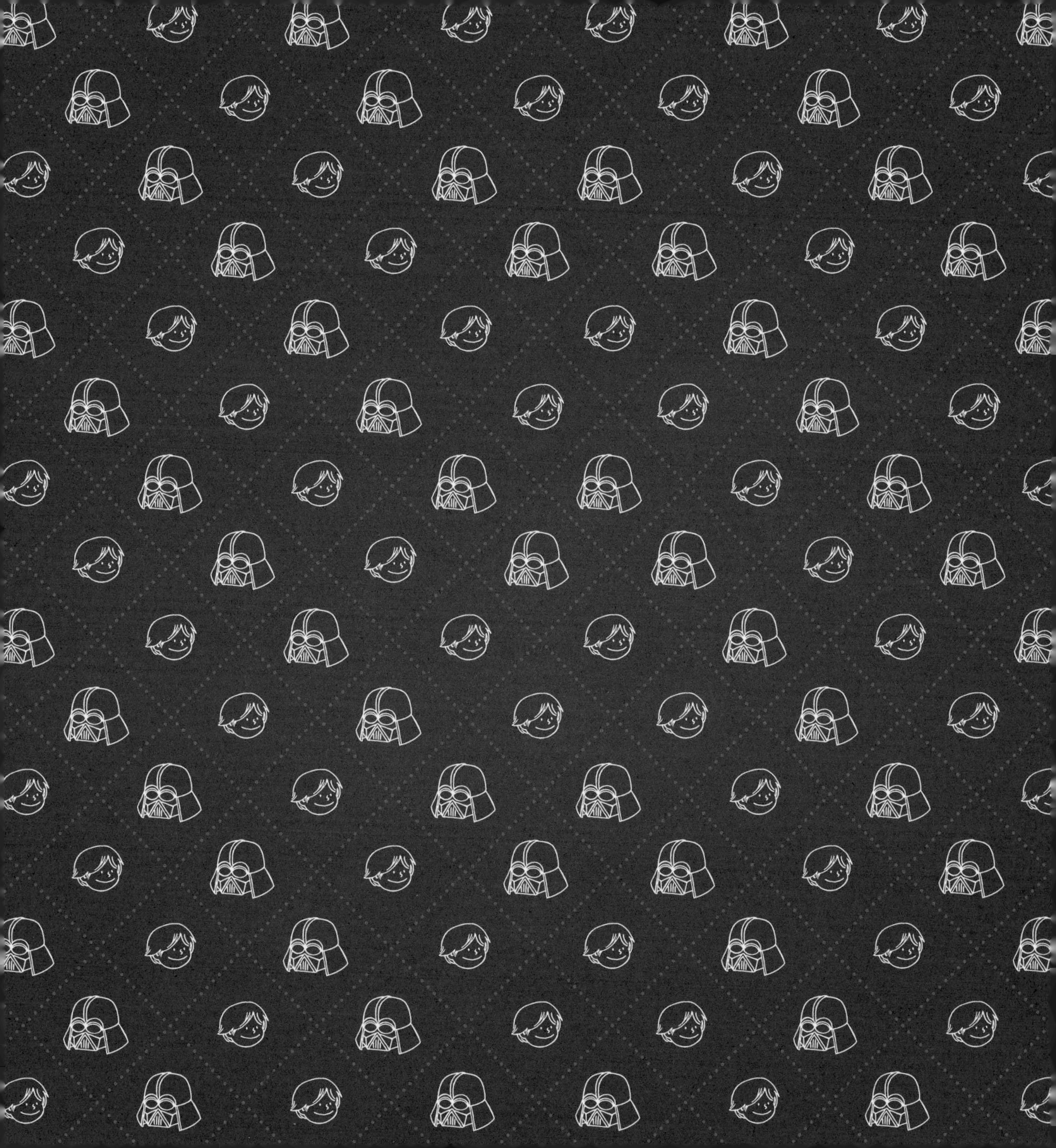